THE HORARY T

THE HORARY TEXTBOOK

John Frawley

To Kirsty,
Thank you for hosting this
most enjoyable weekend!
My best wishes.

John F

22·04·07

APPRENTICE BOOKS

Published 2005 by Apprentice Books
85, Steeds Road,
London N10 1JB
England
www.johnfrawley.com

ISBN 0 9539774 3 9

Cover photograph by Sergio Bondioni, Yellow Brick Studios
Design and typesetting by John Saunders Design & Production
Printed and bound in Great Britain by
J W Arrowsmith Ltd., Bristol

Contents

PART 2

Introduction

My aim in *The Horary Textbook* is to present a clear and comprehensive guide to the craft of horary astrology. Part 1 teaches the techniques that are used. Part 2 shows how these techniques are applied to find answers to all the more common questions that the astrologer is called upon to judge.

The endless variety of questions asked makes it impossible to give a method for tackling each one of them. If ever you wonder how rich life's tapestry really is, set yourself up as a horary astrologer! Whenever I think that I have heard absolutely everything, I can be sure that something yet more bizarre is waiting just around the corner. But the careful study of what is given here will enable you to make a sound judgement on anything that is not.

A companion to this book, *Horary Practice*, is due for publication in the autumn of 2005. That will present a long series of charts on questions of every kind, walking the student through the process of judgement one step at a time – as close as can be to the experience of standing at the elbow of a master astrologer as he works. These volumes will guide any reader prepared to make the necessary efforts to proficiency in this most rewarding of crafts.

Acknowledgements

In writing *The Horary Textbook*, my greatest debt is to William Lilly, master astrologer, *magister meo*, who has taught and continues to teach me so much.

Everyone studying traditional astrology is indebted to Olivia Barclay, who worked so hard to restore Lilly's *Christian Astrology* to its rightful place at the heart of the astrological canon. I was fortunate to study horary with Olivia, and it was she who encouraged me to write, speak and teach on the subject.

Teaching others has taught me even more than being taught myself. How true it is that one does not teach a subject, one teaches people. It is the years of reframing knowledge to make it intelligible to the eager mind of each of these people that gives this book whatever virtue it may possess. To my students, my thanks.

My gratitude, as ever, goes to Victor Laude and Despina Giannokopulou, without whom the road might have petered out long before reaching this point.

Branka Stamenkovic and Tijana Marinkovic have been the most effective of cheerleaders, encouraging me forward whenever the task seemed too daunting. Branka, Yasmin Bolland, Nina Holly, Dolores Quiddington, Richard Redmond and Carol Walsh read the manuscript and provided invaluable suggestions and corrections. What errors remain are mine alone.

Many times I have been asked the horary question, 'Will I make a living as a horary astrologer?' and that the answer to this question is usually 'No' is less because of the skills involved, which can be learned, but because of the sacrifices that must be made. In my case, most of these sacrifices have been made by my wife, Anna, who has stood by me resolutely, never failing in her support and understanding as I have built my career. Were she any less remarkable I would not be in the position to write this book. My thanks to her are endless.

Key

♈	Aries	ruled by Mars
♉	Taurus	ruled by Venus
♊	Gemini	ruled by Mercury
♋	Cancer	ruled by the Moon
♌	Leo	ruled by the Sun
♍	Virgo	ruled by Mercury
♎	Libra	ruled by Venus
♏	Scorpio	ruled by Mars
♐	Sagittarius	ruled by Jupiter
♑	Capricorn	ruled by Saturn
♒	Aquarius	ruled by Saturn
♓	Pisces	ruled by Jupiter

♄	Saturn
♃	Jupiter
♂	Mars
☉	Sun
♀	Venus
☿	Mercury
☽	Moon

☊	North Node of the Moon
☋	South Node of the Moon
⊗	Part of Fortune/Fortuna

☌	Conjunction	same degree, same sign
☍	Opposition	same degree, opposite sign
△	Trine – 120 degrees	same degree, 4th sign round
□	Square – 90 degrees	same degree, 3rd sign round
✶	Sextile – 60 degrees	same degree, 2nd sign round
℞	Retrograde	appears to be going backwards

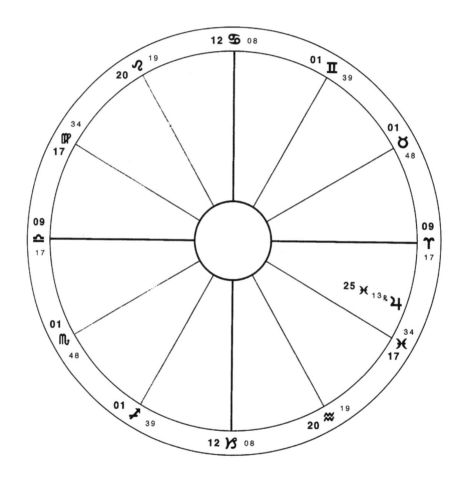

Where is the cat? August 30th 1998, 9.20 am BST, London.

1

Introduction to Horary

Horary is the art of drawing specific answers to specific questions from an astrological chart set for the time the question is asked. It is quick, simple and effective, providing concrete, verifiable answers.

"How quick? How simple?"

Follow this example. You may not yet understand many of the technical terms I use, but the principle of the judgement should be clear. Next door's cat had been gradually moving into my house. When he didn't appear for a couple of days, I was concerned for his safety, so asked the question 'Where is the cat?'

I set an astrological chart for the time I asked this question and for my location at that time. Printing the chart here, I have left out everything not needed for judgement.

I am asking about a cat. This is a small animal, and so is represented by the sixth house of the chart. The planet that rules the sign on the cusp of that house will signify the cat. Pisces is on the 6th cusp, so its ruler, Jupiter, signifies the cat.

Where is Jupiter? In the 6th house: the house of the cat. So where is the cat? In his own house: at home.

Is he OK? Jupiter, the most benefic of planets, is in its own sign, so has lots of essential dignity. Signified by a strongly dignified benefic, the cat is doing just fine.

Jupiter (the cat) is in a water sign, so he may be somewhere wet. But water signs also show places that are comfortable, which, considering the nature of the beast and that he is clearly happy where he is (strongly dignified benefic), must be the more likely choice. So he is probably curled up on the sofa or bed.

Will he come back? Jupiter is retrograde: it is going back where it has been before. So yes, he will come back.

The chart has given a specific, verifiable answer to the question. It has done this using only one planet! Horary is quick; horary is simple.

We can refine this answer by predicting the time of the cat's return. For this

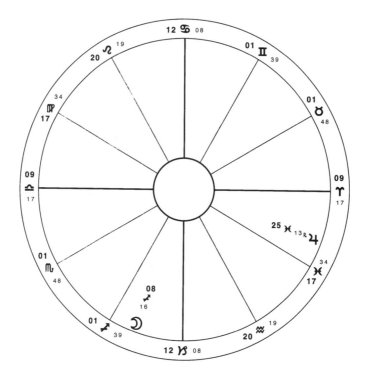

Where is the cat? August 30th 1998, 9.20 am BST, London.

there must be a connection between the cat's significator and something that represents either me or my home. Jupiter is making no such contact in this chart, so we must introduce a second planet. The Moon is natural ruler of all lost objects, especially animate ones.

The person asking the question is shown by the Ascendant and its ruler. The Moon applies to sextile the Ascendant. Just as the 6th can be taken literally as the cat's house, the first is literally my house. The Moon must travel almost exactly 1 degree to perfect this aspect. So the cat will return in almost exactly 1 unit of time. The sign and house the Moon is in as it makes this aspect tell us which unit of time this is. With the Moon in a mutable sign and a cadent house, the unit must be a day. So the cat will return almost exactly 24 hours after the time for which the chart was cast. And so it proved.

Even now, we have only two planets in the chart. Yet we have a precise, timed, accurate prediction. Horary is simple.

Not every chart, as might be expected, is as simple as this one. But many are. A good proportion of horary charts can, with knowledge and practice, be judged at a glance. Horary was the main technique used by most astrologers during the Seventeenth century, and it is a matter of record that an astrological consultation using horary would have taken around fifteen minutes.[1] This time would include the usual social niceties of greeting; the client explaining what he wanted to know and giving any relevant – or, more often, irrelevant – details of the situation; negotiation of an acceptable fee; the astrologer adjusting the chart he had set at the start of his day's work to fit the time this question was asked; him judging the chart and telling the client his judgement; the client, if the answer given was not what he had hoped, quite possibly reacting with disbelief, 'Huh! What do you know?'; the astrologer looking again at his chart and responding, 'I know you have a large red birthmark on your left thigh,' to convince him. All this in fifteen minutes. Even the most complex charts are judged not by any arcane or difficult tricks of method, but by doing a few simple operations over and over again.

It was not only its speed and economy of effort that made horary the mainstay of astrological practice: for most enquiries it was and still is the most appropriate tool. Whatever the situation might be, if the client wants to know something specific about it, use horary. Most answers can be found more quickly and more reliably from a horary chart than from the study of the birthchart; many answers cannot be found in the birthchart at all, no matter how detailed or lengthy the investigation, or how skilled the astrologer. The natal chart will not reveal whether it will rain on the day you've planned a barbecue, whether you should sell your dollars to buy silver, what your sweetheart really feels about you – or where the cat might be. Yet these and issues like them, woven together, make up the fabric of our life.

Most of those who approach an astrologer for a consultation have a particular question in mind. It is of course far simpler to look at a chart that concerns that question and it alone, than to attempt to pick the bones of that question from the birthchart, which shows a lifetime's worth of questions tangled together.

Horary was traditionally regarded as being the student's point of entrance to the study of astrology. One reason for this is that it is much simpler than other branches of astrology, such as natal or mundane. It thus enables the student to achieve with comparative ease a mastery of the techniques that form the bulk of

[1] Keith Thomas, *Religion and the Decline of Magic*, London, 1971. Rep. London, 1991, p. 364.

those used, with greater elaboration, in these other branches. It can be seen as equivalent to mastering one's scales when learning a musical instrument; as such it is a necessary prelude to more advanced study. Unlike mastery of the musical scales, however, horary is of immediate practical use.

"Is horary solely predictive?"

Not at all. It is best known for its ability to provide accurate prediction. It can also be used to investigate the past ('Did the builder steal my ring?'). Its most interesting use, however, is for analysis of a situation. Far more valuable than asking the predictive 'Is my marriage heading for divorce?' is asking the analytical 'What is going wrong with my marriage and what can I do about it?' This too can be done with horary.

William Lilly and first principles

The great master of horary is William Lilly, an English astrologer who lived from 1602 to 1681. His *Christian Astrology*, published in 1647, is, and will remain, the standard textbook.[2] The book you have in your hand leans heavily on it. Where this differs, apart from being written in modern English for modern readers, is in its greater emphasis on first principles. Clarity on the first principles avoids the need for the long lists of minor testimonies, often empirically based, that are so large a feature of Lilly's work.

Minor testimonies do not a judgement make, and can usually be ignored. Consider: if we ask 'Who won that football match?' all that concerns us is the major testimony of who scored the most goals. Who had most possession of the ball; who had the most corners; whose players thrilled the crowd: these are minor testimonies, which do not directly affect the result. In the horary method as I explain it here, I am emphasising the goals scored. This is one example of the Rule of Rules: Keep it Simple!

The reader who comes to horary afresh will forgive those passages where I discuss, clarify or refute points from Lilly. This is necessary for those readers who are familiar with his work.

---

[2] The best modern edition is the Astrology Classics edition, from The Astrology Center of America, Abingdon, 2004. *Christian Astrology* will be referred to as *Lilly* from now on.

Preliminaries

First, inscribe these words of Jerome Cardan on your heart:

He that has too great a conceit of himself will be apt to fall into many errors in his judgement; yet on the other side, he that is too diffident, is not fit for this Science.[3]

This study demands humility. You cannot remake astrology in your own image. You may find much here that differs from what you have previously learned, ideas that you may hold dear. Rather than imposing those ideas onto what is being taught, set them aside for a while, trying what is given here until you see that it works.

The study demands a certain courage. Horary enables us to give clear, detailed answers. There are no helpful clouds of ambivalence for us to hide behind when we get it wrong. We read the chart; we give the judgement; we are proved right or wrong – sometimes quite quickly. The rules given here are your sound support. No astrologer has ever been infallible, but following these rules will allow you to achieve a steadily increasing reliability of judgement.

The reader who has some knowledge of astrology may be tempted to skip the early chapters. Don't! When teaching, I have found even those students with qualifications from the most noted astrological schools often have surprising holes in their knowledge of the basics. Being clear on these is essential. If you do not understand the basic building-blocks, whatever you build with them will be unsound.

This is a book to work with, not a book to read through. The margins are wide to allow room for notes. Pick the examples apart until you are sure you under-stand why I said what I've said. Keep asking yourself, 'Why did he say this?' and 'Why didn't he consider that?' Then practice, practice and practice. Ask your own horary questions. Although, once mastered, horary is best used sparingly, while learning you can ask about every trivial matter that crosses your mind. Questions you would not usually spend time over: 'When will the postman come?' 'Will my mother phone today?' These are all grist to the mill. Look back at your judgements. If one is wrong, pull the chart apart until you have seen why.

Always force yourself to reach a judgement, and write this judgement down. Save the charts so you can examine them once the outcome is known. When answering one's own questions, it is easy to fudge the issue, leaving judgements

---

[3] In Guido Bonatus, *The Astrologer's Guide*, London, 1676; Cardan section, aphorism 2. Book hereafter referred to as *Bonatus*.

hanging in ambiguity. It is also easy to give up, thinking that the chart is beyond you. You will learn nothing that way. No matter how expert you become, horary will continually ask you to stretch beyond what you think you know. For an astrologer as for an athlete, it is the stretching beyond that brings excellence. Push yourself to go beyond your knowledge, and you will be amazed at what you achieve. Remember that even William Lilly described himself as a 'student' of astrology.

You do not need to have a question to judge a horary chart. Take any chart, either one of your own or one from a book, and make up new questions for it. Have some of these questions focus on people other than 'I' (e.g. 'Will my brother's marriage survive?' 'Is my boss going to take that new job?' 'When will my dog find a girlfriend?'). Just don't take your judgements to these invented questions seriously! This is excellent practice: you are learning a language; you will not become fluent without repeatedly trying to speak.

Before you cast a chart, ask yourself what you expect to see in it. How will the situation be shown? You will often be wrong, but doing this will gradually align your thinking with the workings of the chart.

When judging a chart, I find it helps to think in the simplest of terms, as I have shown in the examples here. 'Is he a good guy or is he a bad guy?' 'Good, indifferent, or yuk?' It may sometimes sound like *Learn to Read, Book 1*, but doing this will stop you entangling yourself in abstract concepts. The chart will lead you to all the complexity you need; keeping each step as simple as this will enable you to understand the complexity when you get there. Keep it all down to earth.

Above all, do not beat yourself about the head for getting judgements wrong. The best of footballers can miss a penalty kick. This does not mean he has suddenly become a bad footballer. It does not mean that scoring penalties is impossible. It does not mean that football is nonsense. All it means is that he missed that kick.

2

Getting Started

The person asking the question is the *querent.*
The person or thing asked about is the *quesited.*

Cast the chart for the moment the astrologer understands the question. In the past, the astrologer would usually have been sitting with the client when the question was asked. Today questions are often asked at a distance, both of time and space: by email, phone, post, or recorded on an ansaphone. It is the moment at which the astrologer reads or hears the question that is used for setting the chart, not the time at which the querent poses it.

If I come home to find a letter containing a question lying on my doormat, pick it up, make myself a coffee, then sit to read it, I would set the chart for the time at which I read it: not the time I picked it off the mat; not the time the querent has noted in her letter as the moment she wrote it.

If the question is asked by phone, the chart is cast for the moment the question is asked. This sounds straightforward, and usually is, but some questions have a long labour before they are born. The querent will hesitate, saying 'I want to ask this.... I'm not sure if I should.... Or maybe I should ask that....' This can take longer than the whole of a typical Seventeenth-century consultation. The time taken for the chart is the time at which the querent finally gets to the point, not the time at which the conversation started. It is as if such querents are unconsciously feeling for the correct moment at which to ask: the moment that will provide a chart allowing the correct judgement of that question. This can often be verified by the appearance of datable past events in the chart cast, events that would not have been shown in a chart cast for the time the conversation started.

If the question has been asked, but demands clarification before you understand the core issue, take the time when it is clarified as the time of the question. If you feel you have a reasonable understanding of the question, but when giving the judgement realise that this understanding was faulty, stick with the chart cast for the time you thought you understood it.

If the querent asks further questions on the same issue when you are giving judgement on the initial question, judge these from the same chart. For instance, the initial question might be, 'When will I meet the man I will marry?' and on being given the judgement the querent might add, 'Will he get along with my daughter?' You can read this from the initial chart. If the querent adds, 'And when will I get a decent job?' that is a new question requiring a new chart.

If you are judging your own question, the time to take is the time at which you decide that you will cast a chart to find its answer. This is the equivalent of taking the time at which the querent asks. Don't try to trace the moment when the issue first wandered into your mind: we are using the time when the question was born, not the time at which it was conceived. The time you use may or may not be the time at which you sit down at your computer to cast the chart. If you wake in the night and decide to ask, note the time and use that.

Yes, there is the possibility that the astrologer, having a close working knowledge of the positions of the planets, can carefully select a moment when they are aligned to give the answer desired. Yes, there is the possibility that the astrologer might be daft enough to credit the judgement drawn from such a chart. But we must allow our astrologer a modicum of self-awareness. The Heavens, meanwhile, are a mechanism of the greatest subtlety: attempt to choose such a moment at which to 'spontaneously' ask your question and you will invariably find that they are a good deal smarter than you. The difficult part in judging one's own questions is not the choosing of the time, but the setting aside of one's natural partiality.

The place for which the chart is set is that of the astrologer. In the past astrologer and querent were usually in the same room; today they are often continents apart. As we take the time at which the question is understood, so we must take the place at which it is understood: the location of the astrologer. According to traditional philosophy the question does not really exist until it meets the ear of one who can answer it. Until then it is a no-thing.

Use a computer! There are those of ascetic inclination who see a virtue in casting charts by hand. There is no need for such self-flagellation. The situation today is quite different from the days when the astrologer would have querents queuing for his services, and so could cast one chart when he clocked on for work in the morning and adjust it to fit questions asked throughout the day. If you insist on casting charts by hand you are unlikely to cast sufficient charts for the practice needed to gain proficiency.

For readers who do not have access to a computer, Appendix 1 shows how to calculate a chart by hand without the needless complications usually introduced. This method streamlines the process, making it as quick and painless as is possible.

"Do I need special software for horary?" No! Most advanced astrological software has special 'horary pages', which overwhelm the student in a torrent of information, most of which is irrelevant to the question in hand and much of which is presented in ways that can mislead the inexperienced. I urge you not to use these pages, but only the simplest chart-form on the program, without the lists, tables and other paraphernalia. Following the methods taught in this book, you will soon learn to decide exactly what information you need from the chart, and then to enter the chart looking for that and that alone. This is much quicker and much simpler than wading through a morass of data that you do not want.

Expensive software is not required. Your aim is to get from A to B; you do not need to drive a Rolls-Royce to achieve this. There is freely downloadable software on the web that is completely adequate.[4]

Preparation for judgement

It is my firm belief that no matter how skilled we may be as astrologers, correct judgement is not given unless by grace. Even if all the requisite elements of knowledge are in our head, we cannot make them join together as they should: this is a gift. So I strongly suggest that before entering upon judgement you pray for this grace.

Even if not praying, do something, if only washing your hands, or sitting quietly for a couple of minutes to clear your mind. It is far too easy to read the astrologer when you should be reading the chart; but the purpose of horary is to get a dispassionate view of the situation. You need to put your own views and assumptions aside and be open to what is before you. I find, for example, I am

---

[4] There is free software in both PC and Mac versions at www.astrolog.org, while you can set a chart and print it out at www.astro.com.

often asked questions to which my immediate reaction is 'Don't be silly', but where the chart shows that what the querent is suggesting, no matter how odd it might seem to me, is true. It is vital to remember that you do not know. It is the astrology that knows.

You will find that some charts, like this one about the cat, are crystal clear. Many are not. Sometimes the lack of clarity is caused by the astrologer lacking knowledge or approaching the chart in the wrong way. Sometimes the chart appears muddy because the situation it describes is muddy. Many situations are ambivalent, with no clear answer. As a simple example, a common question is, phrased in one way or another, 'Is this Mr. Right?' A clear answer might be 'Yes – he is your soul-mate!' or 'No – he is an axe-murderer!' More often, the answer is, 'Well, he's OK; you could do a lot worse, and there's nothing much better in prospect'. This too is an answer.

Do not strive for certainty before you give judgement. Some charts are unequivocal; others demand that you tease out an answer. Wait for certainty in these and you will wait forever. But if you have thoroughly assimilated the basic rules, your judgement of such charts will be sound, no matter how cautiously you might edge forward towards it. I have found that it is with judgements like this, where I have felt that I am stepping onto a bridge of gossamer, that my work has been most applauded by clients, for the successful clarification of issues too tangled to resolve in any other way.

There is a common myth that we must find three testimonies in the chart before we can give judgement. This is nonsense, propagated by those who fear giving judgement. If half a testimony is all we have, that is all we have. We must work with what we are given. Few indeed are the charts with three clear testimonies. To continue with the footballing metaphor, we can win 6-0 or we can win by one disputed goal in the last minute: we have still won.

The worksheet

I suggest you copy this worksheet and use it each time you judge a chart. It will help ensure that you have the information you need for judgement, while gradually training you to identify exactly what information you do need.

"Isn't this the same as the software pages you've just told me not to use?" No. Those pages are a waste of time purporting to be a labour-saving device. This worksheet is an educational tool. To fill in this worksheet, you need to look at the chart, and look at it in some depth. Even though much of the information you

WORKSHEET

FOR THE GLORY OF GOD

Querent:

Question:

Time, date, place:

Querent's planets: Quesited's planets:

☽ from: ☽ to:

	Sign	Exalt	Trip	Term	Face	Detr	Fall	Notes
☉								
☽								
☿								
♀								
♂								
♃								
♄								
⊗								

Fixed stars: Antiscia: Major receptions:

put on it is the same as that given you by the horary pages, the act of extracting this information from the chart yourself will show you things that the study of a prepared list will not. As you gain familiarity with the horary process, you will reduce the amount of information you put on this form. After a while, you will abandon it altogether; but do not rush this process.

You may not yet understand some of the terms on this sheet: they are explained in the following chapters.

INVOCATION: to remind us of what we are doing.

QUERENT/QUESTION: the querent's name and the question asked.

TIME, DATE, PLACE: the data on which the chart is set.

QUERENT/QUESITED'S PLANETS: the significator or significators of the querent and of whatever is being asked about.

MOON: the Moon's most recent aspect and its next aspect.

DIGNITIES: enter the glyph for the planet ruling the sign in which each planet falls; that which is exalted there; the triplicity ruler, and so on. Example: if the Sun were at 3 Aries in a daytime chart, the Sun column would read:

$$\sigma' \quad \odot \quad \odot \quad \text{24} \quad \sigma' \quad \text{♀} \quad \text{♄}$$

You may wish to highlight indications of the planet being in its own dignity or debility.

NOTES: anything of significance about the planet, e.g. its being combust, retrograde, in station.

FIXED STARS: list any major stars that fall within a degree or so of the main significators or relevant house cusps. You can allow a couple of degrees for Regulus, Spica and Caput Algol.

ANTISCIA: list the antiscia of any planets that fall on the main significators, or on relevant house-cusps (within about a degree).

RECEPTIONS: list all major mutual receptions between the planets. Reception does not have to be mutual to be significant, but strong mutual receptions can have a significance of their own. By 'strong', I mean reception by sign, exaltation or triplicity. Don't forget negative mutual reception (by detriment or fall): this can be important too.

THE GOLDEN RULES

KEEP IT SIMPLE

No matter how complicated the chart, don't panic. Keep asking yourself the same simple questions about aspect, dignity and reception and you will arrive at the answer.

Resist the temptation to blame the chart for being uncooperative, and then to think that an answer will be revealed if only you add this or that new technique – minor aspects, perhaps, or an asteroid or two. If the answer doesn't appear to be there, this is because you cannot yet see it. Concentrate on what is in the chart, assessing this in these same simple ways, and you soon will.

This refers to Golden Rule number 2, which is:

THERE IS ALWAYS AN ANSWER IN THERE SOMEWHERE

It is often found a few steps after the point at which you decide not to give up.

MIX DISCRETION WITH ART

This is Lilly's oft-repeated phrase for 'use your common sense'.

TALK TO THE QUERENT

If you are not sure of the exact meaning of the question, ask for clarification. If you still aren't sure, ask again. Some querents will ask questions of runic obscurity: make sure you understand before you cast the chart.

If you find a planet is important in the chart, but you don't know what it signifies, ask the querent. If you need to know who is involved in the situation, ask.

It is easy, for example, to work out a detailed judgement about the lost object being with the querent's husband, only to have the querent tell you that she is not married.

YOU ARE ALLOWED TO BE WRONG

Strive to make your judgements accurate, of course. But what we are doing here is remarkable: that we cannot always be successful is no cause to lament. That we can achieve what we do achieve is quite remarkable enough.

3

The Houses

William Lilly rightly says that once the student has the ability to set a chart, the most important thing to understand is the meanings of the houses.[5] Everything that exists can be assigned to one or other of the twelve houses of the chart. If we look at the wrong house to locate whatever our querent is asking about, we shall probably arrive at the wrong answer to the querent's question. A clear understanding of the houses is therefore essential.

The chart is divided into twelve sections. Technically, these are called *mundane houses* (or *earthly houses*) in contrast to the *celestial houses,* which is another name for the signs of the zodiac. Although it is customary now to refer to the celestial houses as 'signs', it is worth remembering that they too are houses. The word 'house' can often be taken literally in the chart, as representing a physical abode, whether it is a celestial (sign) or mundane house. The old texts refer to both signs and houses as 'houses'. Although this is correct, it can sometimes be confusing.

Imagine the chart is a cake. There are many ways of dividing it into twelve slices, giving us the twelve houses of the chart. Do we divide the cake by eye? Do we count the number of cherries in each section and divide it equally like that? Do we divide it according to the appetite of those who are to eat it, making sure each is equally satisfied? Similarly, there are many ways of dividing the chart into houses. These are called *house systems*.

The charts in this book are cast in the *Regiomontanus* house system. I urge you to use this for horary. It is the system used by Lilly, and it works, as can be shown not by the subjective criterion of 'I prefer my birthchart cast by this system because it puts my Venus in this house not that house', but because we can make accurate predictions from the position of the house-cusps it gives, which is the one variable between systems.

---

[5] *Lilly,* introductory pages: To the Reader.

This does not imply that Regiomontanus is the best system for all purposes: I use *Placidus* for natal work. Regiomontanus is well suited to horary. If you were to divide the sky into equal chunks by eye, Regiomontanus is what you would get. It is observer-based, bringing the division of the heavens right down to Earth, which is wholly appropriate for horary, where the question asked by this person right here now is what determines the reality of the chart.

"But why are the houses in the chart different sizes?" They aren't. They are all equal. Consider your own home. This may be equal to someone else's in many ways: because it covers the same number of square yards; because it has the same number of bedrooms; because it can fetch the same price on the market. It is the same with astrological houses: they are equal in many different ways. Regiomontanus houses are all 30 degrees across, but 30 degrees of Right Ascension, not of Celestial Longitude.[6] As the degrees on the cusps (5 Taurus, 12 Gemini, and so forth) are measured in Celestial Longitude, the houses do not appear to be the same size – just as my house may not be the same size as yours in floor area, but it might be in terms of the number of rooms it has.

There is a fashion among those astrologers who study ancient texts to practice horary with *whole sign houses*. Apart from being philosophically questionable, this sacrifices finesse. Use Regiomontanus: it works, and works well.

This distinction between Right Ascension and Celestial Longitude means that charts cast in Regiomontanus will often have some signs sitting on more than one house cusp, while other signs are completely contained within a house, not being on any house cusp. Signs that are completely contained within a house, having no cusp falling within them, are called *incepted* or *intercepted*. Turn to the chart on page 78, where Aries and Pisces are incepted in the 12th house and Libra and Virgo in the 6th. There is nothing of any significance in a sign being incepted, or a planet being in a sign that is incepted. The sign doesn't happen to have a house cusp in it – that's all.[7]

---

[6] Right Ascension is measurement along the celestial equator. Celestial Longitude is measurement along the ecliptic. They both divide the sky into 360 degrees. Imagine there are two motorways leaving a city. One heads due east, so driving 30 miles along that takes you 30 miles east. The other heads a little north by east: drive 30 miles along that and you have travelled perhaps 25 miles east and a few miles north. But you have still travelled 30 miles. Right Ascension and Celestial Longitude are related to each other in the same way.

[7] The same is true in natal astrology.

When using Regiomontanus (or Placidus), a planet in the 5 degrees or so immediately before a house cusp is regarded as being in that next house. Example: in the chart on page 78 the Moon is at 26 Cancer and the 5th cusp at 28 Cancer. The Moon is within 5 degrees of that cusp, and so in the 5th, not the 4th, house.

This 5-degree limit is flexible: use your common sense. If the house before the cusp is a huge house with one or even two incepted signs in it, we would be more free with this 5-degree limit than if it were a narrow house, with perhaps only 20 degrees of longitude from one side to the other.

NB: to be counted as being in the next house, the planet *must* be in the same sign as the cusp, no matter how close it is to that cusp. If the cusp were at 5.59 Taurus, we would regard a planet at 0.01 Taurus as being in that house; if the cusp were at 0.20 Taurus, a planet at 29.50 Aries would not be regarded as being in that house.

Think of this area in front of the cusp as the front garden of the house. You may not be inside the house, but if you are in the front garden you are on that property – and you are definitely not in the house next door. There is nothing fuzzy or ambiguous about this: the planet is either in the one house or in the other.

This 5-degree rule applies only to houses, not to signs. A planet in the last few degrees of its sign is not regarded as being in the next sign.

Throughout this book, when I describe a planet as being *on* a cusp, I mean that it is in the one or two degrees immediately before that cusp. When I say it is *inside* the cusp, I mean it is in the couple of degrees immediately following that cusp.

HOUSE MEANINGS

As between them the houses contain everything in our world, an exhaustive list of meanings is impossible; this list covers the main topics. Part 2 of this book considers questions typical to each house.[8]

If you are to assign things to their correct houses, it is vital to understand the difference between the thing itself and the function of that thing. The thing is

---

[8] For a discussion of why things belong to the houses that they do, see my *The Real Astrology Applied*, Apprentice Books, London, 2002, p. 147 onwards. Hereafter referred to as *RA Applied*.

what it is; its function may vary. Example: my piano is my possession and it is movable, so it is 2nd house. It has nothing to do with the 5th house of creativity and pleasure. To assign it to the 5th makes irrelevant assumptions: that I can play it; that it is playable; that I enjoy playing it. My piano is my movable possession, and so is 2nd house, even if my only use for it is to conceal a damp patch on the wall.

1st house

Its main role is to show the querent. It shows the querent's body, although in a medical question the whole chart can show the body, in which case the 1st shows the head. It shows 'the ship that I sail in': my immediate vehicle, on the analogy of the body being the vehicle of the soul. The querent's name.

The first is 'me'; it can also be 'us'. When one spouse asks about something that the couple plans to do, the chart can either show querent and spouse individually as 1st and 7th houses, or it can show them both as 1st: 'us'. It also shows larger groups of which the querent is a part ('Will we get the contract?') and larger groups with which the querent identifies ('Will we – meaning the football team the querent supports – win on Saturday?').

The 1st shows the general situation in the querent's location. So if I ask 'Will we have a hot summer?' I look to the 1st: the general situation here.

2nd house

It shows the querent's movable possessions. If it cannot be moved (e.g. your house or land) or if it is animate, it cannot truly be possessed. If it's yours, inanimate and can be moved, it belongs here. So your car is shown by your 2nd house: it's yours and it can be moved. It is not 3rd: remember the distinction between the thing itself and the function of that thing.

It is the querent's money, in whatever form that takes: currency, bank account, stocks and bonds. It is the querent's self-esteem, self-valuing, and also esteem for the partner: esteem, or value, seen as a transferable thing.

It is your closest advisors, like the *consigliere* in *The Godfather*: the one who whispers advice into your ear. In a duel it is your second; in court it is your lawyer and the witnesses who testify on your behalf. Your lawyer is 2nd only if acting for you in this case that is being asked about now; otherwise lawyers belong in the 9th, as learned people.

It is the throat and whatever goes into the throat, hence food. It is what sustains the 1st house.

3rd house

Your siblings and cousins. Your daily round; the routine journeys that you make for the mundane business of your life. These tend to be shorter than the special journeys that we make, hence the common label of 'short journeys' for this house. But if I walk round the corner to visit a shrine, that is a pilgrimage, a 9th-house sort of journey, despite its being so short. Your office could be next door to the church you attend, but your journey to your office would be 3rd house, your journey to church 9th.

The knowledge that you need to negotiate your daily round: the '3 Rs'. The elementary school where you acquire this knowledge. The letter that you are sending. The letter you are expecting is usually shown by the 9th (3rd from the 7th); the letter you keep for sentimental reasons is your possession, and so is 2nd. Rumours and gossip.

Being the opposite house to the 9th (the querent's teacher), it shows the querent's students.

It shows neighbours. Sometimes this is in the biblical sense of 'all those I encounter in my daily round'; more often it is specifically those who live next to my home.

The arms, shoulders and hands.

4th house

Your father; your parents in general; your ancestry. Your immovable possessions: houses and property. Your holiday home in Spain is still 4th house: it is your property that happens to be abroad; there is nothing 9th-house about it. Your orchard and all that grows in it – including that potted plant in your living-room. Your home country ('abroad' being 9th house).

'The end of the matter': the way the situation will turn out. This can usually be ignored, except in questions about trials, where it shows the verdict, and illnesses, where it can show the prognosis. If testimonies in other issues are finely balanced, it can be worth taking a look at the condition of the 4th and its ruler; but do this only as a last resort: strive to find your judgement from the main significators.

Being at the bottom of the chart it shows mines and other things under-ground, such as buried treasure.

The chest and lungs.

Note that although the 4th is at the bottom of the chart, it shows north. The convention here is different from that used on maps: the Ascendant is east, Descendant west, 10th house south. Intermediate directions are derived from these points.

The 4th cusp is also known as the IC (*imum coeli:* lowest part of the heavens).

5th house

Pleasure, and the places where we take pleasure: 'banquets, ale-houses and taverns' as Lilly says; theatres, parties, sports.

Children and pregnancy. Not, note, pregnant women: a pregnant woman is a woman who happens to be pregnant, so she has the same house as she does when she is not pregnant (3rd for my sister, 7th for my wife, etc). As this is the house of pregnancy, it is the house of sex (emphatically not the 8th!). But no matter how tenuous might be the querent's relationship with the sexual partner, that partner is a person, and so is 7th house, not 5th. So even if the querent is married, his mistress is still 7th house; what he does with her is 5th. It is that same distinction between the thing itself and the function of that thing. Although pregnancy is 5th, childbed itself is 12th ('confinement'). The book that I have written or picture I have painted is considered as 'my baby': 5th house.

Being the second house from the 4th, the 5th has important meanings as the father's money and the profit from the querent's property.

It shows messengers and ambassadors.

In the body, it covers the heart, liver, stomach, sides and back.

6th house

This is the house of the unpleasantness the world throws at us, the slings and arrows of outrageous fortune, chief among which is illness. It signifies hospitals – a hospital being literally the house of illness. They are not shown by the 12th: they are places to treat sickness, not places to incarcerate the wicked.

The 6th has nothing whatever to do with the querent's job, no matter how menial or how uncongenial that job might be. It is the querent's employees and servants, such as the tradesman who repairs his car. So 'Should I hire this builder?' would be judged from the 6th house.

It is the querent's subordinates at work. It is those who work *for* him; not work he does himself. When Lilly says that the querent's tenants are shown by the 6th, he assumes a master/servant relationship between them. This is no longer current: if I let a flat to someone, that tenant is shown by my 7th house, not my 6th.

It shows small animals, the traditional criterion for a small animal being that it is smaller than a goat, or too small to ride. So this is the house for the lost cat or dog. It is our uncles and aunts (3rd house from the 4th: our parent's siblings), unless we wish to specify our mother's siblings, in which case the uncles and aunts would be 12th house.

It shows the lower belly, bowels and intestines.

7th house

The 7th shows the querent's partners, whether in an emotional or a business sense. Spouses and sweethearts, no matter how brief the relationship might be or how many such the querent might have. Even if the relationship does not yet exist, but is only desired ('Will Kylie go out with me?') or the individual is as yet unknown ('When will I meet the woman I will marry?'), the person is shown by the 7th. The 'ex' too is 7th-house.

The idea of partnership extends to cover doctors, including alternative practitioners, and astrologers, but only if the doctor is treating the illness at issue in a medical question (so he is the patient's partner in returning to health) or if the astrologer is the one judging this horary right now (the querent's partner in arriving at the truth). Otherwise they both belong to the 9th house, as learned people.

Important: if you are judging your own question, you do *not* also get the 7th house! Yours is the 1st, as querent. You cannot be your own partner.

Even more important: although the 7th does in theory show the astrologer who is judging a question, I cannot recall it ever having been necessary to introduce myself into a client's chart. While there are modern theoreticians of horary who encourage such involvement, I cannot see this as anything other than invasive egotism. The chart belongs to the querent: keep yourself and your muddy boots out of it!

Also partners, albeit briefly, are those with whom we do deals, those from whom we buy or to whom we sell. In 'Will I sell my house?' the central issue is not the house, but the prospective buyer, the person with whom I will do the deal: 7th house.

The other class of people with whom we are intimately engaged is our open enemies: 7th house. My opponent in the chess match; the other party in a court case; anyone applying for the same job as me; the team that the team I support is playing: all 7th house. Thieves are regarded as open enemies.

The 7th shows those of greatest significance to us; it also shows those of least. It is the house of 'any old person': anyone who does not belong to one of the other houses. So 'Will that big movie-star get convicted?' or 'Will that guy who's gone missing come home?' are 7th house. Combine this with the idea of doing deals, and the 7th shows Joe Public, the customer, the client. If you are a practising astrologer, your clients are 7th house.

In the body, it is the reproductive system and the pelvis.

8th house

This is the house of death, which in horary means exactly that: death. There is nothing metaphorical here. Its more usual role, however, is, because it is the 2nd house from the 7th, the other person's money. Either the person with whom the querent is doing a deal ('Will he ever pay me?'), the spouse ('Has he really got as much money as he tells me?') or the enemy ('Will I win the bookie's money with this bet?').

As the 2nd shows the querent's self-esteem, the 8th shows the partner's esteem, seen here almost as a separate entity. If the querent in a relationship question is clearly interested in Lord 8 (the planet ruling the 8th house), this often shows a craving for the other person's esteem rather than a craving for the other person's money.

It is the house of wills and legacies, but only in the most general way ('Will I ever be left a fortune?'). In any specific question on inheritance ('Will I get so-and-so's money?'), look to the dead person's 2nd house.

Lilly says the 8th 'signifies fear and anguish of mind'.[9] By this he means that if the querent's planet is found in the 8th, without any reason for being there (such as the question being about death or the spouse's money), this shows that the querent is anguished over the issue. Fear as a thing in itself ('Can I get over my claustrophobia?') is a 12th-house matter.

In the body, it is the organs of excretion.

The 8th has nothing to do with sex. Nothing. That is a 5th-house matter.

9th house

The 9th shows our special journeys. It is the house of God, religion and all things spiritual, including our pilgrimage, our journey to the Divine. As our special journeys tend to be longer than our routine journeys (3rd house) this also covers most long journeys. But it is the specialness, not the length, of the journey that is the distinguishing feature. If I commute from London to New York twice a

---

[9]   *Lilly*, p. 54.

week, this is a routine journey (3rd house). If I then take a weekend off in a spa 20 miles from my home, this is a special journey (9th house). All holidays (holy-days) are 9th, as are foreign countries.

It is our higher knowledge: in essence, the knowledge that is beyond what we need for our daily routine and is taking us to God. It is the schools and universi-ties where we gain such knowledge. It is our teacher, our priest. That monasteries belong in the 12th is a common error: they are not prisons, but houses of prayer – 9th.[10] All learned people are here, as well as their learning. This includes astrologers.

It is the house of dreams, predictions and prophecies, as well as those who predict and prophesy. Being the house of the wise man, it has an important role in marriage questions from certain cultures: it shows the marriage bureau, which fills the role of the local wise man who would once have arranged the match.

In the body, it is the hips and buttocks.

10th house

The 10th shows the king, the boss in any situation, the government, the prime minister or president, the judge in a court case (judge, jury and the whole court system can be taken as 'the judge'). It is honour, success, glory ('Will I win the Olympic gold?'). It shows the querent's mother.

It is the querent's job or career, whatever that career might be – no matter how menial.

There is a connection between the 10th house and marriage. In the modern world this is relevant *only* to arranged or dynastic marriages, and then *only* to the marriage in its formal nature; the actual relationship between the two people is a 7th-house matter.

It shows the thighs and knees. As with all houses, the chunk of body extends through the sign, moving downwards from the cusp. The top of the thigh is shown by the cusp of the house, the knee by the end of the house, just before the 11th cusp. So with the 1st house, for example, the cusp shows the top of the head; the end of house, just before the 2nd cusp, shows the chin. Suppose, then, we need a significator for the querent's knees. We would look to the 10th house (thighs and knees). But if there is a sign boundary in that house, meaning that the end of the house, towards the 11th cusp, is under a different sign from the 10th cusp, it is the ruler of this second sign (the one ruling the end of the house)

---

[10] When Lilly speaks of 'monkery', by the way, he usually means celibacy, not the act of being a monk.

that we would take as significator of the knees. Example: 10th cusp is at 8 Aries; 11th cusp at 15 Taurus. Taurus therefore begins in the middle of the 10th house and covers the end of that house. We would take Venus, ruler of Taurus, to signify the knees, not Mars.

11th house

As the 8th takes key meanings from being the 2nd house from the 7th, so the 11th takes many of its most important roles from being 2nd from the 10th. As such it shows the boss's money, or my job's money: very important, as this is my wages. It shows the advisors or aides of the 10th house. If the 10th shows the king, the 11th might show the prime minister or the grand vizier; if the 10th shows the prime minister, the 11th would show his cabinet. It shows the king's money, hence 'the gift of the king', and so is the relevant house when the querent wants favours from above ('Will I get the government grant?'). As the king's money, it is crucial in questions such as 'How big is my tax bill going to be?'

It shows 'pennies from Heaven': the bounty that drops into our lap without our struggle or desert – so the win on the lottery or the football pools.

The 11th is the house of 'hopes and wishes'. This is rarely relevant except in a negative sense: what is preventing 'When will I marry?' having the answer desired? Lord 11, your hopes and wishes, is getting in the way: whenever you meet someone at all eligible, the deafening sound of wedding bells scares him off. It is said to cover such abstractions as 'trust' and 'praise', although I have never found these relevant in practice.

It is our friends. Be careful here: the modern use of 'friend', at least in England, is much freer than what is meant. Someone with whom I get along well at work is my colleague (7th house), not my friend; the person with whom I exchange amiable banalities in the pub is my acquaintance (7th again). Nor does the 11th show 'social institutions' as the moderns claim. Trades unions, for instance, are ('Should I join the union?') groups of colleagues: 7th house. They are 'us' ('Can we get a pay-rise out of the boss?'): 1st house. They are groups of servants ('Will the union in the factory I own elect a new leader?'): 6th. They are open enemies ('Can I defeat the union that has closed down my factory?'): 7th. They are not groups of friends.

NB: consider this last paragraph carefully. Note how the same thing can be found in different houses depending on who is asking the question and what that question is.

In the body, the 11th is the calves and ankles.

12th house

This is the house of secret enemies, in contrast to our open enemies in the 7th. Note that it is the nature of the way they harm us that makes our enemies 12th house, not whether we know who they are. Witchcraft, spreading malicious rumours, informing on people: these are 12th-house offences, even if the perpetrator is well known. It is the house of secret things, things hidden from the querent.

We do an effective job of being enemies to ourselves, so the 12th is 'self-undoing': the daft things we do to make our lives more difficult than need be. Our vices; sin. Our fears too undermine us, so our phobias are located here.

As an extension of the idea of the 12th as the house of our self-undoing, that in which we imprison ourselves, it also governs prisons.

The 12th shows animals larger than goats. In the body, it governs the feet.

As we saw with the example of trades unions in the section on the 11th house, the house we look to for any person or thing will vary depending on the question. **It is the question that determines the reality of the chart.** If the Prime Minister asks, 'Will I be re-elected?' he is 1st house, like any other querent. If I ask, 'Will the Prime Minister be re-elected?' he is my king, and so is 10th house. If an American asks, 'Will the Prime Minister be re-elected?' the Prime Minister is the king of a foreign country: 10th from the 9th, which is the 6th house. If the Prime Minister's wife asks, 'Will my darling like the socks I bought him for Christmas?' his role is as her husband: 7th house.

TURNING THE CHART

In this review of house meanings I have given several examples of houses that are derived from other houses, such as 'the king of a foreign country (10th from the 9th)' in the last paragraph. Deriving one house from another is called 'turning the chart'.

Example: if I ask the question, 'How is my daughter's career shaping up?' it is no good my looking at the 10th house of the chart, because that is my career, not hers. I need to look at her 10th house. First I must locate my daughter (5th house) and then take the 10th house from that. The 10th from the 5th is the 2nd house of the chart.

What we are doing here is to treat the 5th as if it were the Ascendant and count 10 houses from there – hence the term 'turning the chart'.

When turning, always count the house you start with as '1'. So the 5th house is my daughter's 1st; the 6th is her 2nd house; the 7th is her 3rd house. Until you get used to this, you may find it helpful to put your finger on the house you are starting from, counting '1', and then count round from there. The chart as we usually approach it, with the 1st house showing the querent, is called the *radical* chart. This is 'radical' in its literal sense of 'root'. If I am the querent, I am shown by the radical 1st house and my daughter by the radical 5th.

Follow these meanings round the chart, counting from the radical 5th house. Don't just read this: look at the chart and let your fingers do the walking!

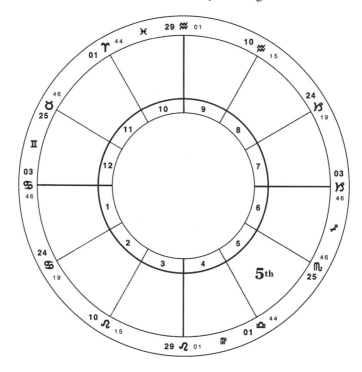

My daughter's bracelet is her 2nd house. 2nd from the 5th is the radical 6th.

My daughter's neighbour is her 3rd. 3rd from the 5th is the radical 7th.

My daughter's orchard is her 4th. 4th from the 5th is the radical 8th.

My daughter's son (hence my grandson) is her 5th. 5th from the 5th is the radical 9th.

My daughter's dog is her 6th. 6th from the 5th is the radical 10th.

My daughter's husband is her 7th. 7th from the 5th is the radical 11th.

My daughter's husband's money is the 2nd from *her* 7th. This is the 2nd from the 11th, which is the radical 12th. Here we have turned the chart twice.

My daughter's piano teacher is her 9th, which is the radical 1st. Her husband's brother is also the radical 1st, because it is the 3rd house from her 7th.

My daughter's career is her 10th, which is the radical 2nd. So is her father-in-law: her husband's father, which is the 4th from her 7th.

My daughter's friend is her 11th, which is the radical 3rd. So is the money she might hope to inherit from her father-in-law: it is the 2nd from the 4th from her 7th. (Her 7th is her husband; the 4th from there is her father-in-law; the 2nd from there is his money.)

My daughter's horse is her 12th, which is the radical 4th. So is her husband's manservant, which is the 6th from her 7th.

You have seen examples here of turning the chart more than once. You can turn it as often as is necessary, but the more you do the more it loses focus: if there is a short-cut, take it. For instance, my daughter's mother is never the 10th from the 5th; she is my wife, which is the radical 7th. This would be so even if I were now married to somebody else, or if we had never married. My daughter's father is not the radical 8th (4th from the 5th); her father is me, and I am the querent: 1st house.

Do not read significance into other meanings of the house you reach when turning. The 8th house (death) from the 4th (my father) is the 11th (my friend). This does not mean that my friend will kill my father; it means only that my father's death is signified by the 11th house.

Turning implies some kind of 'belonging to'. If the object does not, in a real sense, belong to the person, avoid turning the chart. The bigger the thing, the more likely we are to look to the radical, not the turned, chart. If the question is 'How will my brother get on in his new job?' look at the 10th from the 3rd. But if it were 'Will my brother win Olympic gold?' look to the radical – not the turned – 10th. It is still a 10th house matter, but the victory does not belong to the brother in the same way that his job does. Or if it were 'Is my brother's teacher helping him?' the teacher would be 9th from the 3rd; if it were 'Will my brother do well at university?' it would be the radical 9th. In some way, the teacher 'belongs' to the brother in a way that the university does not – even though we might talk about 'my brother's university'.

If, however, the question were 'Will my grandson get into university?' we would have to turn the chart. The grandson is himself 9th house (child's child: 5th from the 5th), so we cannot also use that for the university. We would have to take the 9th from the 9th.

For death and imprisonment, look at *both* the turned and the radical 8th or 12th house. Usually one or other is clearly in play; sometimes both.

Occasionally there is not a cut and dried answer to which house we should look at: in practice, I find that if there is a genuine ambivalence, the chart reflects this and gives the same answer from both possible houses.

We've worked all the way round the chart, turning from the 5th house. Now look at some other examples, taken at random. Work through this list, writing down your answers. Don't just think them: write them down. Then turn to Appendix 2 for the answers. Some of these require you to turn the chart, some don't. Assume that you are the querent, so e.g. your father will be 4th house, your cat 6th. You will never be asked questions about many of these, but every example increases your facility in turning the chart, increasing your fluency in the language of astrology.

Even if you are a hardened horary astrologer, do this exercise and read the answers: there is a lot of important information there.

Your son's pet rabbit
Your father's house
Your pregnant sister
Your new car
Your journey to work
Your boss
The guy who shares your office
The dream your friend is telling you about
Your brothers
Your younger brother, in contrast to your elder brother
Your children
Your younger child, in contrast to your elder child
Your ex-spouse
The local priest

The priest's brother
The priest's sister-in-law
The priest's sister-in-law's neighbour
The king of Spain
Your father's liver
That packet of rice you bought this morning
That wrap of cocaine you bought this morning
The book you borrowed from the library
The book you have written
The person who told the cops about your secret life as a criminal mastermind
Your butler
Your job as a butler
Mines
The man who's come to repair your plumbing
The man who's just whispered a hot tip for the next race into your ear
Your university
Your daughter's university
Your teacher's university
Astrology
Particle physics
Your mistress's brother's Great Dane
The cruise you're thinking of taking
The ship on which you'll be taking it
Your dog's ball
Your mother's friend's child

4

The Planets

Planets acquire meanings in two ways. One is by the houses that they rule; the other is through their natural associations. The first of these is by far the more important in horary.

The planet that rules the sign in which a house cusp falls rules that house, or is *Lord* of that house. So if the cusp of the second house were at 15 Cancer, the Moon, ruler of Cancer, would be Lord of the second, or Lord 2. If the cusp of the fourth house were at 29 Virgo, Mercury, ruler of Virgo, would be Lord 4. This planet is the *significator* of that house. Hence it represents the things of that house in the chart – whichever things are relevant to the question asked. The Moon as Lord 2 might be significator of the querent's money or his lawyer; Mercury as Lord 4 might signify the querent's father or his home. Which meaning it takes will be determined by the question.

It doesn't matter which planet it is: if it rules the house it is significator of the things of that house. This is so even if the planet does not appear to describe that thing. Example: if a boy asks, 'Does my girlfriend really love me?' his girlfriend is signified by the ruler of the 7th house, even if that planet is Mars; the boy himself will be signified by the ruler of the 1st, even if that is Venus. Nor would this tell us that he is effeminate and she wears the trousers. The planets are the actors in the drama that is the chart; when the casting-director is handing out parts he evidently doesn't take much time choosing who gets which.

A house has one ruler and one ruler only. This is the planet that rules the sign on its cusp. This is so even if that cusp is at 29.59 degrees of its sign. There is no such thing as a *co-ruler*: this is a modern abomination.

The planet ruling another sign in that house may, however, be significant; but this will only be if the concept of *next* is relevant to the question. 'Will my next job be any better than the one I've got now?' The ruler of the sign on the 10th cusp will show the present job; the ruler of the next sign, in the usual order of the signs, will show the putative next job. (This *next* could equally well be shown by

Lord 10 about to leave the sign it is in. The sign it is about to enter would then show the next job.)

Sign-rulers

The planets ruling each sign are these:

♈	♂	♎	♀
♉	♀	♏	♂
♊	☿	♐	♃
♋	☽	♑	♄
♌	☉	♒	♄
♍	☿	♓	♃

You will notice that there is no place here for Uranus, Neptune or Pluto. If your previous astrological study has taught you that these planets rule signs, put that idea aside while you are studying horary. You will soon find that using the traditional sign-rulers works.[11]

Alternatives to house rulers

The ruler of the next sign round will never be co-ruler of that house; it can become sole ruler if the Lord of that house is already busy doing something else. Suppose I ask 'Will I get this job?' and find Virgo on the Ascendant and Gemini on the 10th cusp. Mercury, as ruler of both these signs, would signify me (the querent: Lord 1) and the job (Lord 10). We can take the ruler of the next sign to the sign on the 10th cusp to signify the job (following the usual order of the signs). This will usually be necessary only if we need to find an aspect between querent and quesited in order to answer the question, in which case we must, of course, have different significators for them.

Sometimes it is not necessary to distinguish between the querent and the thing asked about. It is common, for instance, when the self-employed ask about their jobs, to find Lords 1 and 10 the same. This makes sense: within the context of the question, person and job are effectively the same. But if the question is 'Will I get the job?' we must have different significators for person and job.

[11] For a full discussion of the recently discovered planets, see my *The Real Astrology*, Apprentice Books, London, 2001, chapter 6. Hereafter referred to as *Real Astrology*.

Sometimes the querent is of less importance to the issue than the quesited, so the quesited can be given the disputed planet. In many questions about third parties the querent has no part in the drama, so does not need to be assigned a significator. 'My friend is ill; will she get better?': we do not need to involve the querent in our judgement at all. 'Where is the cat?': the cat is where it is, regardless of the querent; so if Lords 1 and 6 (small animals: 6th house) were the same, we could use that planet as significator of the cat. Such a question usually has an implied 'Will I see him again and when?': we can still answer this by using the Moon to signify the querent.

Instead of taking the ruler of the next sign, we can use another planet if – and only if – it is within a couple of degrees of the cusp of the house in question and in the same sign as that cusp. This is the *only* time when a planet can be taken as significator because it is in a house: when the house ruler is already in use and the planet is right on the cusp. Otherwise: **planets in a house affect that house for better or for worse; they do not rule it.**

We can also use the *almuten* of the house cusp, but I suggest you keep this for emergencies: only when none of the options above makes sense. I can recall having done this in only one chart. Finding the almuten is discussed on page 51.

The Moon

The Moon is always cosignificator of the querent, unless it is main significator of the quesited. This means that the querent usually has two significators: Lord 1 and the Moon. But if, for example, the question is 'Will I get the job?' and the Moon rules the 10th house, it signifies the job, not the querent. If the Moon signifies the quesited, the quesited has prior claim on its services and the querent must do without it as cosignificator.

In third-party questions ('Will my sister marry this man?') the Moon does not get transferred to the person asked about: it is cosignificator of the querent, not of anyone else. In such questions it is not usually necessary to involve the querent's planets, but the placement of the Moon will often show where the querent's interest lies.

Although both Moon and Lord 1 signify the querent, the Moon is more weighted towards the querent's emotions, especially in relationship matters. Although both Moon and Lord 1 signify the querent, and an aspect from either of them to the significator of the quesited will usually give a positive answer, aspects from the Moon are never quite as convincing as those from Lord 1. In such cases it is reassuring if we can find some supporting testimony.

What does this planet signify?

We begin our judgement with the houses that are relevant to the question, taking the planets that rule them as significators of the things of those houses. These planets are our main players, the actors of the leading roles in the drama. Often, however, another planet will involve itself in the action, whether by aspect, strong reception or placement in one of the relevant houses. How do we find out what such a planet represents?

With great caution. It is here that we face the biggest risk of committing the cardinal sin of the horary astrologer: writing our own stories, our own assumptions, into the chart. Suppose we are judging a relationship question. The rulers of the 1st and 7th houses are our main players. We notice another planet involved in the action, and see that it rules the 9th house. 'Aha!' we think, 'The 9th is the 3rd from the 7th: the wife's brother!' And so we quickly construct a compelling fantasy starring the wife's brother. Only to be to be told that the wife doesn't have a brother, but that the couple's grandson (5th from the 5th = 9th) is central to the issue at hand. Any house can mean a huge number of things, and we are most unlikely to plump on the right one by chance.

When deciding what an unidentified planet might mean, keep your imagination on a short lead and, if possible, bounce your ideas off the querent. Remember it is a consultation: we are allowed to ask the querent whatever questions we need in order to elucidate the chart. Even a completely open question can be useful: 'There seems to be someone else involved in this matter – do you have any idea who that might be?'

Sometimes the house that planet rules will give us its meaning. Often the planet can be taken as 'some other person', its meanings by house rulership being irrelevant. As a general rule, always go for the most concrete of the options available. For example, Lord 10 can signify glory or honour, and sometimes does; it is more likely to signify something less abstract: the boss, the job, the mother.

Once you have decided upon a plausible identification, studying the receptions involving that planet – hence what the other players think of it and what it thinks of them – will usually either confirm this identification or prove it wrong. Then you can either proceed with judgement or think again about what this planet signifies.

NATURAL RULERSHIPS

Rulerships determined by the house a planet rules in that chart, called *accidental rulerships*, are what primarily concern us, but the planets also have their natural associations. Everything is made of all seven planetary influences combined in differing proportions. One or two of these influences will be particularly obvious in any thing that we might consider. Which one of them takes our attention will depend upon the context of the enquiry. The classic example is the rose: it is ruled by Venus, as shown by its beauty; it is ruled by Mars, as shown by its thorns. Or the slug: ruled by Saturn, as being black and nasty and living under stones; by the Moon, as being soft and moist and coming out at night.

These natural rulerships will occasionally be significant in the chart. If we are looking for some lost documents, for example, we might look at Mercury, the natural ruler of documents. In boy/girl questions we will look to the Sun, as natural ruler of men, and Venus, natural ruler of women. The Moon is natural ruler of any lost object, especially an animate one. These natural rulers will sometimes offer information supplementary to what the house ruler tells us; sometimes the chart will emphasise them in so strong a way that we can judge by them alone.

Although the importance of natural rulerships is minor compared to that of the accidental rulerships, it is worth becoming fluent in them. This is best done by putting planets to objects as you come across them in your daily round, as you might learn a language by translating everything you see into that language. Working from the guidelines below, you will soon find it simple: 'Corn Flakes: Sun, as corn is a staple food; Saturn, because they are crispy; Mercury, because they are small and come in great number. Milk: Moon, as a liquid, and because it's white. Sugar: Venus, as it's sweet; Mars, for the energy it gives.'

If you need to find the ruler of an object, go for the essential nature of that object. Consider: what is the natural ruler of a camera? It is a mechanical contrivance: Mercury. It is used to take pretty pictures: Venus. It is used for reportage: Mercury. It works by writing (Mercury) with light (Sun) by means of mirrors (Moon). All this is true. But what is its essential nature? What does a camera do? Its essence is in what it is, not in what it can be used for (taking pretty pictures, reportage), nor in how it does it (machinery, writing with light). A camera's essential function is to capture the ephemeral. So its essence is in capturing, preserving, and its natural ruler is Saturn. Follow this logic with any other item and you will not go wrong.

An exhaustive listing of natural rulerships is impossible: it would mean listing everything that exists. The following should give sufficient clues to enable you to find the appropriate ruler for anything.

Saturn

Cold and dry; diurnal;[12] masculine.

Saturn rules things that are old, black, hard, heavy, dead, decayed, restrictive, dry, cold, solitary, sad.

Examples: root vegetables, because they grow underground. Nightshade, because of its colour and because it is deadly (also Venus for its cosmetic qualities). Liquorice, for its colour and as a root. Mildew. All waste products and refuse. Lead, for its weight; hence also plumbers, who work with lead. Sewermen. Undertakers. Miners. Farm labourers. Gardeners (Saturn was god of agriculture). Discipline. Prisons, ruins, toilets.

Opium, as a narcotic and because it is addictive, creating new barriers. The yew is very saturnine: it has dark foliage; it is poisonous; it grows to a great age; it lives in graveyards. Saturn rules locks; Mercury rules keys. Saturn is natural ruler of fathers in night charts.[13]

Moles, dogs, cats, scavengers, things that live under stones. Sapphire, lapis lazuli. In the body, it rules the right ear, bones, teeth, skin, joints, spleen.

Jupiter

Hot and moist; diurnal; masculine.

Jupiter rules things that are big, expansive, expensive, luxurious, religious, purple, laxative (in contrast to Saturn, which is binding), generous.

Examples: fruit trees, for the abundance of good things they produce. Rich men, aristocrats, judges, priests. Rhubarb. Feasts. Foie gras. Teachers (who have knowledge and pour it out). Gurus. Ivy is ruled by Jupiter because it spreads, by Saturn for its dark colour and association with dark places and decay. Rain. Mercy.

Big animals; animals that are gentle and of benefit to mankind. Amethyst, sapphire (has both Jupiter and Saturn nature), emerald, crystal, tin.

In the body it rules the left ear, lungs, liver, blood, semen.

---

[12] Diurnal planets prefer being above the Earth by day, below it by night. Nocturnal planets prefer the reverse. See p. 68, hayz.

[13] A night chart is one cast during the night; a day chart one cast during the day. In a day chart the Sun will be in houses 7-12; at night it is below the Earth, in houses 1-6. Allow a few degrees in favour of day at both the Ascendant and Descendant, as it is light for a little while before the Sun rises and after it sets.

Mars

Hot and dry; nocturnal; masculine.

Mars rules things that are sharp, burning, cutting, red, abrasive, hot, aggressive.

Examples: soldiers, butchers, tailors, surgeons, barbers, pirates. Anyone who works with fire, hence alchemists, cooks, firemen. Executioners. Peppers, garlic (also by the Moon, for its colour), radishes (also Moon). Nettles, thistles (both also Saturn, as they grow on waste ground). Divorce. Fevers. Lust.

Animals that are fierce or fiery; creatures that bite or sting. Iron, bloodstone, jasper, coral.

In the body, Mars rules the gall bladder and the genitals (especially male).

The Sun

Hot and dry; diurnal; masculine.

The Sun rules things that are unique, royal, golden, life-giving, honest.

Examples: as giver of life, the Sun rules all food, and staples in particular. Citrus fruit, for its appearance, as also sunflowers, marigolds etc. The king of every classification: gold, as king of metals; the eagle, as king of birds; lions, as king of beasts; diamond as king of jewels. Pride. Whoever is in charge. Goldsmiths, minters of money. Amber. Palaces and other grand buildings. The Sun is natural ruler of fathers in day charts.

In the body it rules the vital spirit or life-force, the heart, the brain (seen as the controlling principle) and the eyes – the eyes in general and, specifically, the right eye in males, the left eye in females.

Venus

Cold and moist; nocturnal; feminine.

Venus rules things that are soft, pretty, fragrant, attractive, pleasant.

Examples: flowers (in general: each variety has its own ruler). Soft fruit. Chocolate. Kisses. Marriage. Treaties. Fun. Art, music. Make-up and perfume.

Jewellers, musicians, the person whose main function at work is to look nice, fashionistas, prostitutes, drapers, decorators. Beds, wardrobes. Wives, young women.

Soft and cuddly animals – the typical inhabitants of a children's zoo. Copper, brass, cornelian, azure sapphire, lapis lazuli, beryl, chrysolite.

Venus is natural ruler of mothers in daytime charts.

In the body she rules the kidneys, the sense of smell and the genitals (especially female).

Mercury

Cold and dry; diurnal if preceding the Sun (oriental), nocturnal if following it (occidental);[14] mixed male/female nature, becoming male if with male planets, female if with female.

Mercury rules things that are parti-coloured, ambiguous, dextrous, tricky, mixed.

Examples: sweet & sour sauce, cocktails, pizza. Things that are small and come in great number: berries, currants, aniseeds. Things that grow in husks, on the analogy of the brain within the skull – especially walnuts, which look like brains. Beans, which produce wind (ruled by Mercury, whether bodily or atmospheric). Earthquakes (wind in the Earth). Anything that speaks, or otherwise resembles man: monkeys, parrots, puppets, bees, hyenas (because they laugh). Things that are volatile, such as lavender oil. Siccatives. Things that mimic mental process, hence keys, that undo the lock of a problem. Thieves, servants. Tricksters, con-men, pickpockets. Variety. Virtuosi. Auctioneers, agents and dealers. Merchants. The knowledge needed for any trade. Wits, humorists. The human being. Articulation, talk, lies. Computers. Astrology and astrologers. Clerks, accountants, scribes, messengers, 'media people'. Doctors, medicines. Lawyers (who speak for you). Anyone's 'right-hand man'. Documents, papers, books, magazines.

In the body it rules the tongue, brain (as seat of reason), arms, hands and fingers.

The Moon

Cold and moist; nocturnal; feminine.

The Moon rules things that are liquid, soft, of little flavour or substance, formless, white, new.

Examples: cabbages, for their shape. Cucumbers, melons for their water content. Babies; midwives; the mother, in a night chart. Mushrooms, for their colour, shape, and because they appear overnight. Candles, because they light the darkness. Lost objects. Intoxicants. Changeability, fickleness. Novelty. The

---

[14] See p. 67 for an explanation of oriental and occidental.

common people. Queens, but only as the wife of the king (Sun), not if ruling in her own right, when she would be the Sun. Tramps, pilgrims, beggars, sailors, midwives, barmen, nurses, cleaners.

Creatures that live in water: fish, otters, frogs, ducks, oysters. Or that come out at night: slugs, owls, bushbabies. Pearls, moonstone, alabaster.

In the body she rules the breasts, womb, belly and intestines.

Age

There is a rising scale of age from the Moon, which rules babies, through Mercury, Venus, Sun, Mars and Jupiter to Saturn, which rules the old. This is 'the Seven Ages of Man'.

The outer planets

Uranus, Neptune and Pluto do have their uses in horary, but these uses are limited. They have not a fraction of the importance with which they are invested by most contemporary astrologers. They each have a very few things with which they seem to have a natural connection: Uranus with divorce and other disruption, such as house-moving; Neptune with illusion and deceit; Pluto seems generally and unspecifically malefic.

Treat them much like fixed stars: ignore them unless they are right on a relevant house cusp or in immediate aspect with one of the main significators.

Example 1: if the question is 'Have I got a future with Cedric?' and Uranus is sitting on the Ascendant, it is a strong testimony that the relationship will soon come to an end. If Uranus is floating around in the middle of the first house, however, it means nothing.

Example 2: a client asked a series of questions relating to the sale of her business. Each of these charts had Neptune on the cusp of either the 7th house (the buyer) or the 8th (the 2nd from the 7th: the buyer's money). She was being cheated.

The outer planets do *not* rule signs and they do *not* have any particular associations with any of the signs. The reasoning that suggests that they might is utterly groundless. The reader familiar with modern astrology may be reluctant to abandon these ideas, but if you insist on incorporating them in your charts you will consistently get wrong answers. This is not a matter of opinion.

If the placement of an outer planet demands our attention, it can, like a powerful fixed star, provide a shorthand answer. We will never need to go looking for them ('What is Uranus doing in this chart?') and we will never find them telling us anything that is not equally well shown by the seven planets of the traditional cosmos.

Example: a client asked about her impending divorce. Uranus was on the Midheaven, symbolically halfway between the Ascendant (the querent) and the 7th cusp (her husband). Mars, the traditional ruler of divorce, exactly squared the Ascendant/Descendant axis. Both planets showed the same thing.

Chiron, asteroids, Dark Moon Lilith, Sedna: none of these has any place in horary. No matter how attached to these little fellas you might be, incorporating them in your charts will do nothing but confuse you.

Friends and enemies

If you've read the old texts you will have found lists of which planets are friendly with which, and which are enemies. These lists are irrelevant in horary, because the 'who likes whom' in the immediate context – which is all that concerns us – is shown by the receptions. Example: it is all very well that Mars is in principle a friend to Venus, but that he hates this Venus here right now is all that concerns us when judging this particular chart.

Superior and inferior

The *superior* planets are Mars, Jupiter and Saturn, the *inferior* are Mercury, Venus and the Moon. They are so called because the superior planets have, from the perspective of the Earth, their orbits above that of the Sun (*superior* in Latin = higher) and the inferior have theirs below (*inferior* in Latin = lower). This distinction has no practical relevance in horary.

5

The Signs

The signs of the zodiac are treated quite differently in traditional and modern astrology. Now is the time to reach into your head, locate all you have learned about the signs from the moderns and set that aside.

The signs describe the planets that are in them. In our astrological sentences, the planets are the nouns, the signs are the adjectives and the aspects are the verbs. The sign does not *do* anything: it has no power to act. It simply describes.

The sign a planet is in describes it in three different ways:

1. it tells us how much essential strength the planet has
2. it tells us about that planet's attitude to other planets
3. it has certain qualities of its own.

Point 1 will be considered in chapter 6 and point 2 in chapter 8. Here we shall consider point 3: the divisions of the signs into various groups with shared characteristics.

In most questions most of these characteristics will be irrelevant, just as if I am asking my friend to lend me some money, the fact that he walks with a limp is of no concern. But in some questions these points can be crucial. If the question is 'Will I have a baby this year?' and every significator is in a barren sign, it is most unlikely that we could judge 'Yes', whatever aspects there might be. It is easy to overlook such basic information in the rush to hunt down an aspect.

Note: while the signs do have a set of shared characteristics, they do not have the rounded personalities that they are given in modern astrology. For instance, a planet in Leo is not going to behave in a regal fashion. Leo is a feral sign, and so is inclined to behave like a wild beast – if the context supports this. It is unlikely to manage to be both feral and regal at the same time.

Male and female

♈♊♌♎♐♒ are male; ♉♋♍♏♑♓ female. This division is useful mainly for determining the sex of babies or thieves. It can be helpful when we need to distinguish between various options, as in 'Which of these candidates should I employ?' In such questions we must find a way to distinguish the various candidates, so a division by sex may help.

Elements

♉♍♑ are earth; ♊♎♒ air; ♈♌♐ fire; ♋♏♓ water. Useful mainly in locating lost objects. Can be helpful in vocational questions: 'Should I become an accountant (air, because air relates to the faculty of reason) or a farmer (earth)?' Lord 10 strong in an air sign: testimony in favour of accountancy.

Earth signs are cold and dry; water, cold and moist; fire, hot and dry; air, hot and moist. These few words contain almost everything that is needed for forecasting the weather through horary.

Modes

♈♋♎♑ are cardinal; ♉♌♏♒ fixed; ♊♍♐♓ mutable. The cardinal signs show action that is quick but doesn't last; fixed signs are slow and stable; mutable come and go. This division is useful in many contexts.

The significator of an illness is fixed: it is chronic; cardinal: it is acute; mutable: it will come and go.

'I want to win this dispute, but I don't think it's worth going to court; can I win?' Opponent's significator in a fixed sign: 'No, he'll fight it out'. In a cardinal sign: 'Show him you mean business and he'll give in'.

Mutable signs are less inclined to be reliable or honest.

The cardinal signs are also known as *moveable signs*. Be careful here: moveable and mutable are words easily confused.

Double-bodied signs

The mutable signs are also known as *double-bodied*. This emphasises the duality that is so important a part of their nature.

In questions where someone is considering leaving a steady job to freelance or work part-time, the transition is often shown by the significator entering a double-bodied sign. Duality: freelancing means having more than one boss and sometimes pursuing more than one trade; in part-time work and job-sharing the time or the job is split.

In some questions ('Should *we* do such and such?') it is unclear whether the 1st house should be given to the couple or group, or if the querent should have the 1st and the partner or colleagues should be treated separately and given the 7th. Finding Lord 1 in a double-bodied sign is strong testimony for taking it as significator for the couple or group.

In questions of number (how many babies or thieves), double-bodied signs show more than one.

Note: the double-bodied signs are ♊♍♐♓. These and these only. Regardless of whether you can see the duality in the image of this sign, or if you can find duality in the image of any other sign.

Fertile and barren

The water signs are fertile. Gemini, Leo and Virgo are barren. The other six signs can be regarded as neutral.[15] This relates of course to procreation, but also to other things. If my investments are in a fertile sign they are more likely to grow than if they are in a barren.

Of the barren signs, Gemini and Virgo are also double-bodied, so in questions like 'Will I have children?' they are testimonies for 'No'; but if the judgement from the whole chart is 'Yes', their double-bodiedness will be testimony for more than one child.

Voiced and mute

The water signs are mute; Gemini, Virgo and Libra are loud-voiced; Aries, Taurus, Leo and Sagittarius are half-voiced; Capricorn and Aquarius weak-voiced.

This division is useful in vocational questions ('Am I the singer or the songwriter?'). Another example: a woman asked about her marital problems. Among other testimonies in the analysis, her heart was seen to love her husband while her head disliked him. Her head was in a loud-voiced sign, while her heart was mute – so all he heard from her was the dislike.

---

[15] This is only in horary. In natal work we divide the other six into mildly fertile and mildly barren.

Humane and bestial

The air signs and Virgo are humane. Aries, Taurus, Leo, Sagittarius and Capricorn are bestial, of which Leo and the second half of Sagittarius are feral.

Suppose I ask how my neighbour will react if I complain about the noise he makes: his significator in a humane sign is one testimony that he will behave in a reasonable fashion, in a manner befitting a human being; in a bestial sign suggests he will behave like a beast; in a feral sign, like a wild beast.

Maimed

Aries, Taurus, Leo and Pisces are described as maimed. This may be useful for physical descriptions.

There are many other such divisions, but these are the only ones I have ever found of practical use. Important: all these testimonies are 'all things being equal'. Any single testimony can be outweighed. Use your common sense. For example, fixed signs show stability, but a planet at the end of a fixed sign will show a stable situation coming to an end. 'Will Bugsy squeal?' with his significator at the end of Scorpio, a fixed, mute sign: 'Not now, but he soon will'.

While these testimonies can all be overruled, in some charts the information given by these basic divisions will be all we need for judgement. 'Is my job secure?' with Lord 10 in the middle of a fixed sign. All we need do is glance quickly around the chart to check for contrary testimonies; if we find none we can give our answer: 'Yes, it is'. Judgement can be this simple.

The body

The body is divided among the signs, starting with Aries at the top and working down to Pisces at the toes.

♈:	the head	♎:	urinary system, lower back
♉:	the neck	♏:	genitals and anus
♊:	hands, arms and shoulders	♐:	thighs and buttocks
♋:	the breast	♑:	the knees
♌:	the heart and ribs	♒:	calves and ankles
♍:	intestines and related organs	♓:	the feet

6

Essential Dignity

Horary is commonly presented as being aspect driven. Find your significators, find an aspect between them, and there you have a Yes to the question. This works fine – so long as you don't mind being consistently wrong in your judgements.

The aspect is an important part of judgement, but it is only a part. What the aspect provides is the occasion for an event to take place. No occasion: no event. That is clear enough; but we can have an occasion without an event, or without the event turning out as we wish. We have the occasion: I ask her to marry me; but she can't stand me, so she says 'No'. Occasion alone does not give us a full answer.

For this reason, dignity and reception are of supreme importance. They are the twin keys to judgement.

> **Dignity shows power to act**
> **Reception shows inclination to act**
> **Aspect shows occasion to act.**

There is a clear theoretical distinction between essential and accidental dignity. In theory it is accidental dignity that shows the power to act, while essential dignity shows how pure is the motive behind this action. We do not live in a theoretical world, however, so in practice this distinction is often blurred, even to the extent of disappearing altogether. If the context allows an opportunity for this distinction to manifest, it will – for instance in questions about court cases, where the essential dignity shows who is in the right and the accidental considerations show who is going to win.

Accidental dignity is considered in chapter 7, reception in chapter 8. This chapter is on essential dignity.

The word 'essential' is used in its strict sense: this is dignity that pertains to the essence of the thing. Essence is from the Latin *esse*: to be. It is the is-ness of the thing; its being that and no other; the John-ness in me, that makes me me and no one else; the Malinka-ness in my dog that makes her what she is and no thing else; the you-ness in you that is the intangible but so important quality rendering you different from all others who share your race, sex, size, hair-colour, attitudes, etc. The idea of essence is not accepted in the modern world, because we cannot grab a chunk of essence and weigh it or measure it; it is nonetheless, in the common sense of the word, essential.[16]

Being created by God, who is infinitely good, all things are created good. This includes planets. Evil is not a thing in itself: it has no essence, no being. It is the absence of good, in the same way that darkness is not a thing in itself, but is the absence of light. So although Saturn and Mars are known as *malefics,* the *Greater* and the *Lesser Malefic* respectively, they are not in their essence malign. We just don't much like them, even when they are on their best behaviour. Mars, for instance, rules surgery: however necessary surgery might be, it is not pleasant. When Jupiter or Venus – the *Greater* and the *Lesser Benefic* – is in detriment or fall there is likely to be a pleasing veneer over something unpleasant or harmful. A question was asked about a woman who had suffered a severe allergic reaction to a soft drink. The drink was signified by Venus in Virgo, the sign of its fall: the drink tasted good (Venus) but was harmful (in fall).

The more essential dignity a planet has, the better it conforms to its innate good nature, and so is able to show itself at its best. The more debilitated it is, the more it is deformed from this innate goodness, and so manifests its nastier side. This is true of any planet:

Any planet in its detriment or fall can be malign.
Any planet in its sign or exaltation can behave well.

This is one of the most important rules in astrology. Although it is usual to call Jupiter and Venus benefics and Saturn and Mars malefics, I urge you to treat any planet that is essentially debilitated as malefic, any planet that is essentially strong as benefic.

This strength or weakness is usually contained within the context of the question. A querent asked 'Will I get this job?' and was signified by Saturn retrograde in Aries. Our first thought might well be, 'Would anyone employ Saturn retrograde in its fall?' and this first thought is an important testimony. But it does not mean that our querent is an evil person; it means that she is in a mess, may

---

[16] For a fuller discussion of essence and its relevance to astrology, see *Real Astrology*, chapter 7.

well be applying for the job out of desperation, and is probably little qualified to do it. Always read testimonies in context. Similarly another querent asked when she would find her next boyfriend. Her significators were Venus in Taurus and the Moon in Cancer. This does not mean that she was a candidate for sainthood, only that she was very good-looking and knew it. Context, again.

A direct descriptive relevance within the context can override the positive or negative indications of any dignity or debility, whether essential or accidental. A lost umbrella was signified by Saturn in Cancer. This is a perfect description of the object: it is a barrier (Saturn). What sort of barrier? A wet sort of barrier (Cancer). Even though Saturn is in its detriment, this placement can be taken as descriptive and does not mean it was a decrepit umbrella.

Another example: Jupiter in Pisces is a strongly dignified benefic. But if I ask what the weather will be at the beach, Jupiter, god of rain, in watery Pisces would be a malefic within the context of my question.

The essential dignities and debilities of the planets are given in the following table. Planets gain dignity or debility by being in certain signs or in certain parts of signs. Let us work through this table from left to right. Don't worry – you don't need to memorise it! You will find it is worth knowing the major dignities and debilities by heart; the terms and faces will begin to stick over time.

Sign rulership

Being in its own sign is the strongest essential dignity. Examples: Mars in Aries, Jupiter in Pisces. This is likened to a man being in his own home, in the sense of 'an Englishman's home is his castle'. He is the master there, able to order everything as he wishes, and so is content. Such a planet is well able to manifest its essential goodness. Old texts often have a D or an N next to the planetary glyph in this column, standing for Day or Night. The distinction between a planet's day sign and its night sign is, however, of purely theoretical significance: it has no use in practice and should be ignored.

Exaltation

Each planet is exalted in one sign; some signs have no planet exalted. Examples: Venus is exalted in Pisces, Saturn in Libra. A planet in its exaltation is likened to an honoured guest in someone's home. In some ways the honoured guest is

Sign	Ruler	Exalt- ation	Triplicity		Term					Face			Detri- ment	Fall
			Day	Night										
♈	♂	☉ 19	☉	♃	♃ 6	♀ 14	☿ 21	♂ 26	♄ 30	♂ 10	☉ 20	♀ 30	♀	♄
♉	♀	☽ 3	♀	☽	♀ 8	☿ 15	♃ 22	♄ 26	♂ 30	☿ 10	☽ 20	♄ 30	♂	
♊	☿		♄	☿	☿ 7	♃ 14	♀ 21	♄ 25	♂ 30	♃ 10	♂ 20	☉ 30	♃	
♋	☽	♃ 15	♂	♂	♂ 6	♃ 13	☿ 20	♀ 27	♄ 30	♀ 10	☿ 20	☽ 30	♄	♂
♌	☉		☉	♃	♄ 6	☿ 13	♀ 19	♃ 25	♂ 30	♄ 10	♃ 20	♂ 30	♄	
♍	☿	☿ 15	♀	☽	☿ 7	♀ 13	♃ 18	♄ 24	♂ 30	☉ 10	♀ 20	☿ 30	♃	♀
♎	♀	♄ 21	♄	☿	♄ 6	♀ 11	♃ 19	☿ 24	♂ 30	☽ 10	♄ 20	♃ 30	♂	☉
♏	♂		♂	♂	♂ 6	♃ 14	♀ 21	☿ 27	♄ 30	♂ 10	☉ 20	♀ 30	♀	☽
♐	♃		☉	♃	♃ 8	♀ 14	☿ 19	♄ 25	♂ 30	☿ 10	☽ 20	♄ 30	☿	
♑	♄	♂ 28	♀	☽	♀ 6	☿ 12	♃ 19	♂ 25	♄ 30	♃ 10	♂ 20	☉ 30	☽	♃
♒	♄		♄	☿	♄ 6	☿ 12	♀ 20	♃ 25	♂ 30	♀ 10	☿ 20	☽ 30	☉	
♓	♃	♀ 27	♂	♂	♀ 8	♃ 14	☿ 20	♂ 26	♄ 30	♄ 10	♃ 20	♂ 30	☿	☿

better off than the master of the house: the guest is given the best of everything – he doesn't get last night's dinner warmed up again for his lunch. But there are limits to this strength: the guest cannot wander into the bedroom and start sorting through the cupboards. With the honoured guest, there is a sense of exaggeration: we treat him better than he could ever deserve. This sense of exaggeration is important to an understanding of exaltation.

Consider a cat preparing to fight. He puffs himself up. This doesn't make him any stronger, but it makes him look stronger. He is exalting himself. It is as if the person shown by the planet in exaltation is pretending to be a better version of himself than he is usually able to be. A planet in its own sign is stronger than a planet in its exaltation – except in one specific circumstance. In a question about a contest of any kind, a planet in its exaltation trumps one in its own sign. As the cat knows, it's not only how tough you are, but how tough you look.

Be careful not to exaggerate this sense of exaggeration. Exaltation is very good;

it just isn't quite as good as it makes out. Students sometimes overstate this falling short, making exaltation almost into a debility. It is not: it is most strengthening. Example: the querent's favourite team had been playing above itself, reaching an unexpectedly high position in the league. The team's significator was a planet in its exaltation: very good – but appearing better than it really is.

A planet is exalted all the way through its exaltation sign (so the Sun is exalted anywhere in Aries), but there is one degree where it is super-exalted. This is called its *exaltation degree,* and is shown by the number next to the planetary glyphs in the exaltation column of the table. NB: this number is an ordinal, not a cardinal, so the Sun is super-exalted in the 19th degree of Aries (18.00-18.59) not at 19.00-19.59; the Moon is super-exalted in the 3rd degree of Taurus (2.00-2.59) not 3.00-3.59. 'Will I make the team?' with your planet in its exaltation degree: you'll make the team and be named captain.

There is no practical significance in the exaltation of the Nodes.

Triplicity

The signs divide into four groups of three (hence 'triplicity'): earth, air, fire and water. Each element has its own rulers. You see that the triplicity column is divided into two: there is a different ruler by day and by night.

"How do I know which one to use?" Look at the chart you are judging. The line joining the Ascendant to the Descendant represents the horizon. If the Sun is above the horizon (in houses 7-12) it is daytime; if the Sun is below the horizon (in houses 1-6), it is night. Allow a few degrees in favour of day at either end, so if the Sun is only a couple of degrees below the Ascendant or the Descendant you will count it as day. This is because the Sun's light is visible before the Sun rises and after it sets. 'A few' degrees is all the precision necessary here: the precise number varies with latitude and time of year.

The fire signs (Aries, Leo, Sagittarius) are ruled by the Sun by day and Jupiter by night. Earth signs (Taurus, Virgo, Capricorn) by Venus by day, the Moon by night. Air signs (Gemini, Libra and Aquarius) by Saturn by day and Mercury by night. The water signs (Cancer, Scorpio, Pisces) have Mars as their ruler by day and by night.

"But what has Mars got to do with water?" The water in the water signs is not sweet water, but is the ocean: wild, tempestuous, untameable. It is our desire nature – hence the connection with Mars.

A planet in its own triplicity (such as Jupiter in a fire sign in a night chart or

Venus in an earth sign in a daytime chart) is comfortable. It is literally 'in its element'. Things could be better, but they're pretty good right now. It is in its comfort zone. It is moderately strong, so we have a moderately good version of that planet.

There is another system of triplicity rulers which gives each element three rulers. Both systems date back to antiquity: the idea that the two-ruler system is a modern usurper is erroneous. The 3-ruler system has certain specific uses when judging the natal chart; it is the 2-ruler system, as discussed here, that is to be used for horary.

Term

The next section of the chart divides each sign into five unequal chunks, called *terms.* The Sun and Moon do not rule any terms; each of the other planets rules a term in each sign. 'Term' means boundary, as in the words terminus or terminate. The terms are sometimes called 'bounds'.

The numbers show where the term or bound of each planet's little chunk of power is. As with the exaltation degrees, these numbers are ordinals, not cardinals. Look at the Aries row in the table. The first term is ruled by Jupiter, whose bound is the 6th degree: Jupiter rules this part of Aries up to the end of the 6th degree, which is 5.59 degrees of Aries. Venus takes over from 6.00 degrees until the end of the 14th degree, which is 13.59. Then Mercury's section runs from 14.00 to 20.59; Mars' from 21.00 to 25.59; Saturn's from 26.00 to 29.59. A planet must be in its own little chunk of the sign to be dignified by term. Example: at 7.30 degrees of Taurus, Venus is in its own sign, its own triplicity (if it is a daytime chart) and in its own term. At 8.30 Taurus it is in its own sign, its own triplicity (in a daytime chart) and is not in its term.

The term rulers can be likened to the non-commissioned officers in an army. They have a small amount of power, but nothing so glorious as the officers (major dignities). Still, it is much better being a corporal than being a private (no dignity at all). The terms find their greatest importance when we are progressing the natal chart. In horary they are not so much a positive factor as the absence of a negative. As being a corporal is not so wonderful, but is better than being a private, so a planet in its term is not so strong, but is better than if it has no dignity at all. It is a very minor positive.

I have never seen a convincing explanation of why the terms are as they are. There are several rival arrangements. This one works.

Face

Term is a very minor positive; face is even more minor. The faces divide each sign into three equal chunks of 10 degrees each. The numbers, which are again ordinal, show the boundary of each face. Following along the Aries row, the first face of Aries is ruled by Mars. Mars' face finishes at 9.59 Aries, when the Sun takes over from 10.00 till 19.59, when Venus takes over from 20.00 to 29.59.

A planet in its own face is likened to a man in the porch of his house before being thrown out into the street. His position is not good, but it is better than being out in the wind and the rain: better dignity by face than no dignity at all.

Detriment

A planet in the sign opposite the one it rules is in its detriment (e.g. Mars in Libra, Venus in Scorpio). It is severely debilitated. This speaks badly of whatever is signified by that planet, in a way determined by the context. For example, if a man with a serious illness is signified by a planet in its detriment this shows that he is badly ill, not that he is a wicked person.

Fall

A planet in the sign opposite its own exaltation is in its fall. At the degree exactly opposite its exaltation degree it has the degree of its fall, where it is super-debilitated. Just as exaltation carries the sense of exaggeration, so does fall. With fall it is exaggerated badness. Whether this is better or worse than detriment depends on the context: it can be reassuring to know that the situation is not as dire as you fear. With the planet in its detriment, things look bad and they really are as bad as they seem. With the planet in fall, things seem worse than they are – but they are still bad. There are many contexts in which the idea of 'fall' can be taken literally.

NB: it is common to speak of planets in their detriment or fall as 'weak'. In terms of how much essential dignity they have, yes, they are weak. But this does not translate into weakness of action. In detriment or fall they are nasty or unhappy; whether they are strong or weak – able or not able to act – is shown by accidental dignities more than essential dignities.

Peregrine

A planet that is not in any of its own dignities, nor in its detriment or fall, is peregrine. It is likened to a homeless wanderer, drifting. Bonatti says that this signifies 'one that shall know how to act both good and evil, but be more inclinable to the latter'.[17] It lacks the moral direction implicit in essential dignity (behaving well) and even that implicit in essential debility (behaving badly); it is rudderless. But, by the nature of things, he who is drifting is more likely to fall into doing evil than into doing good.

Being in mutual reception does not stop a planet being peregrine: essential dignity cannot be transferred from one planet to another.

As ever, the context may give a benign meaning to being peregrine. If someone is on a long journey he would be aptly described by a planet peregrine. So would someone casting about looking for a job or a home.[18]

Almuten

Every degree has its almuten. This is the planet with most essential dignity in that degree. By extension, this planet is said to be the almuten of anything that is in that degree, such as another planet, a house-cusp or an Arabian Part.

To calculate the almuten, add the various planetary dignities in that degree, scoring 5 for sign, 4 for exaltation, 3 for triplicity, 2 for term, 1 for face. Example: what is the almuten of 5 Libra in a daytime chart? Venus scores 5 as it is the sign-ruler. Saturn scores 4 for its exaltation, 3 for being triplicity ruler and 2 for being term ruler: total 9. The Moon scores 1 for being face ruler. Saturn scores the most, so is almuten.

In many degrees there are two or even three planets which have equal claim to being almuten. Choose the one that is strongest in that particular chart. For instance, prefer the one on the MC to the one in the 12th house. Or if one is in close aspect to the Ascendant, use that.

There is only one use for almuten in horary, and that a rare one. Taking the almuten of a cusp is one of our options when we cannot use the house-ruler as significator of that house.

---

[17] *Bonatus*, aphorism 55.
[18] My understanding of peregrine has clarified since I wrote *The Real Astrology* (see p. 81). The best description of what it is to be peregrine is in canto III of Dante's *Inferno*.

Dispositor

The dispositor of a planet or Arabian Part is the ruler of the sign in which that planet or Part is. So anything in Aries is disposited by Mars, anything in Taurus by Venus. Mars *disposes* of anything in Aries, Venus of anything in Taurus. In the texts you will sometimes come across disposition by other dignities: Saturn disposits anything in Libra by exaltation. In such cases the dignity is always mentioned.

How much dignity?

Dignities are cumulative. The Sun is exalted in Aries. In a daytime chart the Sun in Aries is also in its own triplicity; so it has more dignity by day in Aries then it does by night, when it does not also have the triplicity rulership.

Although the scoring of 5-4-3-2-1 is adequate for determining almutens, it does not accurately reflect the relative strengths of the dignities. Sign-rulership and exaltation (and also detriment and fall) are very much stronger than triplicity, which is itself very much stronger than term and face. There is not a way of accurately measuring how much dignity a planet has. This lack is not important: we are doing astrology, not arithmetic. In published horaries you will sometimes read statements such as 'Jupiter has a strength of 10' This is meaningless. 10 what? In practice, counting dignity as 'lots', 'some' or 'a little' is quite accurate enough.

Contradictions

You may have noticed that there are apparent contradictions in the Table of Dignities. Mars, for instance, is in its fall in Cancer, yet it is also triplicity-ruler. Venus is in its fall in Virgo, yet in a day chart it too is triplicity ruler. There are many others. This is not contradictory, because the dignities differ in their quality, not only in their strength, so strength is not given with one hand and taken away with the other. Such apparent contradictions reflect ambiguities that are part of daily life: things are not always all good or all bad.

Example: a querent asked about her son's drug habit. The boy was signified by Mars, which was in Cancer – appropriately enough, as the Moon is natural ruler of all intoxicants. Mars is in its triplicity: it is comfortable there. This is only reasonable: if the boy is taking the drugs, it is probable that he likes them. Mars is also in its fall: he is being harmed by them. Fall is far stronger a negative than triplicity rulership is a positive, so the harm outweighs the pleasure. But it is fall, with its sense of exaggerated badness, not detriment: he is being harmed, but not as much as the querent fears.

When lecturing, I find a couple of examples helpful in explaining how dignity works. Imagine that you own a Las Vegas casino. You are sitting in your office, enjoying the feeling of well-being that comes from sitting in your own successful enterprise as you savour a bourbon and a fine cigar. You are in your own sign, so you are able to manifest your best qualities. So when the croupier timidly knocks on your door and apologetically explains that he has dropped $50,000 on the last spin of the wheel, you smile understandingly and toss him the key to the safe. But next morning you awake to find a horse's head in your bed. You are no longer the secure ruler of all you survey: you are not only no longer in your own sign, but have entered your detriment. In your desperation to save your skin, you will not manifest your best qualities. So when the croupier apologetically explains that he has dropped another $50,000, you snap your fingers and send him to sleep with the fishes.

Or consider the typical Sunsign idea of a Libran living-room: all scrupulously neat and tidy, with delicate knick-knacks and every cushion placed just so. Along comes Mars, in the person of Charles Bronson. Placed in that living-room, he will be in an alien environment: he is in his detriment. The tension from being so out of place is likely to make him behave badly, exhibiting the worst sides of his Mars nature.

This does not mean that Mars is a bad thing. If you were a Mexican villager surrounded by bandits you would be delighted to see Mars, in the person of Charles Bronson and his magnificent friends, cresting the hill towards you, six-guns blazing. There, Mars is in its right environment and so can behave at its best. You and your fellow villagers would be far less pleased to see Margot Fonteyn and the *corps de ballet* cresting the hill and coming towards you – even though Venus is nominally a benefic.

7

Accidental Dignity

The manager of a football team must choose which of two players to pick for Saturday's match. Both have lots of essential dignity: they are good players. It is not enough for the manager to consider only how much skill they have: he must consider other factors. One of them knows that a good performance will get him into the England team, so he's fired up. The other's mother died last week, so he's feeling low. One is beginning to show his age and is increasingly slow in motion. The other got kicked last week and hasn't fully recovered. These factors are *accidental* dignities and debilities. It is essential that they are considered in judgement.

Consider: I am the kindest man in the world – I have lots of essential dignity. But I am locked up in solitary confinement – accidental debility. No matter how kind I am, this accidental debility prevents me from manifesting this kindness, just as accidental factors help or hinder our footballers in playing to their best. In principle, essential dignity tells us whether that planet signifies something good or something bad; accidental dignity tells us whether this thing, good or bad, has power to act. There is a planet right on the Midheaven (strong accidental dignity): it has lots of power to act; it is in the driving-seat. In its own sign: it knows how to drive. In its detriment: it doesn't know how to drive. But, being on the Midheaven, it is still in the driving-seat.

In practice this distinction between essential and accidental qualities is often blurred, but starting from this principle and adapting it as necessary will keep you on the right track.

Broadly speaking, the more accidental dignity a planet has, the more able it is to act; the more accidental debilities it has the weaker it is and the less power it has to act. But specific dignities or debilities may or may not be relevant to the issue at hand. My friend has a broken leg, a serious accidental debility. If my question is 'Will he lend me some money?' this debility is irrelevant. If my question is 'Will he play tennis with me?' it is most relevant.

Accidental considerations may or may not be cumulative. Common sense will tell you whether they are cumulative in the question under consideration. If our footballer who is slowing down with age is the same one whose mother has died, these debilities may well add to each other. But if my trousers are held up with a belt, they are not held up any the more if I add a pair of braces.

The list of accidental considerations would be inexhaustible, as each question provides its own list of what is favourable and what is not. If the question is 'Will I become an opera singer?' finding my significator in a mute sign is an accidental debility. If it is 'Will I make a good mime?' it would be an accidental dignity. Here is a checklist of useful considerations. I have also discussed some others that can be safely ignored, for completion and because you will come across these terms in other books. The checklist is usually printed with numbers giving each consideration a score. I have omitted these because of the obsession astrologers have with arithmetic. Give an astrologer two numbers and he will immediately add them up. This is most unhelpful. All these numbers do is give a broad guide to the relative strength of these dignities and debilities, and this I shall give below; putting them in the table causes more confusion than it's worth.

CHECKLIST OF ACCIDENTAL DIGNITY AND DEBILITY

Which house is the planet in?
Is it in its joy?
Is it retrograde?
Is it fast, slow or in station?
Is it combust, under the sunbeams, opposing the Sun or cazimi?
Is it besieged or besieged by the rays?
Is it closely aspected?
Is it on one of the Nodes?
Is it on Regulus, Spica or Algol?
Does the Moon have light? Is it increasing or decreasing in light?
Is the Moon void of course?
Is the Moon in the via combusta?

You'll soon find you notice these things almost without thinking. But for now, work through this list methodically.

House placement

This is important and must be considered. The general principle is 'angular houses strong; succedent houses middling; cadent houses weak'. But the 3rd and 9th houses, although cadent, are regarded – for this purpose only – as being honorary succedents, while the 8th house, although succedent, is as weak as the 6th or 12th.

Listing the houses in order of power is too precious: the angles are all much the same; the succedents (with their honorary members) are much the same; the cadents are much the same. Put simply:

* Angular houses strong
* 6th, 8th and 12th weak
* Others neutral.

The exception to the rule is when the question gives the planet good reason to be in that house. For instance, if I ask 'Will I recover the money I've lent?' and find Lord 1 in the 8th house (2nd from the 7th: the other person's money), it is not weak there: it is the appropriate place for it because I am thinking of 8th-house matters.

A planet in an angular house gains more strength the closer it is to the cusp. If a planet is in a house but not in the same sign as the house cusp (e.g. cusp is at 25 Aries, planet is at 4 Taurus) it is as if there is a layer of insulation between the planet and the house. It is not strengthened as much as it would be if it were in that house and also in the same sign as the cusp. But don't overstate this: a planet in an angular house but in a different sign is still stronger than one in a succedent house.

Remember that a planet within around 5 degrees of the next house cusp, and in the same sign as that cusp, is counted as being in that house.

Joy

This is much less significant, but still worth noting. Each planet joys in one of the houses: Mercury in the 1st; Moon 3rd; Venus 5th; Mars 6th; Sun 9th; Jupiter 11th; Saturn 12th. It is as if it finds that house a congenial place to hang out. Because it likes being there, feels better about itself there, it has a little more power to act. It is also more likely to act according to its own nature – Mercury will do Mercury-type stuff; Mars will do Mars-type stuff. This idea is very close to that behind the essential dignities.

Retrograde

Except for the Sun and Moon, all the planets appear from time to time to be going backwards in the sky: they are retrograde. If a significator is retrograde, this must be considered. It may or may not be an affliction; if it is, it is a serious one.

In many questions retrogradation is exactly what we hope to see: 'Will I get my old job back?' 'Can I get back with Britney?' 'Will the cat come home?' In any circumstance involving returning or going back over something, a significator being retrograde is entirely appropriate, so the retrogradation is not a debility. Even if return is not sought, but still makes sense in context: 'When will I meet a man?' and the aspect is to a planet that is retrograde: 'You'll get back with an ex'.

This is an example of what I would call *the law of sufficient explanation.* If the context of an enquiry explains a debility, it is no debility.

If there is no such favourable spin given by the context, retrogradation is a problem. The planet is going the wrong way: it is against nature. This is a powerful debility, and, being against nature, things are unlikely to turn out well. Consider: the planet has lots of essential dignity, so he's one of the good guys. He's on the Midheaven, so is strongly dignified by house: he has a gun and lots of ammunition. But he's retrograde: with the best will in the world, he's shooting in the wrong direction.

If the planet has only recently turned retrograde, it can be important to consider what it has previously done and is now returning to do again, or what it was about to do but turned away from. Take a look at where it's been and at where it didn't go. But: in retrogradation a planet will either conjunct or oppose the Sun; if the planet you are considering is applying to conjunct or oppose the Sun, do not look at its actions beyond that.

Being direct in motion is usually listed as a dignity. It isn't. This is the usual state of affairs, from which retrogradation is an aberration.

Station

A planet passing from direct motion to retrogradation or from retrogradation to direct motion passes through station: *first station* when turning retrograde; *second station* when turning direct. These are so called because the planet's apparent motion slows to zero, leaving it stationary in the sky. This is extremely important.

Station is a time of great weakness and vulnerability for a planet. Only the strongest of extenuating circumstances will render it capable of action at such times. First station is likened to a man feeling so ill he decides to take to his sickbed: he feels bad, and is going to get worse. Second station is likened to a man getting up from his sickbed for the first time: he feels weak, probably worse than he did than when he was lying down, but he is getting better. I think this fails to state quite how grim second station is.

When considering station, it is vital to look at surrounding conditions. Maybe the planet is turning retrograde to avoid opposing Saturn: this could show the person signified by that planet making a smart move to avoid something nasty. Maybe it happens near the end of a sign: is that planet avoiding losing essential dignity, or is it failing to gain it? Often the retrograde motion will take a planet back into a sign it has recently left: this may well be relevant to our enquiry. What does the change of reception at the change of sign tell us?

Speed

The Sun always moves at almost the same speed (i.e. covers almost the same amount of the zodiac each day). The Moon's speed fluctuates around its average. The other planets slow to zero at station and move faster than their average at other times. This can be of great importance.

The faster the planet is moving, the more power it has to act. This is a question of impetus, just as in physics class: a car travelling at 60 miles per hour does a lot more damage than one travelling at 20.

"How do I know if the planet is moving fast or slow?" I trust that you have taken my advice and turned off the 'helpful' page on your software that gives you this and far too much other information. Either click your chart forward by a day to see how far your planet has moved in that time, then compare this with its average daily motion, or look in your ephemeris to see how far the planet has moved between noon yesterday and noon today. *Raphael's Ephemeris*[19] has a handy table giving the daily motion of all planets out to Mars.

The average daily motions of the planets are:

Moon	13°11'
Mercury	0°59'
Venus	0°59'
Sun	0°59'
Mars	0°31'
Jupiter	0°05'
Saturn	0°02'

---

[19] Foulsham, Slough, annual publication.

This is expressed in degrees and minutes (of arc, not of time). 60 minutes = 1 degree. So the average motion of the Sun, Mercury and Venus is fractionally less than 1 degree per day. But this is their daily forward motion, counting their retrograde periods as negative. A planet can be moving fast but in a retrograde direction. The slower a planet moves, relative to its own norm, the less able it is to act. A planet moving fast and retrograde is well able to act, but in the wrong way: our cowboy is gung-ho about his shooting, which is in the wrong direction.

We don't need to be fussy here: a planet must be significantly faster or slower than its norm for this to be worth noting. A few minutes per day makes a big difference for slow moving Jupiter, but is nothing for the Moon. The Sun is never significantly fast or slow. For the other planets, this table gives a rough guide; but compiling this table was the first time I have ever found it necessary to think about the limits of 'fast' and 'slow', so don't treat this as an exact definition.

	Fast when above:	Slow when below:
The Moon	13°30' per day	12°30' per day
Mercury	1°30'	1°00'
Venus	1°10'	0°50'
Mars	0°40'	0°30'
Jupiter	0°10'	0°05'
Saturn	0°05'	0°02'

This does, of course, have specific reference to questions about speed: 'Can I win the race?' 'Will they process this transaction quickly?' In some cases a planet slow in motion may be exactly what suits you: 'Will I gain by dragging this case out?'

The exception to the 'fast is strong' rule is Saturn. Moving fast is against Saturn's ponderous nature and so for Saturn should be counted as a weakness. But this does not mean its usual slow motion is necessarily a benefit. It often shows things bogged down in one way or another. For example, when Saturn was moving slowly in the fixed earth sign of Taurus I was besieged with medical horaries about either psychic or physical constipation.

Combustion

This is of huge importance. It can decide a judgement on its own. 'Will my team beat their team?' and Lord 7 (their team) is combust: your team wins. End of judgement. There is no greater affliction to a planet than this.

Technically, a planet within eight and a half degrees of the Sun is combust. But combustion varies in its seriousness: a planet eight degrees from the Sun and separating is much less afflicted than one that is two degrees from the Sun and applying. NB: to be combust a planet must be in the same sign as the Sun.

Apart from being utterly destructive, combustion can also show that whoever or whatever is signified by that planet cannot either see or be seen. This can give a positive sense to combustion: 'Can I do such-and-such without applying for a permit?' and the querent's significator is combust: 'Yes. No one can see you: you can do what you like'.

If its significator is combust, a lost object will often come to light when, in real time, its significator leaves combustion.

If this planet cannot see, the person it signifies cannot see reason. The querent whose significator is combust will not take any notice of the judgement. The lamentable truth of this is repeated in chart after chart.

It is sometimes claimed that as Mars, like the Sun, is hot and dry, combustion does not affect it. It does. The idea with combustion is that it is not safe to come too close to the king (unless you are in his bosom); it is no less unsafe if you are a soldier (Mars) than Ann Boleyn (Venus).

If conjunction with the Sun would give a Yes to the question, combustion can be ignored: the poor Sun would never get conjuncted otherwise.

The debate on how combustion affects a planet in that planet's own sign (e.g. Venus combust in Taurus) is an ancient one. Treat it exactly as a mutual reception: the planet has power over the Sun by dispositing it; the Sun has power over the planet by combustion. So the combustion does not harm the planet; the idea of not being able to see or be seen still remains, however.

Although combustion is so destructive, there can be a big difference between combustion with the planet applying to the Sun and combustion when the planet is separating. 'Will I survive this illness?' combust and applying: maybe not. And separating: the worst is past.

Being free of combustion is usually listed as a dignity. It isn't. This is the usual state of affairs, from which combustion is an aberration.

Cazimi

In the centre of combustion there is a tiny oasis called *cazimi*, or *in the heart of the Sun*. To be cazimi a planet must be within 17½' of the Sun's position – though actually measuring half minutes is being far too precious. While combustion is the worst thing that can happen to a planet, cazimi is the best: a planet cazimi is likened to a man who is raised up to sit beside the king. If you are the king's favourite, in his bosom, you have great power. To be cazimi a planet must be in the same sign as the Sun.

Do not think, 'This planet is combust, but it's heading towards cazimi, so all will be well'. Combustion is utterly destructive: there is no moving through it to cazimi. The exception to this principle is if we are electing with the horary chart and the planet we wish to make strong is combust (see chapter 27).

Under the sunbeams

Beyond combustion lies a less harmful area where a planet is *under the sunbeams, under the rays,* or *sub radiis.* This extends from the end of combustion until the planet is 17½ degrees from the Sun. Like combustion, the strength of the effect varies: 9 degrees from the Sun and approaching combustion is serious; 16 degrees from the Sun and separating is trivial.

A planet does not need to be in the same sign as the Sun to be under the sunbeams.

"Why these dimensions?" The Sun's position marked on a chart is that of its centre; but the Sun has a visible disc. The apparent size of this varies, of course, but 35' in diameter is the norm. This is a useful guide to distance when skywatching: the usual diameter of both Sun and Moon is roughly half a degree.

As its disc has a diameter of 35', its radius is 17½'. So a planet within 17½' of the Sun's position is within the Sun's disc (at least, it is by longitude. It may be above or below it by latitude; this doesn't matter). By extrapolation, jumping up a unit from minutes of arc to degrees, anything within 17½° of the Sun is under the beams. Combustion is simply this distance halved.

Opposition to the Sun

The area of 8 degrees or so either side of exact opposition to the Sun is also a place of extreme affliction, not quite so serious as combustion, but not so far short of it. There is no equivalent of cazimi here.

Besiegement

If a significator is placed between two malefic planets it is besieged. Whichever way it turns, there is something nasty there: the rock and the hard place. If a planet is placed between two benefic planets, it is still 'besieged'; but in this case the besiegers are vying with each other to present rich gifts: a cushion and a very soft place. As ever, we must pay attention to the condition of the planets: being stuck between Mars and Saturn in Capricorn, where they both have lots of dignity, it not so bad; being stuck between Jupiter and Venus in Virgo, where they are both debilitated, is destructive.

The closer the besieging planets are to each other, the stronger is the effect of besiegement. If they are not within the same sign, the effects are trivial, unless you have the rare circumstance when all the planets – or all the relevant planets – are in a neat line with the besieging malefics or benefics at either end.

A planet besieged by malefics yet receiving an aspect from a benefic has solace amid his problems: OK, I'm besieged, but the warehouses are full of caviar and the TV's still working. Besieged by benefics and receiving an aspect from a malefic, there is something that blights the promise: I can have the ice cream, I can have the cake, but I've got a toothache.

Besiegement by the rays

Instead of being bodily between the two besieging planets, the significator casts its aspect between them. For instance: Venus is at 5 Pisces, Jupiter at 8 Pisces. A planet at 6 Pisces is in strong positive besiegement. A planet at 6 Scorpio is not besieged bodily, but it casts its trine aspect between Venus and Jupiter: it is besieged by the rays. This is like besiegement, but much weaker.

Aspects

A planet closely aspected by or closely conjunct with another planet is affected by that planet, for better or for worse. The old texts list such contacts with Jupiter or Venus as being strengthening, with Mars or Saturn as being weakening. But this is not always so: as we have seen, Jupiter and Venus in their essential debilities are not helpful, Mars and Saturn in essential dignity are not harmful. Even this statement needs qualifying, because we must also consider what their role is in the chart: death, for instance, may be signified by a strong Jupiter, but Jupiter being a strongly dignified benefic won't make the person any the less dead. Whether the aspecting planet is strong or weak, we must also consider its receptions with the significator: for example, Jupiter in Cancer is strong, a very nice Jupiter; but it is in the detriment of Saturn, so if it casts its aspect to Saturn it will not be much help to it. Reception is treated in more detail in chapter 8.

A clear example of the principle would be a horary for a contest: 'Will my team beat his team?' In such a chart we have only two significators, Lord 1 for my team, Lord 7 for his. If Lord 1 were aspected by Saturn in Aries, a nasty kind of Saturn, my team would be afflicted. If Lord 7 were aspected by Jupiter in Cancer, his team would be strengthened. In this context it would not be necessary to work out what Saturn and Jupiter meant; in some questions it could be, although it is not always possible to do so with confidence.

There is a general rule in all astrology: the closer the stronger. The closer the aspect is, the greater the effect it will have. But we must also consider the strength of the aspecting planet: an opposition from Saturn in the 10th house, where it has lots of accidental dignity, will have a greater effect than an opposition from Saturn in the 6th house, where it has little. For its general effect on a planet you can ignore any aspect that is more than 3 degrees away: beyond this any effect is trivial. More often, though, we are reading aspects as showing future or occasionally past events, in which case they can be relevant at any degree of separation.

The Nodes

The Moon's Nodes are the two points, directly opposite each other, where the Moon's apparent path around the Earth crosses the Sun's.

The Nodes do not cast aspects, nor can they have aspects cast to them. They affect planets only by conjunction. A planet conjunct the North Node is helped, strengthened or increased. A planet conjunct the South Node is harmed, weakened or decreased. Which of these meanings is relevant will be clear enough in context. In some contexts we might think, 'That significator is just separating from the South Node: something unpleasant has happened to that person recently'; in others, we'd read the proximity to the South Node as showing that whatever that planet signifies is being diminished.

Example: suppose I ask, 'Will I win on the horses today?' and find an applying aspect between the ruler of the 8th house (2nd from the 7th: my enemy's money) and my own significator: yes, I will win. If Lord 8 is conjunct the North Node I will win a lot. If it is conjunct the South Node I will still win, but not much. Lord 8, which is the money that I am winning, is increased by its contact with the one, diminished by its contact with the other.

If one of the Nodes falls in a house relevant to the question, it can affect that house. The North Node falling in a house is good for the affairs of that house, or shows the querent benefitting from that house. The South Node falling in a house harms the affairs of that house, or shows the querent losing through the affairs of that house. The effect is much more marked if the Node is close to the cusp.

Examples: 'Will I get the job?' with the North Node in the 10th (the house of work): this does not improve the querent's chances of getting the job, but does show that it will be good for her if she gets it. 'Should I employ this builder?' with the South Node in the 6th (the house of servants): No!

Remember, though, that the Nodes come as a pair: the one is always opposite the other. This means that we can rarely use the house placements of both, else we fall into the trap of thinking that if Mum is good, Dad must automatically be bad; my small animals benefit me, my large animals harm me. The context will show us which end of the nodal axis – if either – we should heed.

Be careful to avoid dragging them into judgement unnecessarily. The chart does not have a dressing-room where they can go to relax when they are not involved in the drama: the Nodes will appear in every chart, but in most charts they have nothing to tell us. If one of them falls into a house that concerns us, we can take note of it; if the Nodes fall in houses that do not concern us, there is no need for us to rack our brains wondering what those houses might mean. Just ignore them.

Although the Nodes do not cast or receive aspects you will often find a significator square to the Nodes (i.e. exactly halfway between them). This seems to show that person torn between two courses of action, often with neither of them being appealing. But this describes his predicament; there is nothing actively malefic about this placement. The planet is *not* affected by being square the Nodes. The idea in some modern books of the degree of the Nodes in any sign as 'a degree of fatality' is groundless.

We have the choice of using the Mean Node or the True Node: the rough position or the exact position. Given the choice, we might as well use the exact position. Most software allows you to set your preference for this.

The Moon

Generally, the more light the Moon has – the closer it is to full – the stronger it is and so the more able it is to act. It is also stronger if it is *increasing in light* (moving from new to full Moon) than if it is *decreasing in light* (moving from full to new). But at full it is weak (see the point on opposition to the Sun, above), so its optimum position is around separating trine to the Sun: there it has lots of light and is still increasing. This point is important if the Moon is the planet whose aspect is showing the event in question.

"How can I tell if the Moon is increasing in light?" Look at the Sun in the chart you are judging. Which is the shorter: the clockwise distance from Sun to Moon, or the anticlockwise distance? If the clockwise distance is the shorter, the Moon is getting closer to the Sun, moving from full to new, and so is decreasing in light. If the anticlockwise distance is shorter, it is moving towards full (opposition to the Sun) and so is increasing in light.

Void of course

It is rumoured that Quentin Tarantino was inspired by make *Reservoir Dogs* by the sight of astrologers discussing the meaning of *void of course*. It is quite simple and need not involve bloodshed.

The Moon is void of course if it does not perfect another aspect before leaving its present sign. If it perfects an aspect immediately after leaving this sign – at 0 degrees of the next sign, perhaps – it *is* void of course now; it *will* not be void of course once it has changed sign. In principle any planet can be void of course, but the term has practical significance only with the Moon. An aspect to the Part of Fortune or any other Arabian Part does not prevent the Moon being void.

If the Moon in a horary chart is void, this is a general indication that not much is going to happen. For instance, if the question is 'Should I emigrate?' a void Moon suggests that the querent is unlikely to do so, whether it is a good idea or not. A void Moon can provide the full answer to a question, either favourably or unfavourably. 'Will I lose my job?' 'Will I win the lottery?' In both cases a void Moon would give the answer 'No: nothing will happen'.

A void Moon is not always the final answer, however. Like any other individual testimony, it can be overruled. If the main significators are strong and applying to aspect, the event can still happen.

The Moon is also void of course if it has a long way to travel before making its next aspect, even though that aspect perfects within that same sign. Example: Moon at 4 Taurus, separating from a sextile with Venus at 3 Cancer. Its next aspect is not perfected till it reaches 22 Taurus. The Moon can be considered void. This often shows a period of stagnation before the querent finds the will to act. There is no set distance here: simply 'a long way'. It has nothing to do with being in or out of orb. I would suggest taking 15 degrees or so as a minimum.

Sometimes there is a clear reason for a void Moon showing nothing happening. A querent had applied for a job on the understanding that the present incumbent was leaving. That person was signified by a void Moon in a fixed sign: she was going nowhere. She didn't leave, so nothing came of the application. In many situations the reason nothing happens is the querent's inaction. As the Moon is usually cosignificator of the querent, its being void can show this lack of will to act. 'Will she marry me?' 'Not if you don't ask her.'

Occasionally the Moon will travel all the way through a sign without making an aspect. At such times it is *feral*, like a wild beast. This is an emphatic version of void of course. Little can be expected from the situation.

The via combusta

Meaning 'the burned-up road' this is the area of the zodiac between 15 Libra and 15 Scorpio. It affects only the Moon, which does not like being there at all. Being here does not make the Moon any weaker, but does distress it. This is primarily of significance in questions where the querent's emotions are important: the Moon's passage through the via combusta shows a period of unpleasant emotional turbulence. Note the Moon's position relative to the via combusta: is it about to enter it, stuck in the middle of it, or about to leave it? So 'Will I be happy if I dump him?' with the Moon at 13 Libra, on the point of entering this area of unpleasant emotional turmoil: 'No' (although this in itself would not be the complete judgement).

"Why this portion of the zodiac?" The idea of the via combusta is connected with the ancient purification rituals around menstruation. That it is between 15 Libra and 15 Scorpio rather than anywhere else in the zodiac is because of the relationship of the Moon (the female principle) here to the exaltation of the Sun (the male principle) in Aries. Ideas that it is determined by ancient placements of fixed stars or the influence of Mars and Saturn over Libra and Scorpio are transparently incorrect.

Fixed stars

The fixed stars are discussed in chapter 11. For the general assessment of a planet's strength or weakness there are only three stars of major significance. These are Regulus (29 Leo), Spica (23 Libra) and Caput Algol (26 Taurus). Fixed stars neither give nor receive aspects: we are concerned only with conjunction. If a significator or relevant house cusp, especially the Ascendant, is within a couple of degrees of conjunction with one of these stars, it will be strongly affected in the following ways:

* *Regulus* gives great power for material achievement. It does not necessarily bring happiness; it does bring success.
* *Spica* is generally fortunate. It doesn't have the will to power that is seen in Regulus, but is a much happier star. It is strongly protective, so is an indication that even if things don't work out as desired, the consequences will not be so bad.
* *Caput Algol* brings difficulties. The usual indication is of losing one's head, whether literally or metaphorically, with unfortunate results. Example: a querent asked, 'I've fallen in love with the man on TV; is there a future in our relationship?' Her main significator was conjunct Caput Algol.

MINOR POINTS

I am including the following only because you may come across these terms in other texts. Some have (very) occasional uses in fine-tuning judgements, but, remembering our golden rule of 'Keep it Simple!' they can all be ignored. We always have testimonies of so much greater significance than these that we can disregard these without fear of error.

Oriental and occidental

Meaning 'eastern' and 'western', these terms refer to a planet's position relative to the Sun. If the planet rises before the Sun it is visible in the eastern sky before dawn, so is *oriental*. If it rises after the Sun if will still be visible in the western sky after the Sun has set, and so is *occidental*.

"How do I know whether a planet is oriental or occidental?" Look at the Sun in the chart you are judging. Which is the shorter: the clockwise distance from the Sun to the planet you are considering, or the anticlockwise distance? If the clockwise distance is the shorter, the planet is oriental. If the anticlockwise distance is shorter, it is occidental. Look at the chart on page 78. Venus, as well as Uranus, Neptune and Pluto, is oriental; all the other planets are occidental. The Moon is increasing in light and will soon be full.

An oriental planet will be more obvious in its actions. If the question were 'Am

I best suited for work on stage or behind the scenes?' this could be a minor consideration; but even there you would find more important testimonies and so could ignore this. That Mars, Jupiter and Saturn are favoured by being oriental, Mercury and Venus by being occidental, is with reference only to natal charts, where the distinction between oriental and occidental is important.

The Moon occidental is increasing in light, oriental is decreasing in light. This is important and is discussed above.

Hayz

Just as animals are nocturnal or diurnal, so are planets. The Sun, as is obvious, is diurnal: it belongs up in the sky during the day. The Moon is nocturnal: it belongs up in the sky during the night. Jupiter and Saturn are also diurnal; Mars and Venus are nocturnal. If Mercury is oriental it is diurnal, if occidental it is nocturnal.

If a diurnal planet is above the Earth (in houses 7–12) in a daytime chart, or below it (in houses 1-6) in a night chart, it is in its *halb*. So is a nocturnal planet that is above the Earth by night or below it by day. Halb is so minor a consideration that it can always be ignored: it pales into insignificance beside other testimonies.

The Sun, Mars, Jupiter and Saturn are masculine; the Moon and Venus are feminine. Mercury takes the nature of whichever planet is (in order of preference) close to conjunction with it, close to aspect with it, or its dispositor. A planet is in its *hayz* if it is in its halb and also in a sign of its own gender.[20] The masculine signs are Aries, Gemini, Leo, Libra, Sagittarius and Aquarius; the feminine signs are Taurus, Cancer, Virgo, Scorpio, Capricorn and Pisces.

Examples: Saturn in Aries is in its hayz if above the Earth by day or below it by night; Venus in Scorpio is in its hayz if above the Earth by night or below it by day. The tricky one is Mars, which is masculine and, unlike the other masculine planets, nocturnal: it needs to be in a masculine sign and below the Earth by day, above it by night.

---

[20] Lilly and authors working from him without other reference state mistakenly that a nocturnal planet should be above the Earth by day and below it by night. Lilly (*Christian Astrology* p.113) is following the French astrologer Dariot, who gives the correct version, but in such a muddy fashion that it is easy to see how Lilly picked up the wrong end of the stick (see Claude Dariot, *A Brief and Most Easie Introduction to the Judgment of the Stars,* trans. Fabian Wither, London c. 1583, reprinted Ascella, Nottingham, n.d., p. 19, although Lilly used a translation published in 1598). The correct version is clearly explained in Abu'l-Rayhan Muhammad Ibn Ahmad Al-Biruni, *The Book of Instruction in the Elements of the Art of Astrology*, trans. R. Ramsey Wright, Luzac, London, 1934; reprinted Ascella, Nottingham, n.d.; para. 496.

Hayz is worth noting in a natal chart, but can be ignored in horary. If you are feeling exceptionally fussy while judging a chart that requires you to quantify something ('How much did the last boss embezzle?') you could take hayz as adding slightly to that quantity.

Latitude

The ecliptic is the Sun's apparent path around the Earth. While the other planets all follow this path, they weave up and down the sky relative to it. Imagine there is a road across the sky, along which the planets travel: the Sun keeps strictly to the white line down the centre of that road, while the other planets wander from side to side. This side to side wandering is movement in celestial latitude.

In the northern hemisphere, which has been regarded as the standard since astrology's birth, north latitude takes a planet higher in the sky, south latitude takes it lower. The higher it is, the less of the Earth's atmosphere its rays need to penetrate to reach us, so the brighter it appears. For this reason, north latitude increases, south decreases. The difference is minor, but if you are estimating quantity you could add it to the mix. If you want to describe someone, a planet having significant north latitude would make that person taller and broader, significant south latitude, shorter and leaner.

You cannot tell a planet's latitude from looking at the chart. Most astrological software has a latitude option somewhere; some ephemerides, such as *Raphael's*, list daily latitude. If you can't find it, don't worry: you are not missing anything important.

Lame, azimene, etc.

Lilly gives a table of degrees that are among other things *deep, azimene, smokey* or *void*.[21] These degrees are based upon the positions of fixed stars, which, although relatively fixed, do yet slowly move. Even by Lilly's day, this table was hopelessly out of date, having been passed down from text to text without anyone thinking to update it or knowing when it was originally composed. It is possible that these points could be of value – if anyone could work out where they are. Until then, leave well alone.[22]

---

[21] *Lilly*, p. 116.
[22] See Avraham Ibn-Ezra, *The Book of Reasons*, 12th century, trans. Meira B. Epstein, Berkeley Springs, 1994; pp. 69-70. Ms Epstein suggests that ibn-Ezra refers to tables composed around 568 B.C., though I suspect they were older still.

Increasing in number

Lilly mentions this frequently, although his use suggests that it is a tag phrase of whose meaning he is unaware. It does not mean, as is sometimes explained, that the planet is passing through degrees of increasing number, such as from 26 Aries to 27 Aries: this is the same as being direct in motion. It refers to the planet's position on its epicycle in the ptolemaic model of planetary motions. The more astrologers relied on ephemerides to plot planetary positions, the more the knowledge of how to calculate this was forgotten. Long before Lilly's day nobody bothered with this; nor should you.

Other points

There are yet more even more minor considerations, but unless you are an especially avid reader of ancient texts you will never come across them. If astrologers did not pass such points down, it was because they knew they were not important; so if you come across a term that is not listed here, you don't need it for horary.

8

Receptions

In a detective film it is not sufficient for the sleuth to prove that the suspect had the opportunity to commit the crime; he must also establish a motive. It is the same in the horary chart. If we are to fully understand the situation described in the chart, and to draw the correct conclusions from it, we must understand the motives of the various people involved.

Event-based horaries revolve upon action, and people do not act without motive. Situation-based horaries often find their entire answer in an analysis of attitude and motivation ('What does he really feel about me?'). So it is vital that we know how to find motive, attitude and values in the chart. This knowledge is found by the study of reception.

The information we need is drawn from the Table of Dignities. When assessing the amount of dignity a planet has, we are concerned only with finding if it is in any of its own dignities or debilities. When assessing receptions, we must consider all the dignities and debilities it is in.

The texts use confusing language for receptions, with talk of planets 'receiving' each other, or 'rendering virtue' from one to another. Far simpler to state simply 'Venus is in the sign of Jupiter', or 'Mars exalts Saturn'.

Let's work through the table again, column by column, supposing our significator is the Moon, at 3 Aries in a daytime chart. It is in the sign of Mars (first column). It is in the exaltation of the Sun, or it exalts the Sun (second column). It is in the triplicity of the Sun (because it is a daytime chart). It is in the term of Jupiter and the face of Mars. It is in the detriment of Venus and the fall of Saturn.

"What does this tell us?" In most contexts, reception can be seen as liking or loving. **The significator – in this example, the Moon – likes or loves to various extents the planets in whose dignities it falls.** At its simplest, we see that in this example the Moon loves Mars and the Sun. It has a further moderate liking for the Sun, because it is in the Sun's triplicity. It has a minor liking for Jupiter and a further, even more minor, liking for Mars. It can't stand Venus and Saturn.

Sign	Ruler	Exalt-ation	Triplicity Day	Triplicity Night	Term					Face			Detri-ment	Fall
♈	♂	☉ 19	☉	♃	♃ 6	♀ 14	☿ 21	♂ 26	♄ 30	♂ 10	☉ 20	♀ 30	♀	♄
♉	♀	☽ 3	♀	☽	♀ 8	☿ 15	♃ 22	♄ 26	♂ 30	☿ 10	☽ 20	♄ 30	♂	
♊	☿		♄	☿	☿ 7	♃ 14	♀ 21	♄ 25	♂ 30	♃ 10	♂ 20	☉ 30	♃	
♋	☽	♃ 15	♂	♂	♂ 6	♃ 13	☿ 20	♀ 27	♄ 30	♀ 10	☿ 20	☽ 30	♄	♂
♌	☉		☉	♃	♄ 6	☿ 13	♀ 19	♃ 25	♂ 30	♄ 10	♃ 20	♂ 30	♄	
♍	☿	☿ 15	♀	☽	☿ 7	♀ 13	♃ 18	♄ 24	♂ 30	☉ 10	♀ 20	☿ 30	♃	♀
♎	♀	♄ 21	♄	☿	♄ 6	♀ 11	♃ 19	☿ 24	♂ 30	☽ 10	♄ 20	♃ 30	♂	☉
♏	♂		♂	♂	♂ 6	♃ 14	♀ 21	☿ 27	♄ 30	♂ 10	☉ 20	♀ 30	♀	☽
♐	♃		☉	♃	♃ 8	♀ 14	☿ 19	♄ 25	♂ 30	☿ 10	☽ 20	♄ 30	☿	
♑	♄	♂ 28	♀	☽	♀ 6	☿ 12	♃ 19	♂ 25	♄ 30	♃ 10	♂ 20	☉ 30	☽	♃
♒	♄		♄	☿	♄ 6	☿ 12	♀ 20	♃ 25	♂ 30	♀ 10	☿ 20	☽ 30	☉	
♓	♃	♀ 27	♂	♂	♀ 8	♃ 14	☿ 20	♂ 26	♄ 30	♄ 10	♃ 20	♂ 30	☿	☿

The concept of liking or loving may seem limited in the contexts to which it is relevant, but it is not. Suppose I am asking when my wages will arrive. If I find that the wages love me (their significator is in strong dignity of mine) I am encouraged: if they love me they will want to be with me. Traditional science saw many phenomena which modern science explains differently in terms of love, a word that had far wider application than is common today. A piece of iron, for instance, loves the magnet.

Just as dignities vary in their nature, so do receptions:

Sign rulership

The planet loves the planet that rules the sign it is in. It sees it for what it is and loves it. Simple and straightforward. The Moon (or any other planet) at 3 Aries loves whatever is signified by Mars.

Exaltation

A planet literally exalts the planet in whose exaltation it falls: it puts it on a pedestal. Exaltation carries the same sense of exaggeratedly good as it does when we are considering dignity. So whomever the Moon signifies in our example sees whatever the Sun signifies as being super-good. You will be familiar with this feeling: it is exactly what you have felt whenever you have first fallen for somebody – you see them as a wonderful being, turning a blind eye to their feet of clay. It is the idea of 'the honoured guest in someone else's house': the guest is treated as if he were the wonderful person that he ought to be; we do not treat our honoured guests according to their true deserts.

Don't overstate this exaggeration: it does not mean that the person who is being exalted is in any way bad; it means only that they are being seen through rose-tinted spectacles. Reception by exaltation is common in horaries cast at the start of relationships. Exaltation, as you have no doubt experienced, tends not to last: the delicious bubble bursts.

A querent asked about a job for which she had applied. Her significator was in the job's exaltation (Jupiter, Lord 1, was in Pisces, the exaltation of Venus, which was Lord 10 in that chart). The querent exalted the job. Note – importantly – that this tells us nothing about the qualities of the job: we need to look at Lord 10 itself for that. But it does tell us that no matter how good a job it might be, it is unlikely to live up to the querent's inflated expectations.

This sense of exaggeration can be a valuable part of judgement, not only when suggesting caution to infatuated lovers. Suppose our querent exalts the person he is thinking of taking to court: he thinks the other guy is more powerful than he really is. We can then look at the other guy's significator to find out exactly how strong a case he has.

Triplicity

If sign-rulership is like love and exaltation like infatuation, triplicity is like friendship: warm and comfortable, but with no grand passion. In most relationship questions, our querents would be hoping for more than this, but in many contexts it will do fine. 'Will I like this job?' and Lord 1 (querent) is in the triplicity ruled by Lord 10 (the job): 'Yes. It won't be the best job in the world, but you'll like it well enough'.

Because of the exaggeration implicit in exaltation, it is often good to find it backed up by some other reception. In our example, the Moon exalts the Sun and is also in the Sun's triplicity, so there is something solid in the Moon's feelings for the Sun, beneath the brittle infatuation.

Term and Face

When considering dignity, we saw how these dignities are not so much a positive as they are the absence of a negative: they are better than nothing. So it is with reception. The Moon here is in the term of Jupiter: whomever the Moon signifies has a minor interest in whomever Jupiter signifies. This is better than indifference, but not by much. 'Will she go out with me?' and her significator is in the term or face of the querent's: 'Yes, she will – if her boyfriend is out of town, her fridge is empty and there's nothing on TV'. Face shows an even more trivial degree of interest than term.

Cumulatively, though, they can be significant. 'Does he love me?' with his significator in the triplicity and term ruled by her planet: it's maybe not the grand amour she longs for, but if she wants a relationship this might yet be an option worth considering.

Detriment

Being in a planet's detriment is the opposite of being in its sign, so this shows hatred. The Moon here is in the detriment of Venus: whomever the Moon signifies has a clear enough view of what Venus is, and hates it.

Fall

This is the opposite to exaltation, so it carries a similar sense of exaggeration, showing loathing rather than hatred. Just as it is common to find the lovers exalting each other in charts cast at the beginning of a relationship, so it is common to find them in each other's fall in charts cast when the relationship is going wrong: fall well describes the exaggerated loathing that spouses conceive for each other at such times.

Nothing

There is no technical term for a planet not being in any dignity or debility of another planet. This shows complete indifference to whatever is signified by that planet. But this is not necessarily the end of the story: motives are not always direct. Maybe she doesn't love him, but wants his money (her significator in sign or exaltation of Lord 2).

Ambivalence

There are many places in the table where a planet is in both dignity and debility of another planet. For example, any planet in Cancer is in both the triplicity and fall of Mars; a planet at 4 Leo is in the detriment of Saturn, but also its term and face. As we saw when considering dignity, this is not contradictory: it reflects ambiguities which are part of our daily experience in relating to people, and which must be understood if we are to give an accurate picture of a situation. For instance: she loathes her husband, but does appreciate that he's a good father to their children; he hates his wife, but likes the home comforts she provides.

The metaphor of liking or loving usually works well, but there are some contexts where concepts of rulership, domination or influence make better sense. For example, in charts about three-way relationships it is common to find the significators of the lover and the cheated spouse in each other's sign: this doesn't mean that they love each other, but shows the politics of the situation, who has power over whom. In some circumstances being in someone's house (celestial house, i.e. sign) shows exactly that: being inside their home.

An example of receptions

Follow this, referring to the table above. Suppose the querent is signified by Mars. She is being courted by Johnny Depp and Leonardo di Caprio, signified by the Sun and Saturn respectively.

Let her significator, Mars, be at 15 Leo, in a daytime chart. Which of the two does she prefer?

At 15 Leo her planet is in both the sign and triplicity of the Sun. What is the Sun? Depp. She loves Depp.

At 15 Leo it is also in the detriment of Saturn. What is Saturn? Di Caprio. She hates di Caprio.

NB: this tells us *only* about her feelings. It tells us nothing at all about whether they are reciprocated.

So what do they feel about her? Let the Sun be at 4 Scorpio and Saturn at 1 Aquarius.

What does Depp (the Sun) feel about her (Mars)? At 4 Scorpio he is in her sign, triplicity, term and face: he is besotted with her.

What does di Caprio (Saturn) feel about her? At 1 Aquarius Saturn is not in any dignity of Mars: he is indifferent to her.

Hmm. So why is he courting her then? What *is* of value to him? Saturn is in the sign, triplicity and term of Saturn. What is Saturn? Di Caprio. So what does di Caprio love? Himself. So he could see her as a trophy, rather than having any real affection for her. A situation which is not unusual, especially in charts about affairs.

But look! In Aquarius Saturn is in the detriment of the Sun. What is the Sun? Depp. Di Caprio hates Johnny Depp. Maybe that is his motive for courting our querent: he wants to spite Depp by stealing the girl he's so crazy about.

Note that, as here, negative reception can provide motivation and is as important as positive reception. As here, the major receptions will usually give us all the information that we need: we rarely need to get involved with the minor receptions.

Mutual reception

So far we have been looking at receptions. The various dignities and debilities in which Mars falls tell us about the attitudes of the person Mars signifies. If Mars is in the dignity or debility of Venus and Venus is also in the dignity or debility of Mars, it is a *mutual* reception. In essence, this is all that mutual reception is: it is reception that is in some way reciprocated.

This reciprocity does not need to be by the same dignity or debility (Mars in the sign of Venus, Venus in the sign of Mars); it can be by any combination of dignities or debilities. Mars in the sign of Venus: he loves her. Venus in the exaltation of Mars: she's crazy about him too. Venus in only the face of Mars: his love is unrequited – she is all but indifferent to him. Venus in the detriment of Mars: his love is less than unrequited – she actively hates him. We can also have ambivalent reciprocity: Mars in the sign of Venus, Venus in both triplicity and fall of Mars. He loves her; there are some qualities she likes in him, but overall she loathes him. As these examples show, considering the particular receptions the planets have for each other will tell us exactly what feelings are between these two people.

Negative receptions (by detriment or fall) are commonly ignored. Don't! They are extremely important. The chart below gives examples of how they work.

Mutual reception by dignity shows us that two planets like each other. If they like each other, they will want to help each other. So mutual reception strengthens planets. Negative mutual reception weakens them.

We cannot, however, give any set value to how much a planet is strengthened, because this varies. It varies according to the strength of the reception and according to the strength of *both* planets.

The more powerful the dignities in which the planets receive each other, the more they strengthen each other. Planets in each other's sign like each other lots, so will rush to offer help; planets in each other's face might grudgingly lend a hand if they really have to. If Mars is in the sign of Venus and Venus is in the face of Mars, Mars wants to help Venus lots; Venus has much less enthusiasm for helping Mars. But if Venus is in only the face of Mars, she may be reluctant to let Mars help her: the smaller the dignity of the reception, the less that planet can accept help, as well as the less it can give it. There is nothing abstract about this: it is simple human experience. If I am stuck in an embarrassing situation, I might gladly let my best friend help me, but would be reluctant to let a mere acquaintance see my need.

To be significantly strengthened by mutual reception, both planets need to be strong. They need to be strong by essential dignity: good guys help each other more than bad guys. They need to be strong accidentally, else they lack the ability to help or – and this is important – be helped.

Consider. Positive mutual reception is like friendship. I can have a strong friendship with someone (major mutual reception), but if he is a nasty piece of work (in his own detriment) he will not help me in my hour of need. Or he may be a lovely person (in strong essential dignity), but lacks the ability to show his friendship by action (accidental debility), as if I were asking him to lend me some money and he wished to do so but could not, because he didn't have any to lend. Or I may be so weak that I cannot be helped: I ask my friend to lend me money to pay my rent; he does so, but I head for the nearest bar and drink it all. His money has not helped me, because of my own weakness.

So even though Mars in Taurus and Venus in Aries have mutual reception by sign, this is not very helpful: both planets are too weak to either help or be helped. The, apparently weaker, mutual reception by triplicity between Mars in Capricorn and Venus in Pisces is much more helpful (all things being equal in terms of accidental strength) because here both planets are exalted, so they are able both to help and be helped.

If you have read other modern books on horary, you may have come across the idea that planets in mutual reception can swap places, so if Mars is in Taurus and Venus in Aries, we can regard it as if Mars were in Aries and Venus in Taurus. This is based on a blatant misreading of Ptolemy, makes no sense (I may be friends with someone, but I don't go to live in his house and he in mine) and must be ignored.

There is another idea that peregrine planets cannot be in mutual reception. Of course they can. A peregrine planet is like a homeless wanderer, mutual reception like friendship. A homeless wanderer can still have friends. He may not be able to help them much, but such friendship is better than nothing.

Receptions in action

Time to look at another chart. I am jumping ahead here, as there are many points in this judgement that are explained in later chapters. For now, pay attention mainly to the handling of the receptions, then look back at this chart for the

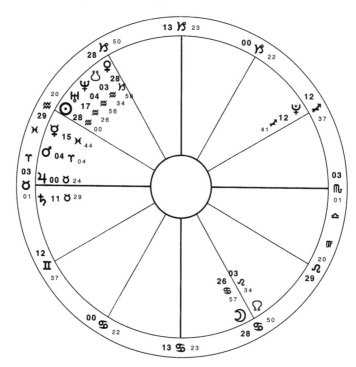

Did he he really love me? February 17th 2000, 9.12 am GMT, London.

other points when you have worked further through the book. I suggest that you read through this judgement several times, following as best you can with what you have learned so far and stretching to comprehend the other points. Work with this, referring continually to the table of dignities: you will learn far more by actively working with these judgements than by passively reading them.

The querent wrote that she had married young, only because she was pregnant. Then she had met another man, who 'told me such wonderful things about myself'. Then she discovered that he was sleeping with another woman. He didn't want to do this, but she was blackmailing him into it. 'Did he really love me? Is there a future in our relationship?'

The chart is set for the time and place at which I read her letter. She, as querent, is given the Ascendant and Lord 1, which is Venus. As querent, she has the Moon as her cosignificator. Because this is a relationship question – and only in relationship questions – we would also give her Venus as significator, as natural ruler of women; but she already has it.

As it is a relationship question, we look to the 7th house. There are two 7th-house people involved in this situation: the husband and the lover. They can't both be signified by Lord 7, so we must choose. Take the one about whom the question is asked, which in this case is the lover: he is given Lord 7 (Mars) and – only in a relationship question – the Sun, because he is a man.

His main significator, Mars, is in the 12th house. So is the Sun, his second significator, because a planet within around 5 degrees of a cusp is counted as being in the next house if it is in the same sign as that cusp. With both his significators in the 12th, the house of things hidden from the querent, we can dismiss any ideas of his blackmail story being true.

What does he think of our querent? To determine this, we must look to see if either of his significators is in any dignity or debility of either of hers. Neither Mars nor the Sun is in any reception with the Moon. The Sun is not in any reception with Venus. Mars is in the detriment of Venus: he hates her.

But she is not asking about his attitude to her now; she is asking what his attitude was in the past. So we must look into the past, which we do by backtracking the planets, sending them back in the direction from which they have come.

Mars, at 4 Aries, has only recently changed sign. It has only recently entered the detriment of Venus: he has only recently started hating her. Before that it was in Pisces. What was his attitude to her then? In Pisces, Mars exalts Venus. He worshipped her!

All the time that Mars was in Pisces, he was exalting her, so yes, he did really love her: he was perfectly sincere in his protestations. But exaltation tends not to last, and once the bubble burst he did not merely become indifferent to her, but began to hate her, no doubt for failing to live up to his glorious illusion. This change of attitude is shown by the change of reception as Mars moves from Pisces into Aries.

When I say 'all the time that Mars was in Pisces', I am not referring to Mars' real-time transit of that sign. Here, Mars' passage through that sign can be read as 'for a long time'.

With practice, you will find you begin to know what a chart will look like before you cast it, from the information you are given in the question. As soon as we read the words 'he used to say such wonderful things about me', we can be sure that we shall find exaltation in the chart.

'Is there a future in our relationship?' Much as we might feel that his blackmail story makes this question redundant, it is important that we answer the question asked and answer it from the chart, not from our own assumptions and prejudices. From what we have seen so far, things do not look promising: he hates her. Mars is not going to turn retrograde and go back to exalting Venus: once the bubble of exaltation has burst it may be replaced by something more enduring, but it cannot be put back together. But his other significator, the Sun, is about to enter Pisces, where it will start exalting Venus. Maybe there is hope.

What does she feel about him? Venus is in Capricorn, the exaltation of Mars. She is still besotted with him. Venus and the Moon both signify our querent, but they show her in different ways: head and heart. Lord 1 shows the querent as thinking being and sometimes as body; the Moon is more the querent's emotions. The opposition between them here shows graphically head and heart at odds with each other, and is common in such charts. People tend not to ask relationship questions when they are happy.

The Moon, her heart, is in both the triplicity and the fall of Mars (the lover). Her emotions still feel warmly towards him; but this warmth is overshadowed by loathing: she must be feeling very hurt.

Venus is in the last degree of Capricorn. It is about to change sign, on which its receptions will change. This change of reception shows that she will undergo a change in her attitudes – as her lover did, as shown by Mars moving from Pisces to Aries. How will her attitudes change? She will stop exalting Mars. As soon as Venus enters Aquarius it is no longer in any dignity or debility of Mars: she will become indifferent to him.

The Moon too is about to change sign. It leaves this troubled ambivalence of triplicity and fall of Mars for Leo, where it too has no interest in Mars. She is very soon to fall completely out of love with him. Is there a future in this relationship? No; largely because she will soon no longer want it.

That has given the brief answer to the querent's questions. We may wish to put flesh on these bare bones by looking a little deeper. What else is going on here?

We might notice that Saturn is playing a big part in this chart. Venus and the Sun are in signs ruled by Saturn; Mars is in Saturn's fall; the Moon is in Saturn's detriment. When Venus changes sign and stops exalting Mars, Saturn is going to become even more important to the querent: in the first degrees of Aquarius Venus will be in the sign, triplicity and term of Saturn. So what does Saturn signify, that will suddenly become so much more significant to her as soon as she stops exalting her lover?

In charts cast about affairs, presenting us with two 7th-house type people, if the lover is given Lord 7 as his significator, Saturn can be taken to signify the cheated spouse. If the querent is exalting the lover, the spouse is usually perceived as 'the great malefic' frustrating their possible happiness. Does this fit with the chart?

There is a weak (peregrine) planet in the first house. This is an affliction to the querent. What is afflicting the querent? Saturn: the husband.

Venus is in the sign of Saturn. This could mean that the querent loves her husband. But if your heart is busy exalting someone, there isn't enough room there to love someone else. So here it makes better sense to read this as the husband having great influence over the querent, or ruling her, or even to take it quite literally: she is in his house.

Saturn is in the sign of Venus. The husband loves her. It is in the exaltation of the Moon. So what does the husband really really want? The thing that he exalts: the querent's heart.

What does the querent's heart think of him? The Moon is in the detriment of Saturn: her heart hates him. And also in Saturn's term: her heart sees some minor redeeming features in him.

Note that the querent's head/heart split, shown by the Venus/Moon opposition, makes perfect sense in her attitude to both the lover and the husband.

Once Venus has changed sign, losing interest in the lover, it will become much more dominated by Saturn. The powerful mutual reception between these two planets will become yet stronger. This must mean a strengthening of her relationship to the husband. Note that we do not need to see an aspect between her and him to show this, because the relationship is already in existence: we don't need to prove an event. Note also that although she is going to become more centred on the husband (moving from sign and term of Saturn to sign, triplicity and term of Saturn) she is not suddenly going to start exalting him (both her planets move into signs where nothing is exalted). As is only to be expected.

The Moon, meanwhile, is entering Leo, which is also the detriment of Saturn. Her heart will still hate him.

Why is her attitude to these two men going to change? Our attitudes do not change of themselves: we do not awake one morning to find that we love this person or hate that. There is a trigger that sets off these changes. The change of attitude is shown by the change of receptions (as here in the changes of sign). The trigger is shown by the aspect happening immediately before this change of reception.

What aspect happens immediately before Venus and the Moon change signs? The Moon/Venus opposition. This must be the trigger – the reason for the change of attitude. What does this aspect mean?

Yes, we can read it as showing her head/heart split reaching a climax; but this doesn't help us much: we are still left wondering why.

When a significator is placed right on a house cusp, it is often there for a reason. It almost is as if the chart puts it there as a way of attracting our attention, of saying 'Hey, look over here!' The Moon is right on the cusp of the 5th house – the house of children. The Moon is ruler of that house, so could be playing a secondary role as Lord 5. The Moon is natural ruler of babies and is in the fertile sign of Cancer. So the Moon applying to Venus must show her getting pregnant. By opposition: she is not happy about this. But it is this that concentrates her mind (Venus) on her marriage. Even though her heart (Moon) will still hate her husband. It is probably in the pregnancy that the position of Jupiter, natural ruler of fertility, so prominent on the Ascendant, finds its significance.

"But who's the father?" The aspect showing her getting pregnant (Moon to oppose Venus) has not yet happened, so the event is still in the future. Had the aspect been separating (perhaps Moon at 29 Cancer separating from opposition to Venus at 28 Capricorn) we would have judged that it had already happened, hence that she was already pregnant. So she is not yet pregnant; the boyfriend hates her; she is still in the husband's house; the chart does not show any other suspects: the husband must be the father.

We saw in passing the boyfriend's attitude to the husband: the Sun is ruled by Saturn; Mars is in Saturn's fall. As with our querent's head and heart, the two significators of the lover show him in different ways. Lord 7 (Mars, here) is him as person, as thinking/feeling being. The Sun, given to him because he is a man, shows him as animal male. When I am lecturing, for the entertainment value, I refer to the division of main significator, Moon (if we are considering the querent) and Sun as head, heart and trousers. This may lack subtlety, but it makes the distinction clear enough. Had our querent not had Venus as her main significator by its being Lord 1, we would have given it to her as significator of woman, in which case it would show animal woman. As it is Lord 1, it plays a dual role here.

So the Sun, the boyfriend's man-stuff, is ruled by the husband (Saturn). No doubt: the existence of the husband probably means he cannot exercise his man-stuff as much as he might wish. His thinking/feeling person loathes the husband (Mars in fall of Saturn). Which is not surprising, because it exalts his own man-stuff (exalts Sun) which is ruled by the husband. So the boyfriend is feeling thoroughly frustrated by the existence of our querent's husband, and is therefore resentful.

You may have noticed that the imminent changes of sign bring some positive reception between our querent and her lover: the Sun will enter Pisces, where it exalts Venus, while the Moon enters Leo, where it is ruled by the Sun. His man-stuff (Sun) will start exalting Venus, which can probably be read here in its role as our querent as animal woman, while her emotions (Moon), still hating the husband, become ruled by her boyfriend's man-stuff (Sun). As we have seen that the relationship between the querent and her boyfriend will not continue, we can read this as a good deal of frustrated nostalgia that they will carry with them, looking back fondly on a passion that found too little realisation.

9

Aspects

Some horary questions are about a state of affairs: 'Am I pregnant?' 'What will the weather be on my holiday?' 'Does he really love me?' These can be judged by assessing the condition of the relevant significators. Most questions, however, ask if or when something will happen. For these, we must not only consider the condition of the significators, but see whether or not they will connect with each other by aspect. If they do, there is at least the opportunity for the event to happen; if they do not, there is not.

If I ask 'Will she marry me?' – though this is surely a question better asked to the person concerned than to an astrologer – finding strong receptions between my significators and hers is encouraging: we love each other. But if there is no aspect bringing our planets together, no matter how we love each other there will be no marriage.

Most questions are concerned with the future, so we are looking for *applying* aspects: aspects that have not yet been made, but will be made in the future. Some questions are about the past ('Did the builder steal my bracelet?), in which case we are interested in *separating* aspects: aspects that have happened.

We are concerned only with the *major aspects*: conjunction, trine, square, sextile and opposition. These are also known as *ptolemaic* aspects, because Ptolemy writes about them in his *Tetrabiblos*, the most influential book on astrology ever written. The conjunction is not technically an aspect, but for all practical purposes can be treated as if it were, so for simplicity it will be treated as such here.

"Why is a conjunction not an aspect?" The word aspect is taken from the Latin word for a glance. A glance, in this sense, is seen as a ray of light passing from the eyes of one person into the eyes of another. In conjunction the two planets are as one, and you cannot glance into your own eyes. Hence conjunction is not an aspect.

There is no place for the so-called *minor aspects* either in horary or anywhere else in astrology. "But Lilly mentions them." Never to any purpose. When he was writing, they were the new hot thing in town. Now that their novelty has worn off they can be ignored.

Aspects can be made only if the signs the planets occupy are themselves in that aspect. Taurus is in trine to Capricorn. So a planet at 29 Taurus is trine a planet at 29 Capricorn. It is not trine a planet at 0 Aquarius. It probably either will be in aspect to it, or recently has been in aspect to it, and either of these may be relevant to our judgement; but it is not in aspect to it now.

To find whether one planet will aspect another, it is essential to know which planet is moving faster. As we saw when considering accidental dignities, the average daily motion of the planets is:

Moon	13°11'
Mercury	0°59'
Venus	0°59'
Sun	0°59'
Mars	0°31'
Jupiter	0°05'
Saturn	0°02'

When I say 'it is essential to know which planet is moving faster', I mean 'which planet is moving faster right now'. This is not always the same as 'which generally moves faster'. You will need to check your ephemeris. For example, as I write this, Mars has recently applied to aspect with Venus – possible only because Venus had just changed direction and was moving so slowly that Mars could catch it. Looking at the chart cold, without consulting the ephemeris, we would assume that Venus was separating from Mars, so any judgement based on those two planets would be wrong. There is usually at least one planet doing something untoward, so checking your ephemeris is *essential*. If you don't, your judgements will be consistently wrong.

It is vital that you know what the planets are going to do, not just what they look as if they are going to do!

Planets do not suddenly change direction while running full tilt along their usual path. Planets gradually slow down until they are apparently stationary, then set off in the opposite direction, gradually picking up speed again.

If you are working from software and do not have an ephemeris, you can check how fast a planet is moving by clicking your chart forward to the same time next day: the difference in planetary positions will give you each planet's daily motion at that time.

The list above is of the planets' average forward motion. More useful for our purposes is a knowledge of each planet's usual speed, whichever direction it is travelling in. We don't need precision here: a rough guide, easily memorable, is sufficient for our purposes. Memorise this list:

Moon	13 degrees
Mercury	A degree and a half
Venus	A degree and a bit
Sun	1 degree
Mars	Half a degree
Jupiter	Barely moving
Saturn	Barely moving

If you compare this with the list of average forward motions above, you will see that although Mercury and Venus are usually moving faster than the Sun, their average forward motion is the same. It is as if the Sun were a man taking two dogs for a walk. The man ambles along steadily, while the dogs race hither and thither, but they all reach home at the same time.

Consider: if the Moon is at 10 Aries, applying to conjunct Venus at 20 Aries, Venus will not have moved far before the Moon catches it. The Moon takes less than a day to travel that 10 degrees, during which time Venus will have moved on only about a degree. So the aspect would perfect at 21 Aries. If it were Mercury at 10 Aries, the situation would be quite different. Every time Mercury moves a degree and a half towards Venus, Venus moves a degree and a bit away from Mercury. It will take Mercury ages to perfect this conjunction; it will not catch Venus before Venus leaves Aries.

Aspects

Most readers will know how to spot an aspect, both in the chart and in the ephemeris, so I have put this information in an appendix for those who are coming to astrology afresh. If you aren't sure, stop now and work through Appendix 3.

In horary we are concerned mainly with exact aspects. Exact means exact. If the aspect fails to perfect by even one minute of arc, it is not exact and the event that it would have foretold will not happen. For instance, if boy marrying girl would be shown by Venus reaching a conjunction with Mars at 22.17 Leo, but Venus turns retrograde at 22.16 Leo, thus failing to perfect the aspect, the marriage will not happen.

To show the event asked about, we need an exact aspect between the main significators. A planet that is not a main significator aspecting one that is may show other influences on the situation, without showing an event. Such aspects need to be close but need not be exact. They can usually be ignored, as with boy marrying girl: that one of them is worried about a tax demand will usually not be crucial to the judgement. But, for example, if the question is 'Will my team win the match?' and my team's significator is closely squared by Saturn, this has an effect: my team is weakened. Keep to a maximum of about 3 degrees apart for this; anything beyond that is trivial.

The old texts use the words *platick* and *partile* when discussing aspects. I'll explain them so you know what they mean, but there is no need to use them yourself. An excess of technical terms brings nothing but confusion. A partile aspect is one where the planets are in the same degree of their respective signs. Venus at 21.05 Taurus is in partile trine to Mars at 21.22 Capricorn: they are both at 21 degrees. If Venus were at 20.59 Taurus, it would not be in partile trine to Mars, because it is not at 21 degrees, even though they are within 1 degree of each other. A degree is, literally, a step (Old French), and you are either on one step or you are on another; there is no fuzzy area between them.

The term 'partile' is superfluous, however. The planets are in the same degree: so what? To give us an event they must perfect an aspect, not merely share a degree; to show influence, they need only be within 2 or 3 degrees of each other.

A platick aspect is an aspect that is not partile. As we are abolishing the term 'partile' we can dispose of 'platick' as well.

The nature of the aspects

Forget all ideas you may have picked up about certain aspects being 'good' and others 'bad'. It is the nature of the planets involved and their attitude towards each other that show this, not the nature of the aspects themselves.

Conjunction

Planets 0 degrees apart. When two planets are conjunct they are as one. The word is from the Latin, where it is a usual word for two bodies coming together as one. But is this a desirable thing or not? In the tenderest of lovemaking or the most savage of rapes the two bodies are together: it is not the union in itself – the conjunction – that is desirable. Only the study of the dignities of the planets involved and, especially, the receptions between them will tell whether the conjunction is a desirable outcome. The chart may show me conjunct the woman of my dreams or conjunct the dole queue: these are both conjunction.

Trine

Planets 120 degrees apart. Trines can happen only between planets in the same triplicity: fire signs trine fire signs, water signs water, etc. This means there is always common ground between planets in trine. So trines show things happening easily. 'Easy' and 'good' are not synonymous! If the brakes on my car fail, it will easily roll down the hill and into the river. Whether this easy contact is desirable or not will be shown by the nature of the planets (nice or nasty) and their receptions (their attitude to each other).

Square

Planets 90 degrees apart. Squares bring things together with difficulty or with delay. These may still be nice things. 'Will she marry me?' with our planets coming together by square may well show a 'Yes', but maybe I'll need to ask her twice, or maybe there will be delays in arranging the ceremony. In many situations, delay or difficulty is only to be anticipated – 'Will I get my tax rebate?' 'Will this house sale go through?' – so a square aspect can be an excellent outcome. The key, as ever, is in the dignities and the receptions.

Sextile

Planets 60 degrees apart. The sextile is the runt of the litter when it comes to aspects. It is by far the weakest of them, but it will usually do the job. Although the sextile is an easy aspect, like a lightweight trine, I'd put more faith in a square with good receptions. But don't overstate this weakness; just be a little more cautious with checking whether the planets are strong enough to act and whether they wish to act.

Opposition

Planets 180 degrees apart. The opposition brings things together only to split them apart again. Or it brings them together with the expenditure of so much effort that the result it not worth it. Or it brings them together with regret. William Lilly says that if 'Will she marry me?' has the significators coming together by opposition, they will marry, but will be 'wrangling and jangling all their lives'. In the modern world, wrangling and jangling are grounds for divorce. 'Will I get the job?' with an opposition between Lords 1 and 10: yes, but you'll wish you hadn't, or you won't stay there long.

If you look at the receptions, it is easy to see why this is so. If two planets are in opposition, their values are totally opposed to each other. If one loves whatever Jupiter signifies, the other hates it; if one exalts whatever Saturn shows, the other loathes it.

It is the condition of the planets and their attitudes to each other – the dignities and receptions – that show whether an aspect is fortunate. Not the nature of the aspect itself.

Let's look at some examples. Whenever I am lecturing in America, my hosts regard a trip to the Indian casino as suitable retribution for England's excesses during colonial days. So suppose I cast a horary to ask if I will win:

* there is an applying trine between Lord 1 (me) and Lord 8 (the other people's money): I win, and win easily.
* there is a square between Lord 1 and Lord 8. I still win, but it takes a lot of effort. Maybe I have to play for hours; maybe there are lots of ups and downs before I show a profit.
* there is an opposition between Lord 1 and Lord 8. I still win (Lord 1 in contact with Lord 8). But maybe I win a pittance – not enough to cover the cost of getting to the casino. Or maybe I win but lose my winnings on the way to my car.
* there is an aspect to Lord 8, and Lord 8 is in its own exaltation and conjunct the North Node. Yippee! The aspect shows that I win; the strength of Lord 8 (the other people's money, which the aspect has shown will come to me) shows that I will win big.
* there is the same aspect, but Lord 8 is in its detriment and squared by Saturn. I still win (aspect) but very little (weakness of Lord 8).

Considerations such as these can be a major part of judgement. 'Should I go for the risky bet/investment at high return, or the safer option at low return?' The answer is here.

Squares become trines

No they don't! Lilly and others would claim that between certain signs a square can be treated as if it were a trine. This is nonsense: if signs were flexible like this, the Moon would not oppose the Sun at Full Moon, the Nodes would not oppose each other, and so forth.

The problem he faced was how some squares bring happier outcomes than some trines. What he lacked was the full understanding of dignity and reception that makes clear why this is so. Getting to see my best friend with difficulty is far nicer than easily meeting someone I don't like. The key is dignity and reception. The importance of these cannot be overstated.

ASPECTS CANNOT BE FORMED IF PLANETS ARE IN THE WRONG SIGN.

If you have come from the world of modern astrology you will be accustomed to regarding a planet at 29 Aries as conjunct a planet at 1 Taurus, or being trine a planet at 2 Virgo. This is not so. Never. Ever. No matter how much you would like it to be so.

Consider conjunction. As we have seen, conjunction is two bodies becoming one. The signs, to give them their correct name, are celestial houses. If you think your body can become one with someone else's body while you are in different houses, you evidently haven't tried it.

Consider the trine. The trine brings together planets that are in signs of the same element. This is why it is harmonious. Suppose I am an accountant, using an office in a big block. There is another accountant in an office across the corridor, and we have a happy relationship: when either of us has a knotty problem with his books, he wanders over to get some help. We may not be the best of friends, but we have something important in common: the same triplicity – we are both accountants.

The office next to that other accountant is rented by a dentist. If I take my knotty accountancy problem across to him, he is no use at all. It doesn't matter how close to the wall of his office he might stand, he is still a dentist. Being within a couple of degrees of that wall does not transform him into an accountant.

So it is with aspects.

It is possible that an aspect may perfect immediately inside the next sign. Example: Moon at 28 Aries applies to Mars at 2 Taurus. There is no connection between them now. None at all. This *is* not an aspect. But it *will be* an aspect.

Such an aspect can show something happening after a change. But we must make sense of this change, as shown by the change of sign and consequent change of reception, if we are to allow this aspect to show the desired event. Example: 'Will she go out with me?' with aspect between you and her perfecting only after your planet has changed sign. Depending on what the receptions show, this might tell us 'Yes she will – but only after you've got a job'. The change of sign shows a change in circumstance, and/or a change in attitude.

Limit this to a few degrees inside the next sign. If the aspect does not perfect within, at most, 3 or 4 degrees of the next sign, the thing will not happen.

Often, the aspect not perfecting until the next sign gives us a 'No'. It is an example of *frustration* (see below). 'What time today will the repairman arrive?' The aspect perfects, but only after a change of sign. 'He's coming, but not today.'

It doesn't matter which planet applies to which. If the question is 'Will my mother come to visit?' this could be shown by either her significator applying to aspect mine or my significator applying to aspect hers. Who goes to whom is shown by the question itself and, if necessary, by the receptions.

Dexter, sinister

In the texts you will read of planets casting 'a dexter trine', or 'a sinister square'. Dexter and sinister are right and left respectively in Latin. They relate to the right and left of somebody standing in the centre of the chart and looking outwards.

A dexter aspect is cast towards the right of this person. This means it is cast against the order of the signs. Example: a planet at 4 Gemini casts a dexter sextile to a planet at 4 Aries.

A sinister aspect is cast towards this person's left, which means it is cast along the order of the signs. A planet at 4 Gemini casts a sinister sextile to a planet at 4 Leo. There is nothing sinister, in the modern sense, about this.

All aspects are two-way streets. If A casts a dexter trine to B, B will cast a sinister trine to A.

These terms have no practical significance. I mention them only because you may find them in other books. Ideas that one is stronger than the other can be ignored, because we are not in the situation of having numerous aspects which we need to compare, and because aspects are two-way streets.

Indirect perfection

As well as having one significator aspect a second significator to show an event, the event can be shown by a third planet connecting the two significators. This is called *translation* or *collection of light*.

Translation of light

Suppose we want to connect Mercury and Jupiter. Mercury is at 10 Cancer and Jupiter at 12 Leo. They are in adjacent signs, so there can be no aspect between them. If the Moon is at 11 Aries, it has just separated from sextile Mercury and is applying immediately to square Jupiter. It carries or translates (which means, literally, 'carries across') the light of Mercury to Jupiter, and so brings about the event. The involvement of the third planet making the connection usually implies the involvement of a third party in the situation.

Translation of light can happen in various ways, all of them variations on the basic theme of a fast planet connecting two slower planets. As in the example here, we can have the situation where a fast planet has separated from aspecting a slower planet and is on its way to aspect another slower planet.

The faster planet may not yet have made the first of these aspects, so it applies to aspect one of the significators and then goes on to aspect the other. This is common in situations where the initiating action has not yet been taken: 'If I apply for this job, will I get it?'

We can have the situation where planet A goes to aspect planet B, then planet B goes on to aspect planet C. This gives a chain reaction, linking planet A to planet C.

Examples of translation:

* Mars at 10 Aries, Venus at 15 Aries. Venus is separating from Mars: this doesn't look hopeful. But the Moon at 8 Aries will conjunct Mars and then go on to conjunct Venus, remaking the aspect and bringing the event.
* Jupiter at 8 Leo, Saturn at 12 Pisces. The Sun at 7 Scorpio applies to square Jupiter and then applies to trine Saturn, translating the light of Jupiter to Saturn.

Collection of light

The two significators both apply to aspect a third, slower planet. It is as if this third planet stands with its arms outspread, collecting the light of the two significators and drawing them together. I want to go out with the belle of the school, but don't dare ask her. Then we both aspect the wicked headmaster, who puts us both in detention, drawing us together. The wicked headmaster has collected our light.

Examples of collection:

* * Mars at 5 Taurus, Venus at 6 Aries. No aspect between them. But they both apply to Jupiter at 8 Cancer, who therefore collects their light, bringing Mars and Venus together.
* * Mercury at 24 Pisces, the Moon at 22 Libra. They both apply to Saturn at 26 Gemini, who collects their light.

It is theoretically possible that we could have a collection where one of the significators has already made its aspect with the collecting planet (I have already been put in detention; all that remains is for the belle of the school to incur the headmaster's wrath). I cannot recall having seen this in a chart, but do be aware of the possibility.

Translation and collection can happen by any aspects or by conjunction. They can be prohibited or frustrated like any other aspect (see below). Like any other aspect, the aspects here do have to perfect: exact means exact.

In translation, the planet doing the translating must be moving faster than the other two planets. In collection, the planet doing the collecting must be moving slower. There is nothing significant about this: it is simply that the situation cannot arise if this is not so.

Contrary to what is said in some texts, there is no set amount of reception needed to make translation and collection work. What we do need is whatever reception makes sense in the context. Example: if my friend goes to ask Bill Gates to lend me some money (translating light from me to him), Bill Gates liking my friend could be more useful than Bill Gates liking me. If my friend goes to ask Susie to come on a date with me (translating light between me and her), Susie's feelings for me are far more important than her feelings for my friend. So with the receptions. It is usually more important that the two significators have reception than that either of them has reception with the connecting planet.

Preventing aspects

Aspects that look as if they are going to perfect do not always do so. In astrology too, there's many a slip 'twixt cup and lip.

Prohibition

A planet getting in the way of an aspect is said to prohibit it. This happens in three ways:

* A is applying to B when it bumps into C. Example: Moon at 8 Taurus is applying to trine Saturn at 12 Capricorn, when it collides with Jupiter at 10 Virgo. I have a date with Julie, but I collide with Lord 6: I get ill and can't go.
* A is applying to B, but C aspects B first. Example: Venus at 12 Libra applies to square Mars at 15 Cancer, but before this aspect perfects Mercury at 14 Virgo perfects a sextile with Mars. I have a date with Julie, but before I get to her door to collect her, some other guy turns up and whisks her away.
* A is applying to B, but before this aspect perfects, C aspects A. Example: Venus at 12 Libra applies to square Mars at 15 Cancer, but before this aspect perfects the Moon at 10 Libra conjuncts Venus. I have a date with Julie, but before I leave to meet her Jane says she wants me back, so I don't go.

Frustration

This is really a particular example of prohibition. A is applying to B, but before the aspect is made, B makes an aspect with C. Example: Venus at 8 Aquarius applies to sextile Mars at 12 Aries, but before the aspect perfects, Mars conjuncts Jupiter at 14 Aries. I plan to propose to Julie, but before I do so she elopes with Alphonse.

   B entering the next sign before A can perfect the aspect can usually be taken as a frustration.

Refrenation

This is an old legal term for breaking a contract. A is applying to B, but before the aspect perfects A turns retrograde, so the aspect fails to perfect. Example: Mercury at 17 Sagittarius applies to square Jupiter at 19 Virgo, but at 18

Sagittarius Mercury turns retrograde, failing to make the aspect. Julie has accepted my proposal, but on the morning of the wedding she comes to her senses and runs away. No matter how close the planets get, if they do not perfect, the event will not happen. A planet turning retrograde usually shows that person changing their mind.

NB: all these points work by conjunction and all aspects. When you read Lilly's description of them and find him speaking of 'corporeal aspects', he means aspects that are body to body in contrast to those that are only orb to orb, i.e. he means that the aspects must be exact. 'Corporeal aspect' does not mean conjunction.

Don't get stressed about these technical terms. All we are saying here is, 'Either we can join our significators in a plausible fashion, or we can't'. The context is the key. The chart is giving us a picture of the situation: if the connection in the chart makes sense in the life, it will work. The touchstone always is 'What makes sense in context?'

Preventions do not always prevent. Consider the example above, where my collision with Lord 6 shows my falling ill and so not going on the date. Perhaps I collide with Lord 6, but dose myself with remedies and go on the date anyway. Whether the prevention stops the event or not depends on three factors:

* the strength of the various planets
* the receptions
* the context. Or, in other words, common sense.

How strong are the planets? If I am strong and the illness is weak, I may well be able to shrug it off. Is the prevented planet strong enough to overcome the prevention?

What are the receptions? The receptions show attitude, and so they show how much the prevented planet wants to overcome the obstruction. Am I crazy with love for my date, or am I going out with her only because I've nothing better to do? The more the planet wants to perfect the aspect, the more it will strive to overcome the prevention.

What is the situation? It is always helpful if we can identify what the preventing planet shows, although this is not always possible. Do this by looking at the houses it rules and then bouncing possibilities off the querent to find one that seems likely. The more we understand the situation, the more we can tell if the prevention will hold or not. Example: boy goes to meet girl. Is their date ten minutes in a coffee-shop or a romantic evening on which he has already invested large amounts of time and money? The illness shown by Lord 6 might prevent the former even if it were only mild, but would need to be far stronger to prevent the latter.

Especially in long-term questions, aspects that would otherwise prevent can be regarded as events happening along the way, but which are not obstacles. So in a general enquiry of 'When will I die?' this encounter with Lord 6 could show a bout of illness, but it will not prevent me dying at some point.

The more we are able to understand the situation, which we can do by a careful analysis of the chart, the more we can suggest ways of circumventing preventions. Here horary goes beyond the merely predictive. 'Yes, she's longing for you to propose; but you'll need to act fast because she's getting tired of waiting and there's this other guy who's keen on her'. 'Yes, you will get the job. Don't let being ill stop you going to the interview.'

Bonatti says that a conjunction cannot be prohibited by an aspect.[23] It demonstrably can, but a conjunction is certainly more likely to be able to overcome the prohibition. As discussed above, consider the planets' strengths and receptions, together with the reality of the situation, to decide whether the prohibition will prohibit.

The Moon's aspects rarely prohibit, unless it is ruling a house which would make sense of the prohibition. If Capricorn rises in the chart for 'Will I get the job?' Cancer will be on the 7th cusp, so the Moon will signify my rivals for the job. If the Moon prohibits an aspect between Lord 1 and Lord 10, then, this prohibition would make sense: my rival gets the job.

Note that a benefic can prohibit as much as a malefic. 'Will I get the job?' My planet is going towards the job's planet, but a strong Jupiter gets in the way. By analysing the chart I see that this means I win the lottery. This is very nice, but it still prevents me getting the job.

You may have noticed that prohibition and translation of light can look much the same. Which is which will be shown by the context and the receptions. Consider: I am in the schoolyard, longing for the glamorous Nancy. I ask my friend to go and tell her that I am pining for her. He walks across the yard to her. But does he give her my message, thus translating light from me to her, or does he chat her up himself, thus prohibiting my aspect to her? His physical action of walking across the yard is exactly the same in either case. Look at his planet and

---

[23] *Bonatus*, aphorism 31.

its receptions. Is he an honourable lad who likes me more than he likes Nancy, or is he morally dubious and crazy about her?

In most horaries we are concerned only with the next aspect a planet makes, or sometimes its next two aspects if there is a translation of light. Do not push planets through aspect after aspect ('The Moon goes to square Mars, then to conjunct Saturn, then trine Venus, then.....'). It is most unlikely that these later aspects will be relevant to the issue.

What this amounts to is: Keep to the point!

Orbs

This is another technical term which must be explained because you will come across it in the texts, but which has no practical use. *Orb* is probably the most overrated concept in traditional astrology.

Each planet is said to have an orb around it. This is like an aura or a force-field, except that it extends not only around the body of the planet, but around the points to which the planet casts its aspects. So if a planet has an orb of 10 degrees, this means 10 degrees around the planet, 10 degrees around its square, its trine, its sextile and its opposition.

The word 'orb' refers to the diameter of this force-field, which has the planet in its centre. The radius of the force-field is called the *moitie* (French for half). The distance to which the orb extends in any one direction is the moitie. It is, of course, the moitie that concerns us, not the orb, just as with a boxer we are concerned with his 'reach', which is how far he can punch with either hand, not how far he can stretch from fingertip to fingertip.

The theory is that when the edge of one planet's moitie touches the edge of another planet's moitie, they are in aspect by orb. Example: if planet A has an orb of 10 degrees, its moitie will be half this: 5 degrees. If planet B has an orb of 8 degrees, its moitie will be 4 degrees. When the planets are exactly 9 degrees apart (the sum of their two moities: 5+4) they are touching by orb – as if we had two boxers just touching each other's glove at full stretch.

"What does this mean?" Absolutely nothing. Which is why you don't need to bother with it.

"Why does it mean nothing?" In the first place, orbs do not come to a sharp end. The planets' auras are not really like boxers' arms which can reach exactly so far and no further. The aura gradually peters away into insignificance. This is why Lilly gives two different lists of the sizes of the planets' orbs, saying he uses whichever he happens to remember, and why I am not giving such a list here: it is a list of what does not exist.[24]

Any two planets in the same sign have an effect on each other, no matter how far apart they might be. Any two planets in signs that aspect each other have such an effect. They *behold* each other. Beholding plays only a tiny role in horary, but is of great significance in natal work – it is probably the most underrated concept in traditional astrology. It is like peripheral vision: two planets may be a long way apart by degree, but if they are in signs that behold each other (literally, that can see each other) it is as if they are in each other's field of peripheral vision. While this may not seem much, any car driver will know how aware we really are of what is at the edges of our visual field.

In horary, we are concerned mainly with planets exactly aspecting each other. Exact means exact, so orb and moitie have no place here. We are sometimes concerned with planets close to each other, casting an influence on each other. But the maximum separation for this to be worth noting, whether by conjunction or aspect, is around 3 degrees: much less than the theory of orb and moitie would have it. On either count, orbs are useless.

There are those who regard the point at which the moities meet as a kind of starting gate: if the planets are not within that distance when the chart is set they cannot go on to form an aspect. Of course they can. This idea has no support anywhere in the texts and is contrary to reason: it is the equivalent of saying that nothing can come from my peripheral vision into my full field of view.

NB: when modern astrologers speak of orbs, they usually attach them to aspects rather than to planets ('A sextile has an orb of X degrees') and they mean the radius of the force-field, not its diameter. Modern 'orb' = traditional 'moitie'.

Now you know what orbs are, you can forget all about them.

Retrograde aspects

The texts are often negative about aspects made when one or, especially, both planets are retrograde. But usually the context shows a good reason for this retrogradation. It is common when the person signified by the retrograde planet is coming back, either literally or metaphorically. If the question were, 'Will I get back with my old boyfriend?' the significators coming together to an aspect with one of them retrograde would make sense in the context.

---

[24] *Lilly*, p. 107.

Aspects between two retrograde planets are rare. If there were a context to support the idea that both parties were coming back (bosses and workers going back to the negotiating table, for instance), this too would not carry any negative indications. Without such a context, however, it must be regarded as against the natural order of things, so giving the sense that matters will not fall out well.

Separating aspects

As we have seen, these show things that have happened in the past. But what if the significators that we are hoping will show an applying aspect (something happening in the future) are in fact separating from aspect to each other?

Judgement will depend on the context. In many questions this can be taken as 'You've come as close to that thing as you are going to, and you're not getting any closer'. If the thing in question is the woman of the querent's dreams, this is not a favourable answer; if the thing in question is death, the querent will be delighted.

Sometimes the context supports the idea that the separating aspect has put events in motion, so if nothing untoward is happening to the significators in the future, we can judge that things are rolling and will proceed to their intended outcome. If the question is 'Will I marry Fred?' when the marriage has already been agreed, a separating aspect could well show the agreement being made. If there is nothing obstructive happening in the chart, the wedding will take place as planned. If the question were 'Will I marry Fred, whom I met for the first time two hours ago?' a separating aspect would be a definite No.

Placement

In some questions, we do not need an aspect. You will find many examples of this in the chapters on chart interpretation. This is common in questions that ask about a state of affairs rather than a specific event: 'Am I pregnant?' Lord 5 (the baby) in the 1st house gives a clear picture of the baby inside the querent: 'Yes, you are'. 'Where is the book?' The lost book is where it is, regardless of what might be happening to it. Its significator's house placement will show its location.

There are other contexts where placement alone will give the answer to an event-based judgement. 'Will I win this tennis match?' with Lord 7 just inside the 1st house: my opponent is in my power – Yes, I will win.

But in most contexts placement shows desire or fear rather than an event.

'Will she marry me?' My significator on the 7th cusp is not a strong testimony for 'Yes'. It shows that I want her to marry me, and so the marriage is more likely than if I don't want her to, but it shows no more than that. 'Will I get the job?' with Lord 1 on the 10th cusp. I clearly want the job, and so am more likely to get it than if I didn't want it; but no more than that. It does not show a Yes.

If something else in the chart shows the Yes, the movement of the significator onto the cusp can show the timing.

Similarly, 'Will I get the job?' with Lord 10 on the 1st cusp does not show a Yes. What a planet on the Ascendant usually shows is the idea of that thing weighing on the querent. The idea of the job, or of getting any job, is weighing on the querent's shoulders.

One of my students set a chart for 'Will my ex come to the family party?' The ex's significator was sitting on the Ascendant, but made no aspect to either the querent or the party (Lord 5). No aspect: he didn't come. But the placement showed that the idea of his coming was weighing on the querent's mind.

Finding the querent's significator *in* the relevant house (rather than on the cusp of that house) still shows only desire or concern. For instance, 'Will I survive this illness?' with Lord 1 in the 8th house shows that the querent is worried about dying, whether he will do so or not. Finding the significator of the thing desired in, rather than on the cusp of, the querent's house is much more positive. 'Will I get the job?' with Lord 10 inside the 1st house: things look good – you have it in your pocket. This is not a certain Yes, but it is strong positive testimony. It shows that the job wants the querent, which is much more encouraging than the querent wanting the job.

If, however, the event is known or assumed, application to a cusp can show the event happening and give the timing. 'When will Granny arrive?' with Granny's significator applying to the 1st cusp confirms that she is on her way and, by the number of degrees her significator needs to travel to reach the 1st cusp, shows the timing of her arrival.

Planets move, house cusps and Arabian Parts stand still. So planets can apply to cusps or Parts; cusps and Parts cannot apply to planets.

10

Antiscia

When I first read about antiscia, the idea struck me as so bizarre that I was sure someone had sucked it out of his thumb. I quickly learned better. These little creatures are an essential part of judgement. If you do not use them, you will consistently get judgements wrong. So pay attention!

The theory

'Antiscion' is from the Greek word for 'shadow'. Every degree in the zodiac has its antiscion degree, and so anything in that degree has its antiscion in that place. We are usually concerned with planets, so the antiscion is the 'shadow' placement of that planet.

Forget any Jungian meanings of 'shadow': there is no such sense here. 'Reflection' might be a better word for it. It is as if the planet has an alternative placement in its antiscion degree. It acts there exactly as it does in the degree where it stands bodily, except that contacts by antiscion usually carry a sense of hiddenness. 'Will I marry Kylie?' and our significators apply to conjunction: 'Yes, you will'. They apply to conjunction by antiscion: 'No, but you will have an affair with her'.

THE CALCULATION

If you already know how to do this, you can skip this box.

Imagine a line drawn between the solstice points (0 Capricorn and 0 Cancer). Imagine that this line is a mirror. The antiscion of any degree, and of anything in that degree, is its position seen in that mirror. So if something is 2 degrees on one side of this line (at 2 Cancer, say: 2 degrees forward from 0 Cancer) its antiscion

will be at 2 degrees on the other side of that line (28 Gemini: 2 degrees back from
0 Cancer).

This reflection around the solstice points shows that the idea is grounded in
reality – it was not sucked out of somebody's thumb. There is a direct connection
between degrees that are the same distance either side of the solstices. Open your
ephemeris at the summer solstice for any year (Sun at 0 Cancer). Pick a number
between 1 and 180. Count that number of days forward through the year and note
the degree of the Sun on that day. Now count the same number of degrees
backwards through the year. The degree of the Sun on that day will be the antiscion of the degree you have just noted. This means that on those two days the time
between sunrise and sunset will be exactly the same.

Each sign reflects onto one other sign:

♈	reflects onto	♍
♉		♌
♊		♋
♋		♊
♌		♉
♍		♈
♎		♓
♏		♒
♐		♑
♑		♐
♒		♏
♓		♎

So anything in Aries has its antiscion in Virgo; anything in Taurus has its antiscion
in Leo. Learn this table.

Once you know which sign the antiscion of something is in, you need to find its
degree in that sign. Original degree + antiscion = 30. The degree the planet is in
bodily, added to the degree of its antiscion, will equal 30. So, to find the antiscion,
we must take the original degree away from 30. Look back at the example above: if
a planet is 2 degrees forward of 0 Cancer, so is bodily at 2 Cancer, its antiscion will
be 2 degrees back from 0 Cancer, which is 28 Gemini. 28 + 2 = 30.

Don't worry! However innumerate you may feel you are, this is not complicated. Each sign consists of 30 degrees. Each degree consists of 60 minutes. 60
minutes = 1 degree.

Instead of thinking of each sign as 30 degrees, call it 29 degrees and 60 minutes.

It's the same thing (because 60 minutes is the same as 1 degree). But it makes the arithmetic simpler.

Follow this example:

Let's say Mars is at 22.35 Taurus. What is its antiscion?
If Mars is in Taurus, its antiscion must be in Leo (from the table above).
What degree of Leo?
Mars is at 22.35 Taurus.
Take this away from 30 degrees.
But to make it easier, call it 29.60 degrees.

$$
\begin{array}{r}
29.60 \\
22.35 - \\
\hline
7.25
\end{array}
$$

So the antiscion of Mars at 22.35 Taurus is 7.25 Leo.
We can check this, because starting degree + antiscion must add up to 30.

$$
\begin{array}{r}
7.25 \\
22.35 + \\
\hline
29.60 \text{ which} = 30.00
\end{array}
$$

Let's do another one.

What is the antiscion of 14.35 Aries?
From the table above, anything in Aries has its antiscion in Virgo.
What degree of Virgo?
Take 14.35 from 29.60.

$$
\begin{array}{r}
29.60 \\
14.35 - \\
\hline
15.25
\end{array}
$$

So the antiscion of 14.35 Aries is 15.25 Virgo.

The common error here is to end up with starting degree + antiscion = 31 degrees. So, until you get used to this calculation, always check by adding the antiscion you've calculated onto the initial degree to make sure they equal 30. If you follow my suggestion of calling 30 degrees 29.60, you will not make this mistake.

If this seems like hard work, believe me: it isn't. In a very short time you will get used to glancing around the chart to see if the antiscia of any of the significators are doing anything interesting. With a little effort at first you will find that checking antiscia happens almost automatically. You do not have to do the whole calculation. It is enough to think 'Lord 1 is at 19 Gemini. Is there anything around 11 Cancer or Capricorn?' If not – forget it. If there is, then you can calculate the antiscial placement exactly.

Contrantiscia

If a planet is at 25.42 Gemini, its antiscion will be at 4.18 Cancer. The point opposite its antiscion, 4.18 Capricorn, is its *contrantsicion.* Contrantiscion is directly opposite antiscion.

You need to know this word, because you will come across it in other books, but I strongly suggest you do not use it yourself. Call it an opposition by antiscion. That is what it is, and this makes its meaning clear. We can do without superfluous technical terms.

Example: suppose my significator in a chart is at 3.17 Leo. Its antiscion is at 26.43 Taurus. If there is a planet at 26 Scorpio, it opposes my significator by antiscion. Or, if you wish, is on my contrantiscion.

In natal charts, other aspects to antiscia have minor significance. In horary they can be ignored. Keep to conjunction and opposition.

If this is your first introduction to antiscia, take a break now and work out where the antiscia fall in your natal chart. You will probably find you have some new and important aspects that you knew nothing about.

How do we use antiscia?

If the conjunction or opposition is going to show an event, it must be exact, just as with a bodily aspect. Don't try moving the antiscion: you'll tie your brain in knots, especially if you are dealing with the antiscion of a retrograde planet. Plot the antiscion on the chart and let the applying planet come to it.

If the antiscion of planet A is conjunct planet B, the antiscion of planet B will be conjunct planet A. This is automatic, so don't get excited about it: 'Look, the antiscion of Mars is on Venus, and wow, the antiscion of Venus is on Mars!'

Often, we are not looking for the aspect to show an event. If two planets are conjunct or opposed by antiscion, they will influence each other. For example, if Lord 10 is the new job I am asking about, and Saturn in Aries opposes it by antiscion, I can see that something nasty is afflicting this job in (by antiscion) a hidden sort of way. For this influence to be significant, the planets need to be close, a couple of degrees apart at most. If this nasty Saturn were on the 10th cusp by antiscion, the judgement would be the same: my job is afflicted in a hidden way.

As this example shows, a planet's antiscion works as if the planet itself were in that place, with the exceptions that

* we are concerned only with conjunction and opposition
* antiscia usually carry a sense of the hidden
* antiscia are less likely to prohibit other aspects.

I have judged many horaries by antiscia alone. The things that will not be shown by antiscia are death and pregnancy.

Use the planet's essential dignities as shown by its bodily position, not the position of its antiscion. If Jupiter is at 23.07 Cancer its antiscion will be at 6.53 Gemini. When considering its antiscion, treat Jupiter as exalted (as it is at its bodily position in Cancer) not as in detriment (as it is where its antiscion falls in Gemini). Antiscia can gain or lose accidental strength, however. In a contest horary one team's significator fell exactly on an angle: this is greatly strengthening, and that team won. I don't think antiscia are affected by falling on fixed stars, but I could be convinced otherwise.

If an antiscion falls right on a house cusp, this shows that this person – if the planet is someone's significator – has an interest in the affairs of that house, or that the house is affected, for better or for worse, by whatever that planet signifies. This is *only* if it falls right on the cusp: if the antiscion is floating around in the middle of the house its effect on that house can be ignored. Example: if I ask 'Will she marry me?' and my significator's antiscion falls on the cusp of the 8th (2nd from 7th: the other person's money) this suggests that I have a major interest in her money. If my significator's antiscion were a few degrees inside that house, it would carry no such meaning.

Worked example

The event in this chart is shown solely by an antiscion.[25] The querent had an email and telephone relationship with a man. She had not heard from him for a

[25] There is another such in *R A Applied*, pp. 26–28.

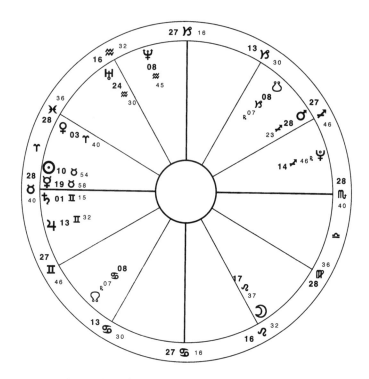

Why isn't he calling? May 1st 2001, 6.21 am BST, London.

few weeks, and he was not answering or returning her calls. She asked, 'Why isn't he calling me? Will I hear from him, and when?' Some of the techniques discussed here are explained later in the book; follow what you can for now, then come back to this chart when you've worked through the practical section.

The querent is shown by Lord 1, which is Venus, and the Moon. As this is a relationship question, we would also give her Venus because she is a woman; but she already has it.

How is she? Yuk! Venus is in its detriment, in the 12th house. She is not happy and she has little power: as we know, because she is having to wait for him to call.

The position of the Moon often shows what the querent is thinking about, especially if this placement is emphasised in some way – as it is here, by being so close to a house cusp. This acts like a highlighter pen, drawing our attention to it. What is she thinking about? Probably having some fun (5th house). It is unlikely that she is thinking about that other major 5th-house concern, children, because the Moon is in a barren sign.

Her boyfriend is shown by Lord 7, which is Mars, and – only in a relationship question – by the Sun, because he is a man.

Does she like him? For this we need to find out her attitudes, which is done by examining her planets' receptions. Look at the table on page 72. Venus is in the sign and face of Mars (him) and the exaltation and triplicity of the Sun (him). The Moon is in the sign and triplicity of the Sun. Yes, she likes him lots!

NB: Venus is in the sign ruled by Lord 7 and is in its own detriment. If Venus were close to the 7th cusp, at, say, 24 Scorpio, it would still be in the sign ruled by Lord 7 and in its own detriment. But that would be a far healthier situation. In that case, she has gone right over to his side of the chart, and Lord 1 will always be in its own detriment on the 7th cusp. Had she been at 24 Scorpio, we could have judged 'She loves him (in his sign), because of which she is very vulnerable (detriment) – as we are if we love someone'. In this chart, however, Lord 1 is in the *other* sign ruled by Lord 7. She has not gone across to his side of the chart. The implication here is that she is unhappy, so she loves him: a quite different dynamic.

Are her feelings reciprocated? Look at the receptions of his planets to find out what his attitudes are. The Sun is in the sign and triplicity of Venus and the exaltation and face of the Moon. The Sun is very keen on her. At 28 Sagittarius, however, Mars has no interest in her at all: it is not in any dignity or debility of either Venus or the Moon. So while the Sun is so keen on her, Mars is completely indifferent. Maybe this is the clue to why he isn't calling her.

Lord 7 and the Sun both signify him; but they signify him in different ways. Lord 7 is him as thinking, feeling person; the Sun is him as animal man. So his animal nature is strongly attracted to her. This is not necessarily only about sex; it also covers the usual imperative to find a mate. As person, however, he has no interest in her at all. Interested or not, with his significators in the 8th and 12th houses, he is not in a good position to act.

Especially unable to act is Mars. Its condition here does not look so bad: it has some essential dignity (term) and is about to enter Capricorn, where it is exalted. But appearances are often deceptive. You *must* be aware of what the planets are doing – not only of what they look as if they are doing. You *must* check your ephemeris. Mars is in first station: scarcely moving as it turns retrograde. It fails to reach the promised land of its exaltation. Station is a time of great vulnerability.

So Mars (the boyfriend as thinking/feeling being) is in a very vulnerable position. Why? The planet's being so close to the house cusp points us to the answer. On the cusp of the 2nd house from his own 1st house (which is the querent's 7th house), he is concerned with his money. How is his money? Look at the ruler of that house, Jupiter. It is in its detriment. His money is in a mess.

So we see that her boyfriend is bogged down (Mars not moving) amid his financial worries. Which is why he hasn't called her, even though we can reassure the querent that he is indeed still strongly interested in her.

Will he get in touch? To judge 'Yes' to this we need an aspect. The Moon (her) does apply to Mars (him); but this aspect is prohibited by Mercury: the Moon squares Mercury first. Even were this not so, we would much prefer to join one of her planets with the Sun (the bit of him that is keen on her) rather than with Mars (the bit of him that isn't).

The Sun is at 10.54 Taurus. Where is its antiscion?
From the table, Taurus has its antiscion in Leo. Hmm – that's where the Moon is: this might be interesting. But where in Leo?

$$\begin{array}{r} 29.60 \\ \underline{10.54 -} \\ 19.06 \end{array}$$

The Sun's antiscion is at 19.06 Leo. Keep the antiscion still, letting the planet apply to it: the Moon applies immediately to conjunct the Sun. Great news, because (judging essential dignity from the bodily position, not the antiscion) they have powerful mutual reception. He will be back in touch.

When? With the Moon at 17.37 Leo, it must travel a degree and a half to reach the Sun's antiscion at 19.06 Leo. So he will call in 1½ somethings. 1½ whats? 'Years' is obviously not a relevant answer to this question: for our smitten querent 'years' might as well be 'never'. As he hasn't called her for weeks, 'hours' is probably too small a time unit. Which leaves us with days, weeks or months.

Following the sign + house formula,[26] 1½ degrees in a fixed sign in a succedent house would give us weeks. But we could take just the fixity of the sign, which would give our longest unit: months. The judgement given was that he would call, possibly in a week and a half, more likely in a month and a half. He phoned her in a month and a half.

Note that his calling her is shown *only* by the antiscion. Ignore that and the judgement is wrong. These little creatures are important!

---

[26] See chapter 13 on timing.

11

The Fixed Stars

The fixed stars are what we commonly call 'stars', in contrast to the 'wandering stars', or planets. As a trip outdoors on a clear night will show – at least, if you are not in a city – there are any number of these. A hundred or so among them have significant astrological use, but of that hundred or so only a handful need to be noted in horary. The fixed stars become more significant the higher up the astrological scale we go: they are useful in natal astrology; they are invaluable in mundane astrology; horary queries are generally beneath their concern.

The stars that that can have a major bearing on horary judgement are:

Algol	which is at	26 ♉
Alcyone		29 ♉
Aldebaran		9 ♊
Regulus		29 ♌
Vindemiatrix		10 ♎
Spica		23 ♎
Antares		9 ♐

These placements are as precise as we need, and are accurate for the time of writing, which is 2005. Despite being 'fixed', the stars do move, albeit very much more slowly than the planets: roughly one degree every 72 years. After 2010 you can regard Regulus as being at 0 Virgo. If a significator or relevant house-cusp is within a couple of degrees of one of these stars (limit this to 1 degree for Vindemiatrix), this may be important – if the star carries a meaning relevant to the context of the question.

We are concerned *only* with conjunction to fixed stars: no aspects. Planets are either on stars or they are not: do not (in horary) think of planets moving onto stars. Example: if the question were, 'Can I hold my marriage together?' Lord 7 on Vindemiatrix would be an indication that the querent's spouse wants a divorce. That Lord 7 will be on Vindemiatrix when it has moved forward 5 degrees does not mean that the spouse will be wanting a divorce in the near future. Such movement should be ignored. The exception to this general rule is when we are using horary to elect a time to act.[27] In that case a planet moving onto Regulus, for instance, might well show the optimum moment.

Ignore antiscia falling onto fixed stars.

Algol

Caput Algol. Medusa's Head. This is the most unfortunate of the stars. In horary, the general idea with it is of losing one's head. This can be literal, but do keep any impulse to grand opera that you might have out of your horary judgements. Yes, such gory events do happen; but they tend not to, especially if the question is 'Will I get the job?' or 'Can I buy this flat?' The losing of heads can usually be taken metaphorically.

Example: the querent was concerned that a nanny she was thinking of hiring might not be able to cope. The nanny's significator was on Caput Algol, exactly confirming the querent's fears: the nanny could lose her head.

Algol being in Taurus, the Moon or Venus will have lots of essential dignity if placed on it. In this example, the nanny's significator was the Moon. Lots of dignity, so she was a decent person, but still unable to cope.

Alcyone

This is the main star in the cluster that is the Pleiades, or the Weeping Sisters. Weeping is the main idea here: there will be regret; things will not turn out well.

Like all star clusters, the Pleiades afflict the eyesight, so this may be an indication that whoever's significator is on Alcyone cannot see clearly, or is deluded.

Aldebaran

The South Eye of the Bull. This is the brightest star in the constellation of Taurus (even though by zodiacal measurement it is in that part of the zodiac that is called Gemini).[28] It is associated with the spring equinox, the start of the year, so the idea here is of inception, of a positive start.

---

[27] See chapter 27.

[28] For a discussion of the distinction between the signs of the zodiac and the constellations that bear the same names, see *Real Astrology*, chapter 5. For now, the important point is that the signs and the constellations are different and must not be confused.

Example: if the question were 'Should I look for a new job?' finding Aldebaran on the Ascendant would be an indication that it is time to start a new cycle, so 'Yes, a new job could be appropriate'.

Regulus

Cor Leonis. The Heart of the Lion. This is the brightest star in Leo. Any star that is the 'heart' of its constellation is the epitome of the idea which that constellation expresses, so Regulus is the most Leo bit of Leo: super-Leo. It is highly auspicious for material achievement, and in horary its significance can usually be limited to that. It is not necessarily happy, but it does bring success.

If the question were, 'Will I get the promotion?' finding the querent's significator on Regulus would be a strong positive testimony. If the question were, 'Does she love me?' or 'Will Puss come home?' that a significator is on Regulus is unlikely to add anything to our judgement.

Vindemiatrix

The Gatherer of Grapes. The Widow-Maker. This has a strong association with divorce and separation. So if the question were, 'Is there a future in our relationship?' finding Vindemiatrix on the Ascendant would be an immediate testimony of 'No'.

It is also associated with the story of the Sorcerer's Apprentice – you have probably seen this in *Fantasia*. Overstretching. Assuming powers you are unable to control. Stupid for stupid's sake: doing something daft even though you're aware that it's daft. 'Should I open a spiritual school?' with the querent's significator on Vindemiatrix: 'Only if you wish to damage yourself and others'.

Spica

The Virgin's Spike. This is the brightest star in the constellation of Virgo. It is associated with Our Lady, so is strongly protective. Spica rising is not necessarily an indication that all will go as is hoped, but even if things don't work out, you will be OK at the end; you will be looked after.

Spica can be most fortunate, bringing bounty, but it doesn't carry quite the sense of material achievement of Regulus. It is, however, much the happier of the two stars.

Antares

Cor Scorpionis. The Heart of the Scorpion. As Regulus is the Leo-most bit of
Leo, this is the Scorpio-most bit of Scorpio (even though it is currently placed in
Sagittarius). This is the star that is Blake's

> *Tyger, tyger burning bright*
> *In the forests of the night.*

It is very powerful, but – as we might expect from Super-Scorpio – not the most
benign of stars.

Being directly opposite Aldebaran, star of the spring equinox, Antares is
associated with the autumn equinox. So as Aldebaran is about inception and new
cycles starting, Antares is about closing down and cycles ending. This is by no
means always negative. Suppose the question were, 'Should I take early retire-
ment?' Antares on the Midheaven (or the Ascendant) would be an indication
that a cycle is closing and it is time to move on.

Other stars

Other stars can be important in specific contexts. Suppose a woman were to ask,
'Should I join the army?" and Lord 10 were on Bellatrix ('the female warrior'):
this would be important testimony. But to deal with all these possibilities here,
the fixed star chapter would be longer than the rest of the book, which would
greatly exaggerate the overall importance of the stars in horary judgement. I plan
to devote a future book to the fixed stars; in the meantime, I would suggest that
there is a greater danger in overstating their significance than there is in ignoring
them. Fear not, ignorance of their meanings will not keep you from sound judgement: there will always be other testimonies.

If you wish to investigate the stars further, I commend Vivian Robson's *The
Fixed Stars and Constellations in Astrology*.[29] This is based on traditional sources,
though much diluted. If studying his book, ignore all his references to Alvidas
and Wilson. For horary purposes, ignore also his specific notes for each of the
planets falling on stars. In natal work, being specific like this makes sense: we can
say 'Your Saturn is on Regulus, therefore....' But in horary it is not 'your Saturn',

---

[29] London (?) 1923. Available in a new edition under the Astrology Classics imprint of The Astrology
Center of America.

which is one facet of you, but 'your significator', which is all of you: it is not 'your Saturn is on Regulus' as much as 'you are on Regulus'. So keep to the general meanings of the stars.

Robson's list of stars gives their positions in 1920. To bring these up to date you will need to add 'a degree and a bit' to the positions he gives. The stars have their own individual motions as well as the general progression of 1 degree in 72 years (50″ in one year). These individual motions are tiny, but are sufficient to make exact calculation from 1 degree in 72 years inaccurate.[30] But there is no benefit in computing these positions to the minute. By 2015, we can raise the 'degree and a bit' to 'a degree and a half'. When studying Lilly's charts, subtract 4 degrees from Robson's positions, 5 from the positions I've given above.

If you involve other stars in your judgements, perhaps because you are already familiar with them, be wary of taking them too literally. Sometimes the context will demand a literal interpretation, as with the female warrior above. Usually it does not, so regard them instead as giving a descriptive tone. A star on the Ascendant of a horary chart can be seen as the illustration on the cover of a novel: it does not reveal the details of what will transpire, but it does give a general indication of the novel's theme. If you want the details, read the book – or, in our case, judge the chart. The story will be told by the chart whether you look at the cover or not.

Example: I had been advised by the vet that I should have my dog spayed. I cast a chart to see if this was wise. Fixed stars all have the nature of one or more planets. All the relevant significators in this chart had stars of Venus/Saturn nature on them: limitation (Saturn) of her female reproductive system (Venus). But this told me nothing that I didn't already know by the nature of the question.

The soul of horary is quick, efficient judgement. You do not need the majority of the fixed stars for this. You may be tempted to race off and explore their use. Better far to work with simple tools and produce a sound result. In horary, less is truly more. Burning this maxim upon your heart is a more important lesson than learning the manifold details of the legion of fixed stars.

The main stars afflicting the eyes, physically or metaphorically, are:

---

[30] You have probably seen TV programmes showing how the shapes of the constellations change over thousands of years: that is these individual motions at work.

The Andromeda nebula	which is at	27	♈
Capulus		24	♉
The Pleiades		29	♉
The Hyades		5	♊
Ensis		23	♊
Praesepe		7	♌
Copula		25	♍
Foramen		22	♎
Aculeus		25	♐
Acumen		28	♐
Spiculum		0	♑
Facies		8	♑
Manubrium		14	♑

Other than where noted above, however, I suggest ignoring these unless the question specifically directs you to them ('Am I in full possession of the facts here?' 'Is this eye operation a good idea?')

12

Arabian Parts

I used to use Arabian Parts a lot in horary. I now use them less and less, as I find that in most charts they tell nothing of major significance – and in horary we are not concerned with minor significance. Yet there are circumstances when it is worth taking a look at one of them. In most questions, an Arabian Part will not give the main answer. So resist the impulse to calculate ever more recondite Parts in the hope that one will suddenly transform your judgement. It won't.

An Arabian Part is a point in the chart that gives information about a specific subject. There are hundreds of such Parts, cast for anything from apricots to the death of kings to facilitating fraudulent marriage. The Part is calculated by taking the distance between two points (usually two planets) and extending that distance from a third point (usually the Ascendant). The most valuable and most often used of Parts is the *Part of Fortune*, or *Fortuna*. This is cast by measuring the distance from the Sun to the Moon and then extending that distance from the Ascendant. If the Sun is at 10 Taurus and the Moon at 25 Taurus, there are 15 degrees between the Sun and Moon, so Fortuna will be 15 degrees from the Ascendant, travelling anticlockwise.

Most software will present you with a list of Arabian Parts for any chart. But if you are still using the page of the software that gives you this and other information, you haven't been paying attention: stop it! Calculating Parts is not difficult, but the exercise involved may be sufficient to deter you from using them unnecessarily.

More importantly, the way the Parts are presented in computer programs is wrong. What the software gives is a list of whichever Parts happen to be in close aspect to a planet in that chart. If the Part of Lentils is conjunct Saturn it will appear on the list – regardless of the fact that the question is 'Will she marry me?' and lentils have nothing to do with it. That some random Part happens to be in aspect to a planet is irrelevant. It does not mean that the Part is therefore significant in that chart.

The correct use of Parts is to decide which Part we are interested in, calculate it, and then see what it and – most importantly – its dispositor are doing. They may or may not be in aspect to a planet.

THE CALCULATION

If you already know how to do this, you can skip this box.

All our degree measurements (6 Aries, 17 Cancer, etc) are measurements of celestial longitude. They tell us how far round the ecliptic a point is. A planet at 12 Taurus is in the second 30-degree chunk of the zodiac (which chunk we call Taurus) and is 12 degrees into that 30-degree chunk.

When we are measuring the distance from one planet to another, counting how many degrees there are between them, we are measuring their distance apart in celestial longitude. But thinking, 'The distance between them is 3 signs and 17 degrees' is clumsy and invites error. It is much easier to work in *absolute longitude*. This is the distance something is from 0 Aries, but is expressed as a number of degrees, not as so many signs and so many degrees. Our example planet at 12 Taurus is at 42 degrees of absolute longitude. To reach it, starting from 0 Aries, we must travel through the 30 degrees that make up Aries, then another 12 degrees of Taurus: 42 degrees in all.

The absolute longitude of 0 degrees of each sign is:

♈	0	♎	180
♉	30	♏	210
♊	60	♐	240
♋	90	♑	270
♌	120	♒	300
♍	150	♓	330

Learn this table.

So a planet at 14 Leo has an absolute longitude of 120 degrees (0 Leo) + 14 degrees = 134 degrees. A planet at 8 Pisces has 330 degrees (0 Pisces) + 8 = 338 degrees.

The business of finding the distance between planet 1 and planet 2, then adding this distance to the Ascendant (or some other point) can be expressed more simply as Asc + planet 2 – planet 1.

Suppose we wish to calculate the position of Fortuna in a chart where the Sun is at 17.34 Leo, the Moon is at 4.52 Libra and the Ascendant is 22.36 Virgo.

The formula for Fortuna is Asc + Moon − Sun.

Asc is 22.36 Virgo.
o Virgo is 150 degrees, + 22.36 = 172.36
Moon is at 4.52 Libra.
o Libra is 180 degrees, + 4.52 = 184.52
Sun is at 17.34 Leo.
o Leo is 120 degrees, + 17.34 = 137.34

Asc + Moon: 172.36
                         184.52 +
                         _____
                         356.88

Note the number in the minutes column: 88 minutes. There are only 60 minutes in one degree, but ignore that arithmetical nicety here. If you avoid changing the minutes up into degrees (leaving them here as 88) you ensure that you can take away the third part of the formula without problem. Treat each side of the point as a separate sum, even if you have over 100 in the minute column. This will keep you clear of the usual errors with this calculation.

Asc + Moon: 356.88
− Sun: 137.34 −
                         _____
                         219.54

So Fortuna is at 219.54° of absolute longitude.
Look at the table of absolute longitudes to find the biggest number that is less than 219.54.
It is 210, which is 0 Scorpio.
So Fortuna is in Scorpio.
Take this 210 away from its absolute longitude of 219.54:

                         219.54
                         210.00 −
                         _____
                           9.54

So Fortuna is at 9.54 Scorpio.

Note: you can add or subtract 360.00 at any time during this calculation if it will make the sum easier. If you find that the number you have to subtract is bigger than the number you got by adding the other two together, add 360 to the number you got from the addition. If the number you end up with when you've finished the sum is bigger than 360, subtract 360 from it. If your final total gives you a number of minutes greater than 60, subtract 60 from it and add 1 to the number of degrees.

Let's do another one. Suppose we want to find the Part of Resignation and Dismissal, the formula for which is Saturn + Jupiter – Sun. Suppose Saturn is at 17.54 Aries, Jupiter at 4.58 Taurus, the Sun at 20.17 Sagittarius.

Saturn + Jupiter:	17.54	
	34.58 +	
	51.112	note the minutes column
	51.112	
- **Sun:**	260.170–	we can't do this, so add 360.00
	51.112	
	360.000+	
	411.112	now we can subtract the Sun
	411.112	
	260. 17 –	
	151. 95	

So the Part is at 151.95° of absolute longitude.
This is degrees and minutes, though, not degrees and decimals. So now we must adjust the minutes column: 95 minutes = 1 degree and 35 minutes.
So 151.95 = 152.35.
What is the biggest number less than this in the table?
150. So the Part is in Virgo.

$$152.35$$
$$150.00 -$$
$$2.35$$

So the Part is at 2.35 Virgo.

As a little practice will soon show you, this calculation is far simpler than it might seem. I have had many students professing their innumeracy, but all have learned to do this without too much anguish.

Using the Parts

It is a general principle that Parts don't do, they are done to. They don't cast aspects (a Part is nothing but a point in space: it has no light and so cannot cast an aspect); they have aspects cast to them. Suppose Jupiter is exactly square the Part of Marriage: whatever Jupiter signifies is putting a strain on the marriage; this does not show that the marriage has any effect on Jupiter.

That said, certain Parts in certain circumstances can act as if they were casting aspects. If my significator applies to oppose the Part of Resignation and Dismissal, this is testimony that I may lose my job. What the Part is doing here is marking the time of an event, much as a milestone marks a place on a road, rather than showing the event itself. If the milestone tells me it is 100 miles to town, I may decide to stop for some dinner; this does not mean that the milestone has made me stop for dinner. But this is a quibble: in the chart the link between Part and action can be regarded as direct.

If you are taking an aspect to the Part to show an event, stick to conjunction and opposition. Other aspects are unlikely to give the event unless there is strong, congruent testimony elsewhere.

Consider the strength of Parts as with a planet: they are affected by combustion, aspects from planets, and so forth. Be cautious with gauging strength from house placement: if the Part of Work to be Done is in the 12th, does it mean it is weak, or does it suggest working with large animals?

Keep to the point. Do not introduce Parts unless they are directly relevant to the context. If the question is 'When will I marry?' the Part of Death conjunct Lord 7 does not mean you will marry an axe-murderer. It does not mean anything at all: it is not relevant and should not be used. If the question is 'I am terminally ill; will I marry before I die?' the Part of Death might well be relevant.

Turned charts

If you are turning the chart, turn the Parts too. If I am asking, 'Is being a ballerina really my daughter's heart's desire?' it is no good my looking at the radical Part of Vocation. It is not my vocation that is in question; it is hers. So we must turn the Part, casting this Part from her 10th cusp, not mine.

The Part of Fortune

Although this is the most important Part in natal astrology, and will be displayed on the chart by most software as a matter of course, its role in horary is limited. It rarely tells us anything that is not shown elsewhere.

The formula for Fortuna is Asc + Moon − Sun. It is common practice to reverse this formula in night charts (Asc + Sun − Moon). I strongly advise against this: use the standard formula by day and by night. Most software allows you to choose whether to reverse by night or not.

Fortuna can show the querent's treasure – whatever that might be in the context of the question. So if Fortuna is right on a house cusp, this can show that the affairs of that house are important to the querent. 'When will I marry?' with Fortuna on the 5th cusp might suggest that the querent's 'treasure' is having children. The Part needs to be within a degree or two of the cusp to carry this meaning.

As Fortuna is the querent's treasure, it can signify the missing thing in a lost object question. But it usually doesn't: Fortuna is a long way down our list of possible indicators.

It can have a role in questions about money. The more general the question, the more likely it is to have this role. 'How do my finances look over the coming months?' with strong Jupiter trine Fortuna: very rosy! In a more specific question, such as 'Will I make money by buying this flat to let out?' even so rosy a testimony would have only a secondary significance. For the main line of the judgement, look to the house given by the question (in this case the 5th: 2nd from the 4th, hence profit from property).

As a general principle, if you notice that something is happening to Fortuna, such as an exact aspect, this can be worth considering, although it is unlikely to be of major significance. You don't need to go looking for it specially ('I wonder what Fortuna is up to.').

The Part of Marriage: Asc + Desc − Venus

This Part plays an important role in many relationship questions. I use it more than all the other Parts put together.

This Part tells us about the quality of the relationship between two people, and of their attitude towards it. It also tells, metaphorically, of the relationship's attitude to each of them: if reception shows that this Part hates one partner, we see that the relationship harms that person.

It does not relate solely to formal marriage. Being cast from the Asc and the Desc, it does relate solely to the relationship between those persons signified by the 1st and 7th houses. If Lord 7 is the married querent's lover, the Part of Marriage describes her relationship with the lover, not her marriage.

Consider this example:

> Lord 1 is Mars at 19 Virgo, showing the querent
> Lord 7 is Venus at 12 Gemini, showing the querent's wife
> The Part of Marriage is at 5 Virgo.
> It is a night chart.

Do the spouses like each other?

Check the receptions to find out (chapter 8).

Mars is in the face of Venus. Venus is in the face of Mars.

So there is a mutual reception between them, but only by face. This is very weak – scarcely a flicker of affection.

Mars is also in the fall of Venus: the querent loathes his wife.

But Mars and Venus share a powerful interest in Mercury: Mars is in Mercury's sign and exaltation; Venus is in its sign and triplicity. Whatever Mercury signifies is of major importance to both of them.

What is Mercury?

The Part of Marriage is at 5 Virgo, so Mercury is the dispositor of the Part of Marriage. Mercury signifies the marriage.

So we see that although the partners don't like each other, they both value their marriage. This is common, especially in charts of the 'Will our marriage survive?' type. It is also common in such cases to find that the dispositor of the Part of Marriage is itself disposited by Lord 5: what is important to the marriage? The children.

In relationship questions, if you find that both parties share a strong interest in an as yet unidentified planet, you will usually find that this planet disposits the Part of Marriage. It is as if there were three distinct entities involved: the husband, the wife and the marriage itself.

The dispositor of an Arabian Part signifies that thing. The dispositor of the Part of Marriage signifies the marriage; the dispositor of the Part of Surgery signifies the surgery; the dispositor of the Part of Wheat signifies the querent's wheat.

This is important: it is this that enables us to discover the attitudes of the people involved towards that thing, while the condition of the dispositor will tell us at least as much as the condition of the Part itself about the condition of that thing.

Some examples of what this can show us:

* 'Have I got a future with Bob?' with querent's significators showing no interest in Lord 7 (Bob) but in major dignities of the dispositor of the Part of Marriage. 'You don't seem to like Bob that much. The chart suggests that you want a relationship, and he's just the guy who happened along.'
* 'When will I find a husband?' with Lord 1 having recently entered the sign ruled by the dispositor of the Part of Marriage. The querent has only recently decided that she wants to marry. This is common in questions where the marriage will be arranged.
* 'Is she leaving me?' with Lord 7 at 29 degrees of the sign ruled by the dispositor of the Part of Marriage. She is at the very least about to lose interest in the marriage, and is quite possibly physically leaving. Which it is will be shown by other testimonies. But perhaps her planet is in station, turning retrograde before it leaves the sign: 'She's seriously thinking of going, but she'll change her mind'.
* 'Will our marriage be long and happy?' with the dispositor of the Part of Marriage placed at the beginning of a fixed sign and having lots of essential dignity. 'It will be long (fixed sign) and happy (essentially strong).'
* 'Will my mother approve?' with Lord 10 (Mum) in the fall of the dispositor of the Part of Marriage. 'No!'
* 'Will we have children?' with Part of Marriage and its dispositor in fertile signs: strong testimony for 'Yes'.

What the Part of Marriage does not do is give the answer to 'When will we marry?' The timing will not be given by an aspect from one of the partners to the Part of Marriage or its dispositor. We need an aspect between the two people. This Part shows the relationship, not the event of the marriage.

The Part of Marriage of Women: Asc + Saturn – Venus
The Part of Marriage of Men: Asc + Venus – Saturn
The Part of the Marriage Partner: Asc + Desc – Lord 7

I mention these Parts only so you don't get confused when you come across them elsewhere. They are relevant only to arranged marriages, and despite my having done many horaries on that subject, I have never found them helpful there either. Keep them for natal work. The first two of these Parts reverse their formulae by night, so Marriage of Women by day is Marriage of Men by night and vice versa.

The Part of Divorce: Asc + Desc – Mars

There is an idea that the formula for this Part is that for the Part of Marriage reversed. This is wrong: divorce is not the opposite of marriage.

Unsurprisingly, one or both spouses are often found in major dignities of the dispositor of this Part in questions where divorce is a live option. One partner may well exalt it, regarding the divorce as the solution to all problems; the other may be in its fall, hating and fearing the idea.

Unlike the Part of Marriage, this Part does relate to a specific event, so an aspect to it can give that event and its timing. Significator applies to conjunct the Part of Divorce: 'You'll get divorced' (other testimonies agreeing, of course). Significator applies to oppose the Part of Divorce: 'You'll get divorced, but wish you hadn't'.

'Will our divorce affect the children?' with Lord 5 and the dispositor of the Part of Divorce in each other's detriment: 'You bet! They hate it and it hates them'.

Do not cast this Part unless the question states that divorce is a serious option! No matter how the Part might be placed, if divorce is not an option it will not be relevant, as if an actor playing Hamlet wanders on stage during a production of *Othello*. It doesn't matter how convincingly he might ad lib: he's in the wrong play and should be ignored. This is true of all Parts.

The Part of Resignation and Dismissal

This is a rarity among Parts, being calculated from the positions of three planets: Saturn + Jupiter – Sun. Look at this in questions of the 'Will I keep my job?' variety.

Like the Part of Divorce, this relates to an event, so an aspect to this Part can give us that event. If the question were 'Should I resign?' the querent's planet applying to oppose the Part of Resignation and Dismissal would suggest, 'It looks as if you may, but you'll regret it'.

Suppose the dispositor of the Part of Dismissal is sitting on the Ascendant: the idea of being sacked is weighing on the querent. In itself, though, this testimony shows only that the idea is weighing on him; it does not show him being sacked.

"Are Parts accurate?" At the moment polls closed in the British general election on May 1st, 1997, the Moon (natural significator of the people, or the electorate) was exactly – to the minute of arc – on the Part of Resignation and Dismissal in the birthchart for the Conservative Party, which the electorate was dismissing.

The Part of Vocation: MC + Moon – Sun
The Part of Fame: Asc + Jupiter – Sun

Although these are most useful in natal work, it can be worth looking at them in horaries on vocational questions. The Part of Vocation is the same as Fortuna, except that it is extended from the Midheaven instead of the Ascendant. As it is based on Fortuna, I advise against reversing the formula in night charts. The Part of Fame does reverse by night.

Although it would be a rare horary where it carries this meaning, Fortuna is the soul, which is why it carries the idea of being the querent's treasure, 'the pearl of great price'. The vocation is what the soul is called to do, hence the Part of Vocation being the same arc as Fortuna, extended from the MC, which (10th house) shows our action. This Part can give insight into our querent's deepest longings in the direction of action.

'I'm gonna die if Dad makes me become an accountant!' with Mercury opposing the Part of Vocation: we can see why. Accountancy is opposed to the nature of the querent's soul. Part of Vocation in a fertile sign on the 5th cusp: 'Maybe you should stay at home and have children'. Common is a strong emphasis on the 2nd house: 'You need to stop living on air and earn some serious money, for the good of your soul'.

The Part of Fame is also called the Part of Work to be Done. This is perhaps the better name for it, because it does not necessarily make us famous, but it does carry the sense of 'a man's gotta do what a man's gotta do'. This is at a more material level than vocation. If that is the soul's calling, this is 'You're in this time, this place, and have these abilities; this is what needs to be done'.

The Part of Death

There are several formulae for this. The ones I use are Asc + 8th cusp – Moon and 8th cusp + Saturn – Moon. This is not to suggest that other formulae are wrong, but two is quite sufficient.

Be careful how you use this. Death is an important event in the life: we do not have to scrape up minor testimonies in order to show it. Do not take an aspect to the Part of Death as sole testimony that someone will die.

In questions directly about death I no longer use these Parts. If the person will die it will be shown by other testimonies (aspect to Lord 8, for example). I have yet to see a chart where death was shown only, or even primarily, by a Part. If you do not exercise a little restraint here your horary charts will have more dead bodies than a Hong Kong cop movie.

Keep these Parts for questions where Death is a shadowy figure lurking in the background: will he walk out on stage? A political exile asks, 'Is it safe for me to go back to my country?' with the Parts of Death or their significators very much in play: 'Too risky'. This is not a clear testimony of 'No, you'll be killed'; it is enough to warrant caution.

Similarly with 'Should I have this operation?' Finding the Part of Death on the Midheaven (dominating the chart) or in the same degree as the Part of Surgery: 'No, too much risk'. The Part on its own will not show that Death carries you off; it can show that you're coming closer to him than is wise.

The Part of Surgery: Asc + Saturn – Mars

This reverses by night, giving Asc + Mars – Saturn. In most horaries on surgery we can take Mars, its natural ruler, to signify the surgery. If Mars is the significator of either the querent or the ailment, we need another option, which this Part can provide. Even if we are able to use Mars, it is worth casting this Part to see what it has to tell us.

Be careful! Even at its best, surgery is not nice: don't expect to see happy planets in friendly aspect. Finding the significator of the illness ruled by the dispositor of this Part is most encouraging: the surgery has power over the illness. The illness dispositing the Part of Surgery or its ruler is most unfortunate.

People ask about laser surgery on their eyes. Finding the Part of Surgery or its dispositor on a star that afflicts the eyes (see page 114) would be a negative indicator. Look also at the relationship between the Part, together with its dispositor, and the Sun and Moon, the natural rulers of the eyes.

Reversing the formula for this Part gives the *Part of Sickness.* This is one option for the significator of an illness, but we have better. I suggest leaving this for natal work.

Parts of Commodities

Wheat, olives, cotton, grapes: these and more all have their Parts. In days long past a staple of the astrologer's trade was queries on when to market one's crop, or whether to plant this or that. These Parts are invaluable for deciding such questions – though in the modern world such questions are few and far between. Strong Jupiter trines the Part of Maize; weak Saturn opposes the Part of Wheat: go for maize next year. Lord 8 (2nd from 7th: the other people's money) conjuncts the Part of Cucumbers in two degrees: take your cucumbers to market in two days and you'll make a killing.

   As this is a textbook and not an encyclopaedia, I will not list these Parts here. If you are asked such a question – and among the thousands of horaries I have done I can recall but one – refer to al-Biruni, who gives a comprehensive list of Parts.[31] If you need the Part for a commodity he does not list, study the way his other formulae are constructed, then substitute the natural ruler of the commodity in question.

Other Parts

If you feel the urge to incorporate other Parts in your charts, see al-Biruni for their formulae. Working with his table, the arithmetic is Place 3 + Place 2 – Place 1. But if you feel the urge to incorporate other Parts in your charts you probably have not understood the basics of horary. Let's build the house before we start sticking fancy bits on the outside. You don't need them! Extra techniques will never substitute for a lack of work on the basics. So do some more work on the basics.

---

[31] Al-Biruni, op. cit., paras 476-479.

13

Timing

Brace yourself: this is the tricky bit. Querents do not want to know only if things will happen; they have the habit of wanting to know when things will happen. So we must be able to time our predictions.

This is possible with great accuracy: I have timed predictions to the minute, although it would be foolish to do this for clients – it is amusing, but serves no practical purpose. Sometimes the judgement of timing is clear, so clear that it can be as simple as anything else we have considered. More often, however, it does involve balancing considerations and possibilities.

The Method

Assume that you have set a horary and judged that there will be an event: 'Yes, such and such will happen'. This event will usually have been shown by an aspect. It is usually this aspect that gives us the timing of that event.

Occasionally we have to look elsewhere for the timing, either because the event-giving aspect provides no timing that could be true, or because the event is shown by something other than an aspect. Look back at the lost cat chart in chapter 1. The event – the cat's return – was shown not by an aspect, but by Jupiter being retrograde. Jupiter was making no significant aspect, so something else had to show the timing of the cat's return. In this case, it was the Moon's application to an aspect with the Ascendant.

The appropriate aspect, once identified, can show us the timing of the event in various ways.

All timing is with reference to the moment for which the horary is cast. This is 'time zero'.

Using past events

If it is available to us, this is by far the most reliable and most accurate method for timing. It depends upon the chart showing us a past event. Suppose the question is 'When will I marry again?' and we know that our querent divorced three years ago. The chart shows her significator separating from Mars, the natural ruler of divorce. If it is 5 degrees separated from Mars, we know that on the scale of this chart, 5 degrees = 3 years. So if her significator now applies to aspect the ruler of the seventh house, signifying the future husband, in 10 degrees, judgement is simple: 'You will remarry in 2 x 3 years = 6 years'. It is as if the chart carries its own scale of calibration, as we might find the scale marked on a map.[32]

Sign and house

Unfortunately, few charts show past events. Or, as in principle I suppose that they all should, few are they that show them with sufficient clarity for this to be of use. So we need to find other methods. This is when it starts to get complicated.

Timing, for reasons that I do not understand, is the one area of horary where students display the utmost resistance to absorbing knowledge. Pay attention! This works.

We have our aspect. If we have an aspect there will be a number of degrees between where the applying planet is now and where it will be when the aspect perfects. Unless this is one of those charts where we can take the timing from a past event, this number is the number of time units (hours, days, years, etc) between the time of question and the time of the event.

Take the number of degrees that the applying planet must travel before perfecting the aspect. Suppose the aspect is Sun at 10 Taurus applying to Mars at 14 Leo. How far must the Sun travel to make the aspect?

The answer is not 4 degrees.

Mars is not standing still, waiting for the Sun to catch up. Mars is moving too.

What concerns us is not the distance the applying planet must travel to reach the position of the other planet as it is in the chart.

What concerns us is the distance the applying planet must travel to perfect the aspect. For this, you will need to consult your ephemeris.

---

[32]   The chart discussed in *The Real Astrology* pp. 4-7 gives an example of this.

My students can be recognised by having the words CONSULT YOUR EPHEMERIS branded onto their foreheads. Branding is painful, so please pay attention here. *It is where the aspect perfects that matters.*

The Sun at 10 Taurus applying to Mars at 14 Leo would typically perfect when the Sun is at about 17 Taurus, not 14 Taurus. The Sun has had to travel 7 degrees to perfect the aspect, not 4.

It is this 7 degrees that is important.

So: ask yourself

* where does this aspect perfect? (from your ephemeris)
* how far does the applying planet have to travel to reach this point?

We have now identified the number of degrees. This tells us how many time units will elapse before the event. Now we must find which time unit is relevant. Is it hours, days, weeks, months or years? If you have read Lilly, you will have found that he brings nothing but confusion here. First, he gives two contradictory scales of timing; second, he pins both to fixed units. The suggestion that, for instance, angular houses = years is most unhelpful. If the question is 'When will my boyfriend phone?' years is not a relevant concept. Put Lilly away and listen up.

Any question carries its own timeframe, which will usually have a short, a medium and a long possibility. For the love-struck teenager demanding 'When will my boyfriend phone?' minutes as short, hours as medium and days as long might be the options. For the older querent asking 'When will I meet Mr Right?' years must be the longest option, giving months as medium and weeks as short. The three units will follow consecutively one from the other: we do not have minutes, months and years.

"But this assumed timeframe limits the possibilities of what the chart can tell us." No. We can have perfection in less than one degree, so our decision that years, months or weeks is the reasonable range of choice for 'When will I meet Mr Right?' does not clip Cupid's wings. A perfection at less than one degree on our fastest option could still give us 'This afternoon!'

Yes, the choice of the right selection of time units (fast/middle/slow) is sometimes open to debate; but less often than you might think. Usually, it is obvious enough. In cases of doubt, remember that the maximum theoretical separation of an aspect is a little under 30 degrees (planet at 0 degrees of a sign perfects an aspect at 29 degrees of that sign). This gives a maximum of a little under 30 of any time-unit. For example, 'hours' might seem unlikely as a fastest unit if you are thinking only of a couple of hours; but think of a maximum of 29 hours – more than one day – and you see that it holds wider possibilities.

Once you have chosen the range of short, medium and long units, decide which of these is the appropriate one by considering the sign and the house in which the applying planet stands. Ignore the sign and house in which the planet applied to stands. We are concerned *only* with the applying planet. *Only* with the applying planet. Students resist this, and persist in factoring in the house and sign of the planet that is applied to. If you feel I am labouring this point, remember that I speak from long experience of teaching. Only, only, only!

Finding the applying planet in a fixed sign will give the longest time-unit, cardinal the shortest and mutable the middle from what we have decided is the reasonable timeframe for the question

That is simple enough. It becomes more complicated when we introduce the houses, as there is an inbuilt contradiction. Of their nature, angular houses equate with fixed signs and so indicate the slowest time unit. Cadent – as might be expected from a house that is literally 'falling' – gives the fastest; succedent the middle. Combining house and sign will give us, for instance, long + long, which must indicate our longest unit. Or short + short, which is our shortest. Any other combination will give our middle unit.

Yes, the system is heavily weighted in favour of the middle unit. This probably says something about the nature of things; but if the chart wishes to show us the fastest or the slowest it is quite capable of so doing.

Now for the contradiction: angular houses of their nature are slow. But a planet in an angular house has a good deal of accidental dignity. Accidental dignity increases the planet's power to act. So if that planet wants to act, it is well able to do so, and is therefore likely to act quickly. So angular houses are fast.

The key is the word 'wants': the issue of *volition*. If things are unfolding as a natural process, whatever is in an angular house will unfold slowly. If whatever or whomever the angular planet signifies is, within the context of the question, in a position to act, and if (and only if) the receptions indicate that it wants to act, it will act quickly. This inherent (apparent) contradiction is the reason for Lilly giving two apparently contradictory tables.

Example: I ask 'When will the cheque arrive?' and find the significator of the cheque in an angular house. There is nothing the cheque can do to expedite its own arrival. The question of volition is irrelevant. The angular house would suggest a slow time unit.

On the other hand, when Indian women ask the question 'When will I meet the man I will marry?' it is common to find their significators in angular houses. Once they have taken the decision that it is time to marry, there is a good deal that they can do to expedite the process, in contrast to Bridget Jones, who can only wait until Cupid squeezes himself into her life. If these angular significators provide us with an applying aspect, and if (as the fact that she is paying to ask the question would lead us to expect) their receptions show that she wants the match, we can take this angularity as showing a fast unit, *because she has power and wishes to use it.*

The reverse is also true. For things unfolding of themselves, like an apple falling from a tree, cadent houses show things happening quickly. But if volition is at issue the person signified by the cadent planet has little power to act, so cadency will slow matters down.

Memorise this table:

	Shortest	Medium	Longest
Sign:	Cardinal	Mutable	Fixed
House:	Cadent	Succedent	Angular
But:	Volition can make angular fast and cadent slow		

Examples: 'When will I get a better job?' Years must be our longest unit, so months will be medium and weeks fast. The querent's planet in a succedent house and a cardinal sign applies to perfect the aspect in 6 degrees. Our answer will be '6 somethings'. Succedent is medium; cardinal is fast. This is not fast + fast, which would give our fastest unit (weeks); nor is it slow + slow, which would give our slowest (years); so it must be medium. You will get a better job in 6 months.

'My flat is on the market. When will I sell it?' Days, weeks or months would be reasonable. The buyer's significator (Lord 7) applies to perfect the aspect in 5 degrees. It is in a fixed sign and an angular house. Slow + slow. This would give a timing of 5 months, our longest unit. BUT: remember about volition! It is angular, so the buyer has lots of power to act. Does he want to act? Check the receptions: 'Oh good – the receptions show that he is eager to buy'. He is willing and able, so we can treat his angularity as fast. Fast (angular with volition) + slow (fixed) gives us a medium unit: 5 weeks.

Even with the variable nature of angular houses, this is really not so complicated. In the majority of charts, this is all you will need to give accurate timing. But not in all charts: there are variations.

Much as I emphasised that what concerns us is the distance the planet must travel to perfect the aspect, and much as this is usually true, there are some charts where we do treat the planet applied to as if it were standing still. I gave the example above: 'The Sun at 10 Taurus applying to Mars at 14 Leo would typically perfect when the Sun is at about 17 Taurus, not 14 Taurus. The Sun has had to travel 7 degrees to perfect the aspect, not 4. It is this 7 degrees that is important'. Sometimes, however, we would take the 4 degrees from the Sun to where Mars is now, ignoring the fact that Mars too is moving. This is done when:

* regarding the second planet as moving would give a timing that is not possible within the reality of the question
* we have two testimonies of timing in the chart, and treating the planet applied to in this aspect as if it were standing still brings these testimonies into agreement (i.e. both showing the same timing).

In some charts, we consider only the sign of the applying planet, not its house. "Which charts?" The charts where we consider only the sign of the applying planet, not its house. I would like to be able to quote a rule, but have never found one. They just look like 'sign-only charts'. Given enough practice, you will develop an eye for them. It may be that a preponderance of them have the planet in a fixed sign, and so give the longest time unit. That, at least, is my impression; but treat this suggestion with caution. See the chart on page 106 for an example.

So far we have taken number of degrees = number of time units. This is usually accurate enough. For added precision, we can adjust this number. If the applying planet is moving significantly faster or slower than its usual speed, it will take a greater or lesser time to cover the same number of degrees. We can, if we wish, adjust the number of units up or down accordingly. Don't be too precious here: the planet needs to be *significantly* faster or slower than usual for this to be worth considering. A couple of minutes of arc per day is a great deal for Jupiter; it is inconsequential for the Moon.

I have timed predictions with an unnecessary degree of accuracy by carefully calculating the exact proportion by which the planet is faster or slower than average; but there is little point to this. 'A bit' is quite accurate enough an adjustment. Striving to tell our client that she will meet Mr Right at 3 minutes past 10 on Monday 28th serves only our ego. 'Around the end of the month' is all the accuracy required. Use your common sense: if the event will happen later this week, it is reasonable that we should predict the day; if it will happen in twenty years' time, selecting the year is quite accurate enough. Do resist the impulse to show off. If you predict, 'You will marry in 3 years' time' and she does, you will be seen as a great astrologer. If you predict, 'You will marry on August 17th in 3 year's time,' and she marries on August 18th, you will be the astrologer who got it wrong.

NB: if the applying planet is moving faster or slower than usual, this will affect *only* the number of time units; it will not affect our choice of what time units they are. If we have worked out the timing to be 6 weeks, adjusting this by planetary speed might make it 5 weeks or 7 weeks; it will not make it 6 days or 6 months.

Double-bodied signs make things slower. This too will affect only the number of time units, not their nature. 'A bit' slower is as accurate as we can or need be. In practice, it is not usually necessary to consider these factors, work though they do.

If the aspect is to a retrograde planet, so that both planets are applying to perfection, the event can happen faster than the number of degrees would suggest. How much faster? Again, 'a bit'. In such cases it is probably best to use the number of degrees to give an outer limit of time, qualified by 'probably sooner'.

If the chart shows two aspects indicating that the event will happen, these aspects will usually, as we might expect, show the same time. 'Close enough' is good enough. If one shows 12 units and the other shows 3, a correlation of 12 weeks = 3 months is sufficiently close to add confidence to our prediction.

Disregard real time. It is a common error among students, no matter how hard they are beaten, to cling to the idea that if the ephemeris shows that the aspect will happen next Tuesday, the event shown by that aspect will happen next Tuesday. It won't! What the ephemeris shows us is time from our perception, which is an illusion; what the planets show us is as close an approximation as we may easily get to what time truly is. Work from the symbolic methods of timing, as discussed above.

When ephemeris time does become relevant is when our questions are on general indications over long periods of time, or when we wish to look beyond the immediate limits imposed by the question to see what may happen over a longer period. This is often to reassure the querent that all is not lost.

Examples: suppose the question is 'Can you give some general indications for my business over the next few months?' and we find that the querent's business is signified by Jupiter, which will enter its own sign in three months' time. We might judge that things will start looking up around then. My experience is that the querent will usually respond, 'Oh yes – that's immediately after the big trade show,' or some such, and that such indications will prove accurate.

Or, suppose the question were 'Is this really the man of my dreams?' and the chart gives an obvious judgement of 'Are you mad?' We might look further, noting that in a couple of months the querent's significator moves out of its detriment and into some interesting mutual receptions, and so add 'But by the autumn you'll be feeling much better in yourself, and so be able to enter a relationship that nurtures you, rather than grabbing someone unsuitable out of desperation, as you are doing now'. Or words to that effect.

When considering the longer term, a planet's passage through an entire sign shows one of the natural time-units, usually a month or a year. So if, for instance, the querent's business were signified by Venus, placed at 28 Leo, in a question about long-term prospects, we might judge (other testimonies concurring), 'You may feel you have the world at your feet now (Venus on Regulus), but you are entering a sticky period (into Virgo). The next year (passage through Virgo) looks set to be a story of considerable potentials (Venus in triplicity) never quite unfolding (Venus in fall). Overall, the downside during this period is going to be significantly more than the up; but after that (Venus into Libra) all falls happily into place. So grit your teeth and hang on in till then.'[33] Don't look beyond the next sign or two; if we do that we find everything happening to everybody.

This looking ahead must be done sparingly. Those new to horary are often tempted to race planets around the chart as if it were a Snakes and Ladders board; this impulse is better curbed. In all but a few charts, we are concerned only with a planet's next aspect and nothing beyond that.

Lilly gives several examples where a 'real time' transit is significant. So if Mercury applies to Jupiter he judges not 'It's four degrees till perfection: it will happen in four weeks', but 'My ephemeris shows this aspect happening next Tuesday at 3.56: it will happen then'.[34] Don't try this at home! Please.

If you really must dabble in this kind of thing, it is best kept to side issues. Example: we have decided that our querent will marry his girlfriend in six months' time, judging from the six degrees needed to perfect the aspect between them. We note that both planets are in major dignities of the ruler of her fourth

---

[33] The medical chart on p. 128 of *RA Applied* shows an example of this.
[34] See *Lilly* pp. 385-8 for an example.

house, showing that her father has a major say in this matter. We note also that at 11.52 on Friday 28th, our querent's planet transits the twelfth cusp, there being a mutual reception between the ruler of the twelfth and the significator of the girl's father. The twelfth being the house of animals larger than goats, we advise that at 11.52 on the 28th he attend the market, where he will be able to purchase the very camel that will persuade the father to allow his daughter to wed.

On the subject of transits, let us deal with the idea that if something in the horary chart conjuncts something in the querent's nativity, the chart is 'radical' or somehow more real. I ask a question about love, and find in the horary that Venus is right on my natal Ascendant. Does this make the chart 'radical'? Of course not. It shows that Venus is transiting my Ascendant, and I, not surprisingly, am thinking about love. No more than that. Let us not forget that this with which we deal is a congruent system: it all fits together, in the most intricate and endlessly remarkable of ways. That Venus is on my Ascendant may show that I am thinking about love – a fact that might be obvious from my going to an astrologer and asking 'Does she love me?' – but it tells us nothing about whether this love is reciprocated. These considerations serve only to confuse the issue. All charts are 'radical', and we are well advised to keep the querent's nativity well apart from his horaries, lest they breed monsters.

A particular instance in which the 'real time' movement of the planets can be significant occurs in lost object questions. In the chart for such it will often be found that the significator of the object is combust: the object cannot be seen. Assuming that all else in the chart is indicative of a recovery, we can reach down our ephemeris, note the exact moment at which the planet leaves combustion, and judge, 'You'll find it then'. This may present the odd picture of thousands of people around the world throwing up their hands in glee as they recover cherished possessions at exactly 8.22 GMT, but it seems to work with the reasonable degree of reliability that is all we ask.

When a date is specifically mentioned in the question, it is often of significance, so it is worth checking the planetary placements on that date against the horary chart. As a general rule, if we restrict the querent to few words, whatever those few words are will usually be important; if those few words relate to timing, let us look at them.

A querent was desperate for her son to be accepted into a school, which prospect was looking increasingly unlikely. Her ambitions to place him in a private school had excluded him from the acceptable state school options, while he had been turned down from the private school she wanted, for reasons which she believed were unsound. The boy had an entrance exam at another school, and an appeal at the school desired, both on named dates. How would he fare?

His significator, Lord 5, was Jupiter. The schools were shown by the ninth house and its ruler, the Moon. The exam was on the 18th of May. By transit, the Moon, Lord 9, was on the 5th cusp of the horary chart on that day. This is a positive testimony, but there was no mutual reception with Lord 5. At this school the boy passed satisfactorily, but with no scholarship. The appeal at the second school was due on August 10th. On that day, the boy's significator, Jupiter, transited the 9th cusp, where, it being in Cancer, it was exalted – so the boy is there and is highly thought of. Will he get the scholarship? Yes. And so it proved.

Similarly, if the question contains a given bound of time, this too will be reflected in the chart. It can be taken that the end of the relevant planet's present sign is the end of the given timeframe. If I ask, 'Will I win the lottery this year?' and find my significator conjuncting the ruler of the 11th house (pennies from Heaven) immediately after it leaves its present sign, I would judge, 'No; but I will early next'.

Finally, there are those welcome questions that admit of only one possible time unit. 'When will such and such happen today?' is the most common of these. 'Minutes' is usually not an option, because we know the event cannot happen within 29 minutes. 'Days' is impossible, because we are concerned only with today. 'Hours' is our only option. Yippee!

The golden rule in matters of timing, as in all else in astrology, is that we do not have to be perfect. We are allowed to judge, 'It might be in three days; but weighing all the evidence I think it more likely to be in six.'

14

What is the Question and Who is Asking It?

Perhaps the most important part of horary judgement is done before we even cast the chart. This is the determining of what question is really being asked.

Questions often come swathed in clouds of irrelevant detail. There is a skill in cutting through these swathes to reach the bones of the issue. You have probably had the experience while watching a film of suddenly realising, 'Hey – this is *Romeo and Juliet*, dressed up!' or 'This is *Snow White* set in modern New York!' You have noticed that beneath its disguise the bones of the plot are those of *Romeo and Juliet* or *Snow White*. So it is with horary: there are certain standard questions which recur again and again in different guises.

* Does she love me?
* Will I get the job?
* Will I win?
* Am I bewitched?
* Will the king be deposed?
* Will I get the gift from the king?
* Can we do the deal?

Keep your ears open and you will quickly recognise them when you hear them. Allow yourself to be sidetracked by irrelevant details and you will end up answering a question that has not been asked.

Similarly, the fact of who is asking the question is not always as clear as it might seem. There are direct questions posed by the person concerned. There are direct questions asked by someone about somebody else. So far so simple.

Then there are questions asked by someone acting as mouthpiece for someone else. Suppose Erika wishes to ask me a question, but we do not have a common language. She has a friend who speaks English, so she asks the friend to ask the question on her behalf. The friend is not asking her own question about Erika; she is relaying Erika's question to me. I must ignore the friend, treating this exactly as if Erika herself were asking me, so Erika will be given the 1st house as querent.

Be clear on the distinction:

* the friend asks her own question, 'Is my friend Erika going to marry Rudolph?'
* the friend relays Erika's own question, 'Will I marry Rudolph?'

In the first example, Erika would be given the 11th house; in the second, she would be given the 1st.

Then there are questions that arise in conversation, it being unclear who is really asking. I am chatting with my friend about his work prospects. The question comes up, 'When will I get a better job?' But who is really asking it? Is it my friend, is it me, or is my friend articulating the question that I am forcing into his mouth? Be wary of such situations, especially when you are eagerly pressing everyone you know for horaries so you can practice your skills. This is one advantage of professional practice: the fee changing hands makes it quite clear who is the querent.

There are those who would rigorously limit the scope of horary enquiry. 'You can't ask that: it's too trivial'. 'You can't ask that: it's too important.' Between what is trivial and what is important, precious little survives.

With a very few small restrictions, you can ask anything. Trivial? So who am I to tell you that your concerns are trivial, and apply a cosmic veto to them? Maybe in the great scheme of things 'Who will be president?' is of more moment than 'Where is the cat?' but in fact it is my bystander's curiosity in the former of these that is trivial; the whereabouts of Puss most certainly is not. Compared to the rise and fall of empires, our grandest concerns are as nothing – and yet salvation is gained or lost in an instant, so the matter of any instant cannot be trivial.

It is claimed that we cannot ask 'important' questions, such as 'Who will win the election?' because so many people are asking this same question and the same question cannot be asked more than once. Let us consider this statement, 'The same question cannot be asked more than once'.

It is true; but it is not true in the way in which it is meant. Fundamental to astrology is the fact that every instant is different. THIS instant is different from THIS instant. Each is different, and whatever happens in it will be distinct to that instant. Take this away and we have no astrology. So it is not undesirable to ask the same question twice – it is impossible. Even if the question has the same words, it is not the same question.

Nor is there any reason why someone should not ask the same question of more than one astrologer. Doctors can give second opinions; so can astrologers. Truth is a sturdy beast; it does not run away if more than one person looks at it. Each separate question on the same subject is like a cross-section of the same situation, as a zoologist might take cross-sections of a worm to put under the microscope. Different cross-sections, but still the same worm, so still the same answer. If fifty or five hundred people ask 'Who will win the next election?' the cosmos, which is an infinitely subtle mechanism, will find fifty or five hundred ways of showing the same answer. No matter how many people examine individual stills from *Gone with the Wind*, Rhett Butler always leaves at the end of the story.

A querent will ask what is apparently the same question at different stages of a situation. Common is 'Should I throw him out?' followed by 'Should I really throw him out?' and 'Will I be OK if I throw him out?' These consequent charts can be seen to relate to each other in exactly the same ways as birthcharts of family members relate to each other. The same patterns occur, and usually, in question after question, the querent edges towards a position from which she feels able to make a decision one way or the other.

Other querents will ask similar questions about different situations. 'Will I get a job from this audition?' 'Will I get a job from tomorrow's audition?' The first few of these will have clear results. After a while, however, the charts become more and more vapid, almost as if the cosmos is losing interest in the situation and saying, 'If you haven't taken the hint by now, I'm not going to keep performing for you'. Typically, these charts will start showing minor events that are going to occur on that day ('Oh look, your father's coming to visit you') but say little of significance about the job situation. It is possible that this reflects either querent or astrologer losing interest in the repeated questions, or the nature of the true question changing as the querent despairs of having a successful audition. In the latter case, the querent is not so much asking for information as hoping that the consultation will work magic. It will not.

Questions like this verge on the mechanical, and the mechanical is one real limit to what can be asked. There must be some spark of genuine interest in the question, even if the question is a 'trivial' one and hardly of life-changing significance. There is no such spark of genuine interest in, for instance, 'Will 1 come up on this week's lottery?' 'Will 2 come up on this week's lottery?' etc.

Then there are such products of the fourth-form as 'Is horary true?' and 'Is the Bible the word of God?' A moment's reflection should make clear why these cannot be asked.

Supplementary questions are fine. 'When will I marry? Will we have children? Will he get along with my family? Will he have a good job?' These can all be judged from the same chart. But it is best to discourage questions on different issues: 'When will I marry? When will I get a better job? Where is the cat?' Sometimes querents will have two or three issues weighing on them, so if necessary these questions can be answered from the same chart. But the asking of many unrelated questions suggests that none of them is the real issue. It is better to ask the querent to reflect on what is most important and then ask that.

The default option

Always be aware when judging charts of what the 'default' is – what happens if nothing happens. If I ask 'Will she marry me?' five minutes after I saw her for the first time, there would need to be strong testimony to give a Yes. If there is no such testimony the answer will be No. If I awake on the morning of our wedding and ask the same question, there would need to be strong testimony of something going wrong to make the answer No. In the absence of such testimony, things will go as planned: the default option is that the marriage will go ahead. In the first instance, if nothing happens there will be no marriage; in the second, if nothing happens to disrupt them, events will roll along as planned and the marriage will take place. Similarly with questions on other subjects.

The Considerations before Judgement

This is another of those topics that we must cover only because you will read about it elsewhere.

In ages past, when the astrologer was working for the king, upsetting his employer with an unpleasing judgement could be fatal. But twisting the judgement to give a pleasing answer was little better an option, as events would soon show that the judgement was wrong. The astrologer needed a diplomatic way of fending off unwelcome questions, so a list of 'considerations before judgement' was developed. This list is sufficiently comprehensive to ensure that it gives an excuse for not judging any chart that might endanger the astrologer.

When a king whom not even his mother could love asked, 'Does the princess of the next country love me?' the astrologer could draw up the chart, confident he would find Saturn in the 7th house, or Lord 7 debilitated, or fewer than 3 degrees (some lists state 5) or more than 27 degrees of a sign on the Ascendant, or, or, or. This would enable him to explain, 'I'm sorry, your Highness. I'd love to judge this chart, but I can't. See – here, it says so in my textbook'.

The only one of these considerations that is more than an empty excuse capable of impressing ignorant monarchs is that about the number of degrees of a sign on the Ascendant. If an early or late degree of a sign is there, the Ascendant is close to changing from sign to sign. As the Ascendant represents the querent, it is crucial that the astrologer has the right sign on it, otherwise he will use the wrong planet to signify the querent and arrive at an incorrect judgement. Nowadays this is not a problem: timekeeping is so accurate that we can always know which sign is rising. In the past this was not so – Lilly grumbles about overcast skies making it impossible to do more than guess at the correct time.

The one consideration that is more than an excuse is no longer current. The considerations that are excuses are no longer needed – unless you find yourself working for a short-tempered king, in which case I suggest you pull any excuse out of the air and say it is handed down in the secret oral tradition in which you were trained. So you can forget these considerations.

There are astrologers who make much of them, deliberating long over whether a chart is 'radical', by which they mean 'capable of being judged'. These astrologers have their own translation of that famous Hermetic dictum, running 'As above, as every now and again so below'. Every chart can be judged. Astrology does not stop working.

I am not going to list the considerations here: my experience with students is that in too many cases once the considerations have been inserted into the head it is impossible to completely flush them out again. Better not to insert them into the head. You will not miss them.

15

First House Questions

Questions relating only to the first house are rare. The hero recovering consciousness and asking 'Where am I?' would be an example, but I have yet to be consulted in such circumstances.

An actress asked if she would be more successful if she gave up her stage name and reverted to her own name. One's name is a 1st-house matter, so Lord 1 signified the name. It was retrograde: going backwards, which fitted with her idea of reverting to her own name. But was this a wise decision?

Suppose her planet were Venus, at 2 Gemini, retrograding back into its own sign. Going back will make it much stronger: 'Yes, change back to your own name'. Suppose her planet were Venus, having just turned retrograde, at 28 Aries: it would have been about to enter its own sign, Taurus, becoming much stronger; but it has turned away and is not going to do so: 'No, the change is harmful; persevering in your present direction will bring you success'.

Testimony could also be given by accidental factors. Perhaps her planet was retrograding away from the South Node and applying to a dignified Jupiter: changing the name is the better option. Retrograding out of the angular 1st house into the cadent 12th: the change is harmful and will remove her from view.

THE SHIP THAT I SAIL IN

Contemplating my car, and asking 'Will it get me to Glasgow?' I am seeing my car as what Lilly calls 'the ship that I sail in', hence 1st house. Similarly with 'Will my flight arrive safely?' The analogy is with the body (1st house) seen as the vehicle of the soul. If I ask 'Will someone buy my car?' I am seeing the car as a movable possession, not as a vehicle, so it is shown by my 2nd house. In the first question its role is as a vehicle; in the second its role is as a possession, which happens to be a vehicle.

I do not need to be in the ship at the time of asking the question; nor, indeed, to be in it at all. If I ask 'Will my treasure-ship reach port safely?' the ship is 1st house, even if I have never set foot on it. It is as if my soul has sent my body off on an errand.

Such judgements are simple: take Lord 1 and see if anything nasty is going to happen to it. For serious accidents, the prime suspects would be aspects from debilitated Mars or Saturn, or from Lord 8; combustion; conjunction with the South Node. Milder afflictions, such as an aspect from debilitated Venus or Jupiter, would be troublesome but not disastrous. The lack of any such affliction would promise a safe journey.

PHYSICAL APPEARANCE

Describing the querent's appearance from the chart might seem one of the more pointless of astrological operations, especially if querent and astrologer are in the same room. Lilly found it useful:

* when the Ascendant was in an early or late degree of its sign
* when he needed to convince the client of his abilities.

In the first of these cases, finding that Lord 1 accurately described the querent, who would have been sitting in front of him at the time, was confirmation that he had set the chart with the correct rising sign, and so could proceed to judgement. With modern methods of timekeeping, we no longer need such confirmation. As for the second case, while it must be satisfying to see clients' reactions on hearing the whereabouts of their hidden marks and scars, I would advise against performing such gymnastics to convince clients of your abilities. Imagine a surgeon being asked, 'I'm not sure that heart operation you've done will be effective; can you whip out my gall bladder to show me you know what you're doing?'

So there is no need to describe the querent. We are, however, sometimes asked for a description of another person, usually the future marriage partner, sometimes a thief. In that case, take the description from the main significator of that person. Qualify the basic characteristics of that planet by the ruler and other major dignities of the sign it is in. This is no place for precision: I hate the thought that we might tell the querent that her husband will be 6′ 3″ and she refuses the perfect spouse because he is 6′ 4″.

There is a problem with the racial determination of appearance. We can follow the astrological rules and describe the man as having curly red hair and freckles, but if he is Japanese we are unlikely to be right. Hair, skin and eye colour are primarily racially determined, and I know of no way of finding which race a person might belong to from the chart. Suppose Miss English Rose asks us to describe her future husband; our description of 'black hair and sallow complexion' could well fit the Japanese guy she ends up marrying. But the usual context of such an enquiry is with an Indian or Pakistani woman who will be marrying someone of her own race. In such situations the chart seems to take 'black hair' for granted, feeling under no obligation to involve Saturn in the description.

The following guidelines are all that is needed:

Saturn: tall and slim. Can give darker hair and complexion.
Jupiter: big, both in height and build; fleshy, especially if in water signs.
Mars: short, muscular, solidly built.
Sun: tall and well-built, but not as big as Jupiter. Big hair.
Venus: short, soft-bodied (in contrast to the muscularity of Mars).
Mercury: mid-height or a little above; slim; straight hair.
Moon: fleshy; not tall. Generally bigger if waxing than if waning.

Suppose the person's significator is Mars at 4 Libra. Mars is short, and is ruled by Venus, which is also short. It is in strong Saturn dignities (at 4 Libra it is in the exaltation and the term of Saturn), which will add some height. This can only qualify our basic Mars testimony, however; so while it can make him taller, it will not make him tall. He will be about mid-height or slightly above. Mid-height for his race. The Saturn influence will also make him slimmer. Mars is in its detriment, so he will not have the muscle that Mars usually shows; both Mars and Saturn are lean, so he will be non-muscular, but in a lean, non-flabby sort of way. Had Mars been in Taurus, again in its detriment, the other major dignity (besides Venus) would be the Moon. In Taurus Mars would again lack its usual muscle, but would be bigger built and more fleshy than Mars in Saturn-influenced Libra. Mars in a Venus sign, as also Venus in a Mars sign, is sure to be attractive.

This description is quite sufficient. 'You'll know him by the dragon tattooed on his left forearm,' sounds good in a novel, but the aim of astrology is not to make the astrologer feel clever.

Close aspects to the main significator can show the details of appearance: a Mars square, for example, showing a visible scar; a gentler aspect from Mars showing patches of pigmentation on the face. But I suggest that such details are better left for confirming what the querent may tell you about the person. If the querent says, 'The one I suspect of being the thief has a big scar on his cheek,' we can refer to the chart, note the Mars square and reply, 'Yes, that would fit: bring him in for questioning'.

Conjunction with the fixed stars listed on page 114 will show affliction to the eyes, although in an age of contact lenses and laser surgery this is less useful for description than once it was.

Although the planets show a fixed rising scale of age, from babies (Moon) to the most aged (Saturn), for purposes of description these should be regarded as comparatives. That the husband is signified by the Moon shows that she will marry someone younger than her, not that she will marry a baby; Saturn would show that she marries someone significantly older, but not necessarily ancient. The Sun, Venus and Mars can all, in this context, be taken as showing much the same age.

If you feel you cannot live without checking the querent's marks and scars, this should be done off the first, heartfelt question. We cannot expect the stars to show the same arrangement of bodily blemishes every time a regular client asks a horary. Look first at the sign rising. Which part of the body does this signify? (see page 43) There will be a scar or mark there. The degree of that sign that is on the Ascendant will show where in that part of the body the mark lies: at 0 degrees it will at the top of that part, at 29 degrees it will be near the bottom.

Treat the cusp of the 6th house and the position of the Moon in the same way, by sign and degree, showing two more marks. A debilitated planet in the 1st house will show a mark on the face, the whereabouts on the face being shown by its degree. Close aspects to the Ascendant from Mars or Saturn will show marks according to the planet's sign and degree – but do keep these aspects close. The more debilitated the planet is, the larger the mark. If the significator is above the Earth, the mark is at the front or on the visible area of that body-part; if below the Earth it will be hidden. If the dispositor of the planet showing the mark is in a masculine sign, it will be on the right; if in a feminine, on the left.

Lilly says that these rules not only convinced his clients, but had a major part in persuading him of the veracity of astrology.[35] On the odd occasion I've used them they have worked well enough.

[35] *Lilly* p. 148.

16

Second House Questions

LOST, STOLEN AND STRAYED

Finding a lost object by casting a horoscope is spectacular. Not finding it is an excellent way of losing credibility quickly. My success rate with these questions is far below what I have with horaries in general. The problem lies in translating the symbolism of the chart into life. In most questions, we have a limited range of possibilities – 'Yes, he'll marry you' or 'No, he won't', at an extreme of simplicity – but a lost object can be anywhere. As we are usually dealing with places which we haven't seen, we have little information to work with when deciding what the planets represent. Mars in one room might represent the fireplace, in another it might be the gun-cabinet. I find I am often looking at the chart, seeing exactly where the object is in astrological terms and knowing that it would be so obvious – if only I knew where it was. Which, of course, I don't.

And when locating a lost object, we must be exactly right; in many other questions we have an amount of leeway. Explaining to your client, 'You almost found it,' is unlikely to impress.

I would love to be able to give you Frawley's Foolproof Method, with a guarantee of 100% success; but I can't. Frawley's Non-Foolproof Method, as I explain it here, works well enough. It will find some objects with astonishing accuracy; it will fail to find others in the most frustrating manner. As with all astrology, however, we should celebrate what we can do, not lament what we cannot.

Main significators

The object will be shown by either the 2nd or the 4th house if it is inanimate, either the 6th or the 12th if it is animate.

With an inanimate object we have the choice of the 2nd, the house of our movable possessions, and the 4th, the house of buried treasure. Treasure need not have been buried deliberately: it can be that document you put down which someone has buried under a pile of magazines. Some modern texts make much of a distinction between lost objects (2nd house) and mislaid objects (4th). The authors who can make such a clear distinction between losing something and mislaying it have subtler minds than mine. Nor, in practice, do we need to invoke the distinction between lost objects and buried treasure. Whatever the circumstances of the loss, look to the rulers of the 2nd and the 4th, and use whichever of them best describes the object.

Example: 'Where are my keys?' with the chart showing Cancer on the 2nd cusp, Virgo on the 4th. Mercury, ruler of Virgo, is the natural ruler of keys: Mercury will be the significator.

If the querent asks about somebody else's lost object, so you must turn the chart, always take that person's 2nd house, whether it appears to describe the object or not. 'Where is my daughter's watch?': the ruler of the 6th house (2nd from the 5th) will signify the watch.

If the object is signified by the same planet as the querent, give the disputed planet to the object. In these questions the most important point is the where-abouts of the thing; its relationship to the querent is secondary.

If you are looking for a lost animal, take the 6th if it is smaller than a goat, the 12th if larger. We are concerned here with generic distinctions: my Great Dane may be bigger than my Shetland pony, but dogs are small animals (6th) and horses are large ones (12th).

If you are looking for a missing person, use whichever house shows that person's relationship to the querent, e.g. 5th for a missing child, 6th for a missing employee. The 7th is said to be the house of fugitives; it is more reliable to use the specific house for that individual. Keep the 7th for missing spouses or for 'any old person'.

Other significators

The Moon is the natural ruler of all lost objects, especially animate ones. But keep with the main significator, as above, as far as you can: looking at two planets for location will only confuse you. In most lost object charts we don't need to consider the Moon. As a secondary significator, it is useful for timing recovery when the main significator is not making any aspects. For an example of this, look back at the cat chart in chapter 1.

Yes, this does mean that the Moon can signify both the object and the querent, sometimes both in the same chart. This is not as confusing as it sounds, because it will represent each of them at different stages of the judgement.

Sometimes the natural ruler of the object can be used, whether it rules the relevant house or not. Do this if the chart thrusts this planet on your attention, or if, considering both the planet and the sign it is in, it perfectly describes the object. A client asked 'Where are my pistols?' and the chart showed Mars (gun) in Virgo (Mercury sign, so small gun; double-bodied sign, so more than one small gun) right on the Ascendant.

Fortuna, which shows the querent's treasure, in whatever sense fits the context of the question, can occasionally be useful. I suggest you ignore it until you get really stuck. Even then, you will more often reach a judgement by persevering with the main significator.

Will it be found?

If it will not be found there is not usually much point describing where it is, no matter how fervently the client may demand that you do.

The strongest testimony of recovery is an applying aspect between the object and the querent, or between the object and Lord 2 (if the object is signified by something else), showing it returning to the querent's possession. We see here the two roles of the Moon: recovery of my lost cow could be shown by Moon (querent) applying to Lord 12 (cow); it could also be shown by Moon (natural ruler of lost objects) applying to Lord 1 (querent). Be open to either possibility.

The Moon applying to its own dispositor is a good testimony of recovery.

Having at least one of the Lights (the Sun and Moon) above the horizon (the Ascendant/Descendant axis) is helpful. This is quite literal: if there is no light we cannot see to find anything.

If Lord 1 is combust the querent can't see. If the object is combust it can't be seen. But combustion doesn't last forever: especially if the planet has already made its conjunction with the Sun and so is moving out of combustion, this is a positive sign for recovery.

The object's significator being close to an angle increases the likelihood of recovery, even without an aspect. So does a clear location: in such cases we would often not even bother looking for an aspect. 'Where is the teddy-bear?' 'In the 5th house: in the child's room'. With such information we can get up and go to look for it, without wasting our time hunting aspects.

The 1st or 2nd house favoured by the presence of a strongly dignified Jupiter or Venus, or the North Node, is mildly encouraging testimony.

Lilly says that if the object's significator is in its detriment or fall, the object will be damaged or only partly recovered. This is true on occasions, but I have not found it generally so.

Has it been stolen?

Probably not. Lilly gives a long list of testimonies showing that the thing has been stolen;[36] apply these rigorously and you will find cause to hang anyone. Most things are lost because we cannot remember where we put them; but as soon as we find they have gone, thoughts of theft, or any other way of pinning the blame on someone else, crowd to our mind. The wise astrologer will not encourage this. I strongly suggest that you do not invoke a thief unless the querent raises the possibility of theft. This follows the usual rule: **Don't write extra characters into the story unless you really must.** Imagine yourself a TV scriptwriter, and remember that every new character you introduce is another actor who will have to be paid!

There are three testimonies which would provide evidence of theft:

* a separating aspect between the suspect and the object, showing that the suspect has come into contact with the object. Similarly with the general significator of a thief (see below).
* a close conjunction of suspect and object, showing that the object is with the suspect. This can be by antiscion.
* the object being in the suspect's house, especially if just inside the cusp.

If there is any doubt at all that the object may not have been stolen, I would be most reluctant to cry 'Thief' without one of these testimonies.

Examples: 'Did the builder steal my bracelet?' with Lord 6 (the builder) separating from aspect to whichever of Lord 2 or Lord 4 signifies the bracelet. Yes, he did. No such aspect: no, he didn't. Note: this must be a separating aspect. An applying aspect, which shows something that hasn't happened yet, cannot signify a theft that has already taken place. Lilly gives a chart about some stolen money.[37] Lord 2 (the querent's money) is conjunct the significator of the thief by antiscion (antiscion implying something secret or hidden). Had the builder and

---

[36] *Lilly* pp. 331–6.   [37] *Lilly*, p. 394.

the bracelet been conjunct, bodily or by antiscion, this would show that the builder still had the bracelet.

If the querent *knows* that the object has been stolen, things are different. We do not then need to prove the fact of theft. Questions where theft is certain are discussed below.

Where is it?

Once you have identified the significator of the object, look to the chart to find out where it is. Remember: this planet *is* the missing object; where the planet is, there the object will be.

By far the most reliable way of determining this is by house meanings. In my experience, this is the only method worth using. As with the lost cat in chapter 1 ('Where is the cat?' 'In the cat's house.') so with most other questions. 'Did I leave my keys at my friend's house?' with significator of the keys in the 11th house (friends): 'Yes, they are with your friend'. A querent had lost the stone from a ring. The significator was conjunct the Ascendant, showing that the stone was very (very!) close to the querent. It had fallen into the lining of his jacket.

It is tempting to take what the querent says as truth. Don't! If the querent knew what was going on the object would not be lost. The querent's statements must be treated with extreme caution. Always remember: **The truth is in the chart, not in what you are told.** My experience is that the most common locations for lost objects are:

* exactly where the querent tells you it definitely isn't
* with the children
* with the spouse.

If the chart supports one of these, ignore all protestations to the contrary.

If the significator is in the 7th, our first choice must be that it is with the spouse. The 7th is the house of the thief, so this could mean that a thief has it; but remember the comments on theft, above. There are a lot more spouses than there are thieves. Do remember, though, that the 7th is not only the house of the spouse. It is also the 3rd from the 5th, making it the house of the child's sibling: the younger brother or sister. Always go for the most obvious option first, which in this case is the spouse; if that doesn't produce the object, you can move on to the younger child. You do not have to get it right first time: this is a consultation, not a magic act.

Ask the querent for a list of suspects. If the object is lost at home, who lives there? If outside the home, where has the querent been? Does the querent work? Whom has he visited? You are entitled to ask these questions.

For the basic 'Where is it?' the Moon being void of course is irrelevant: the object must be somewhere, even if that somewhere is 'destroyed'.

In the home

1st house: the front door or entry hall (entrance to the chart); the querent's own place in the home.

2nd house: the kitchen (2nd rules the throat and hence what goes into it). The storeroom or larder. The cloakroom (in the strict sense of the word: see 8th house) or wardrobe. The room next to the entrance. **Any house can be read as being next to the room shown by the house adjacent.**

3rd house: in an office, this would be the post-room. The communications hub. Corridors, halls and landings.

4th house: the informal room of the house (in contrast to the 10th: the formal room). The granny flat. The cellar (bottom of the chart).

5th house: the child's room or nursery. The games room.

6th house: the servants' quarters, hence the utility room. The dog kennel.

7th house: the spouse's lair.

8th house: the toilet (2nd being where food comes in, 8th being where it goes out). The bathroom (where dirt is removed).

9th house: the study. The chapel, shrine, meditation room. A landing or upstairs corridor (higher version of the 3rd house).

10th house: the home office. The formal room of the house (when Lilly calls this 'the hall' he means the great hall where you entertain visiting royalty, not a corridor). The attic (top of the chart).

11th house: the guest room (where your friends stay).

12th house: the garage (where the horses are kept) or stables. The junk room.

Above the Ascendant/Descendant axis can mean upstairs; below it downstairs.

Within the room

Once you have decided on a room, look at other factors of the planet's placement for further information.

Significator in an:

* Earth sign: on, near or under the floor.
* Air sign: high up, maybe on a shelf or hook. Somewhere light. By the window or TV.
* Fire sign: somewhere hot. Near the walls.
* Water sign: somewhere wet. Somewhere comfortable.
* Mutable signs can show that it is inside something – in a box or cupboard.

A planet on the cusp of the house or at a change of sign within that house will show the object is near the door. Near to the following cusp can show it at the opposite end to the door.

Look at close aspects to this planet. Conjunct the Moon: it's next to the fish-tank. Opposed Saturn: it's opposite the clock.

This is, as noted above, the biggest problem with locating lost objects. Everything in the universe is described by only seven planets. We might imagine that the Moon signifies a fish tank; it could be a candelabra, a white sofa, or any one of a million other possibilities. That said, connections with Mercury often show that it is with books or knick-knacks; connections with Venus, near clothes (especially women's), bedding or soft furnishings. I haven't noticed similar major indications with the other planets.

Outside the home

Being in an angular house can show that the object is close at hand or near where it ought to be. In a cadent house it may be a long way off. In a succedent house, somewhere between the two. How far 'a long way off' is will be determined by the context: 'Where is my globe-trotting son whom I haven't heard from?' is likely to be further away than 'Where is the cat?'

Give priority to the natural meaning of the house, however. If the object is in the 9th and we know the querent goes to college, it may well be at her college, even if that is very close to home.

In some cases we do not know if the missing object is inside or outside the home. Being in the 9th might show that it is a long way off, possibly in a 9thhouse sort of place (church, school). Or it could show that it is at home in a 9th-house sort of place: in the study or near a shrine. Being in the 10th: is it at work, or is it in the feasting-hall at home? I do not know any way of distinguishing which it will be. Try the most likely; if that doesn't work, try the alternative. Remember: you do not have to get it right first time.

There are several methods of determining direction in the chart. The only method with any reliability is based on the North South East West that forms the fundamental structure of the chart: the Sun rises in the east (Ascendant), travels through the south (MC) to set in the west (Descendant), returning to the east by way of the IC, which is north. Midway between north and east is, of course, north-east. Involving the signs only confuses matters: it may offer the promise of refining the direction, but in practice gives only contradiction. North by west is a refinement; north by south is a nonsense. NB: remember that in the chart, unlike a map, south is at the top.

Direction-finding is meant only for use outdoors, locating lost people or animals: don't use it within the home – unless the querent's house has its east and west wings.

If you are asking about somebody's whereabouts, remember that in the turned chart that person's home will almost always be shown by their 1st, not their 4th – as with the cat in chapter 1. 'Where's my brother?' with Lord 3 (my brother) in the 3rd (the house of brothers): he's at home.

Fido's significator in the 12th is an indication that he may be in the pound (12th being the house of prisons).

Theft

Some questions on theft have a specific suspect: 'Did the builder steal my bracelet?' with the implication that if he didn't, the querent probably lost it. In others, the thief is 'person or persons unknown'.

If there is a specific suspect, use the ruler of that person's house in the usual way, e.g. Lord 3 for the neighbour, Lord 6 for the builder. If there is no specific suspect, the choices for significator of the thief, in order of preference, are:

* a planet that is peregrine, in its detriment or its fall, *and* is in an angle or the 2nd house
* Lord 7
* Mercury, the natural ruler of thieves.

If we know that the object is stolen, we do not need to have a separating aspect between thief and object to prove this.

Once we have the thief's significator, we can draw a description in the usual way (see page 143). If we are taking Mercury as significator because it is natural ruler of thieves, we cannot, of course, use Mercury for the description – not all thieves look mercurial. In this case, use its dispositor.

The significator in a double-bodied sign is a good indication that there is more than one thief.

Unfortunately, unless the thief is known to the querent there is not much point in describing him.

Where is my shawl?

The querent, an elderly woman, had been wearing an antique, black shawl, which she had hung up somewhere, but she couldn't remember where. Lord 2 or Lord 4? Saturn, Lord 4, well describes something black and antique.

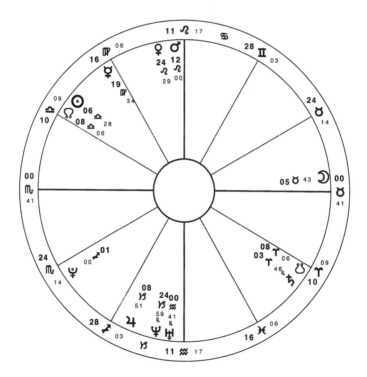

Where is my shawl? September 29th 1996, 9.22 am BST, London.

Where is Saturn? In the 5th. So the shawl is in a place of recreation. If the querent's children were possible suspects, the obvious suggestion here would be 'blame the kids', but they were not.

Describe the place of recreation. Saturn is in a fire sign, so a fiery place of recreation. A restaurant would fit.

OK – let's say it is in a restaurant. There may be other options, but this seems reasonable, so we can pick it up, run with it and see where it gets us. We now need to describe/locate the restaurant. So we go one step deeper into the chart. Saturn is the shawl. Its being in Aries has told us it is in a restaurant, so the ruler of Aries *is* that restaurant.

Mars is exactly on the MC. On an angle: close to home. Within one degree of an angle: very close to home. We might have taken the 10th as a workplace, and judged that the restaurant was very close to the workplace, but the querent was retired.

Aries has told us it is in a restaurant. The planet ruling Aries shows us where this restaurant is. It does this by its placement – as if the restaurant itself were the lost object. The sign this planet is in will describe the restaurant. If Mars were in Capricorn, an Indian restaurant; in Cancer, a Chinese; in Leo, French or Italian.

The shawl is in a French or Italian restaurant very close to the querent's home. 'Oh yes – there's a French restaurant just next door. I was there the other night.' And that is where the shawl was found.

Note here a clear example of a general principle in all traditional astrology: **Planets *are,* signs *describe.* Planets are nouns, signs are adjectives.**

Important point: here, we have taken successive steps deeper into the chart. Suppose the situation were different. Suppose Mars were itself significator of the lost object and the querent worked in an office. Mars is in the 10th: she's left it at work. Where at work? Mars is right on the cusp: near the door. Mars is in a fire sign: is there a heater near the door? Or maybe right by the wall.

"What's the difference?" If the significator tells us the object is in a specific place, we don't need to locate that place. So we can take other indications as showing its location within that place. But Saturn in the shawl chart showed us only that the shawl was in some place of recreation. This gives us a range of possible locations, so we must choose one out of this range – we are still looking for the specific place. Look at the cat chart again. The cat is in the cat's house. There is only one cat's house relevant to the question: we need look no further. Had Mars been the object in this chart, showing it to be in the office: there is only one office, so we don't need to look further. Out of the broad span of 'places of recreation' we must choose one, so we do need to define the range as is shown above.

We've taken the sign Saturn is in to describe the kind of place of recreation: it's in a fire sign, so it's a fiery kind of place, such as a place where things get cooked. Suppose Saturn had been in an air sign. We can't be overly literal about this: a hot-air balloon is an airy place of recreation; more likely would be a cinema or theatre, a café, where people meet to talk, maybe a chess club. Air is the mental faculty, so could describe anything that engages that. Similarly, a watery place of recreation could be a swimming-pool, but is more likely to be a pub. Take this as a general rule: be flexible.

MONEY

Although the 2nd is the house of money, when people ask about money it is not usually the 2nd that is of chief concern. They are asking not about their own money, but about someone else's money that they would like to have. Where we find this other money in the chart depends upon the context of the question. Who's money is it?

It is usually either 8th house or 11th house. 8th, being 2nd from the 7th, is the money of spouses, business partners, clients, enemies and 'any old person'. The 11th, being 2nd from the 10th, is the money of the job, of the boss, or of the king. It is also 'pennies from Heaven'. So:

* 'When will I get my wages?' 11th house
* 'Will this job pay well?' 11th house
* 'Will I get a tax rebate?' 11th house
* 'When will this client pay me?' 8th house
* 'Will I win on the horses tonight?' 8th house
* 'Has my sweetheart got any money?' 8th house
* 'Will I win the lottery?' 11th house

And:

* 'Can I earn a living from astrology?' 10th house (see chapter 22)
* 'Will I inherit Dad's cash?' 5th house
* 'Will I profit by buying this house?' 5th house (see chapter 18)

Let us pick our way through this maze, one step at a time.

Stocks and shares

This is the most straightforward, so we'll dispose of this one first. There is a myth that stocks, bonds and shares are 8th house matters, as 'other people's money'. They are not: your stocks are your own money (2nd house) in a different form. When you buy stock your money no more becomes someone else's than it does when you change your cash into a foreign currency. It remains your money, which may increase or diminish in value.

So questions about investments should be judged from the state of the 2nd house and the condition and actions of Lord 2. Change of sign is often crucial here. 'Should I switch my savings from A to B?' Lord 2 is leaving a fertile sign and entering a barren: 'No, your savings won't grow'. Lord 2 leaving a sign where it is peregrine and entering one where it is dignified: 'Yes, your savings will benefit'.

As a general rule, where Lord 2 is going shows the future *if the change is made.* So Lord 2 applying to the South Node is testimony not to change; applying to the North Node is testimony for change. But be prepared to be flexible if the chart suggests otherwise. For example, suppose that Lord 2 is near the end of a sign when it hits the South Node, and that in the next sign it will be dignified. We can take its meeting with the South Node in the present sign as what will happen if the situation stays as it is, and its movement into the next sign as the prospective change. In this example the querent would benefit by changing: stay put and his money will suffer (Lord 2 conjunct South Node). The chart has given us an overriding indicator of change in the change of sign.

If the querent is asking about a specific commodity, it is worth looking at the natural ruler of that commodity. 'I'm thinking of selling gold and buying dotcom shares', with the Sun (gold) about to conjunct Saturn and Mercury (computers) about to enter Virgo: 'Buy the dotcoms!' Be careful, though: this applies only to specific horaries; it does not mean that every time the Sun conjuncts Saturn the price of gold falls!

If your querent is thinking of cornering the market in cucumbers or some other product, you can also look at the Arabian Part for that commodity, considering both the Part and its dispositor.

Getting paid or repaid

We need to be clear about where the money is coming from. This is usually obvious enough: if you work for a company, your wages are shown by the 2nd from the 10th, which is the 11th. But sometimes it is necessary to think about the nature of the working relationship. Is it an employee/boss relationship, or is it a client relationship? For example, if you decide to work as an astrologer, the person who comes to you for a consultation is your client: 7th house. For 'Will he pay me?' you would look at the 8th to show his money. This is also the case if your client is a company. If the company takes you onto its payroll, as its in-house astrologer, however, your wages are 11th house. So also for any freelance work you might do for AstroCharts Inc. Your general question, 'Can I make a living from astrology?' concerns the 10th house, because it is the 2nd from the 9th and as such shows profit from your knowledge (chapter 22). Do not use that approach in any enquiry about a particular payment.

If the question concerns the amount of the payment, look at the ruler of the house that shows the money, considering its essential and accidental dignities. The stronger the planet, the greater the amount. Look also at afflictions or benefits to the house in question: for example, strong Jupiter on its cusp is good news; weak Saturn is not.

NB: in any question concerning only the *amount* of money, we do not need an aspect. But if there is one, we must consider its nature. The idea of profit assumes that it is coming to us: it wouldn't be profit otherwise. So also with wages. Suppose Lord 11 is strong, and applies to Lord 1 by square: 'The wages are good, but there may be delays in your getting them, or you may have to press for them'.

More often, such questions are less about the amount involved and more about the 'when' or 'if' of its arrival. Here we do need an aspect: no aspect, no arrival. Look for an aspect between the significator of the money and either the querent (Lord 1 or Moon) or Lord 2. The 2nd can be taken as the querent's pocket or bank-account, so an aspect from the money to Lord 2 shows it arriving in the querent's pocket. It doesn't matter which significator applies to which: the question assumes that the money is coming to the querent.

If you have lent money to someone, it is now that person's money. If you ask, 'Will he pay me back?' it is that person's 2nd house that is of interest (so 2nd from the 3rd if I lent it to my brother; 2nd from the 11th if I lent it to my friend). Look for an aspect between the ruler of that house and either Lord 1, the Moon or Lord 2. If there is no aspect showing repayment, a favourable aspect between the person's own significator and the querent's can show an agreement being reached. Watch out for severe afflictions to the significator of the person's money: you won't be paid, because he has no money. No matter how strong it might be, the significator inside its own house is also bad news: he may have plenty of money, but it is staying in his pocket.

Gambling

I once sent an article to an American astrology magazine, including judgement on a horary 'Will I win on the horses today?' I received a heated letter in reply, berating me for my foolishness in even considering such a question, because it is impossible to know whether someone has won or not. As astrologers are beings far above vulgar concepts of profit and loss, I should explain that if you end up with more money than you started with, you have won; if you end up with less, you have lost.

Gambling is often regarded as a 5th-house activity. But if someone is asking a question about gambling, the point at issue is the profit to be made; I have never been asked 'Will I have a good time at the racecourse?' Having a good time is a 5th-house matter; turning a profit is not.

The bet is a contest between you and the bookmaker, so he is your enemy (7th house) and his money is his 2nd, which is the radical 8th. It is his money that you want, so success will be shown by an aspect between Lord 8 and either Lord 1, the Moon (assuming the Moon does not signify either the bookie or his money), or Lord 2. Again, it doesn't matter which planet applies to which.

Provided there is such an aspect, the strength of Lord 8 will show how much the querent will win, relative to his stake. This can help decide on the bet. Suppose the querent has decided to back a certain team. The bookie might offer a range of bets on that team's victory, each at different odds. If Lord 8 is strong, showing a good win, the querent can take the more adventurous bet at longer odds. If Lord 8 is weak, he should stick to the safer, short-odds option.

With such questions – and with those about investments – the querent should be persuaded to do his homework first. The chart will be more reliable if he has expended some effort in selecting the proposed bets.

Lotteries are not a contest. At least, they are a contest only if the querent has developed a scheme to outwit the lottery company: then it becomes 'us against them' and should be judged from the 8th house, as above. Lotteries are seen as the querent holding out his hands to see if good fortune will fall into them: pennies from Heaven. As such, they are judged from the 11th house: does Lord 11 aspect the querent or his pocket? If the querent is asking only about a jackpot win, Lord 11 would have to be exceptionally strong to allow a 'Yes'.

If the querent is asking about winning prize-money with his own horse, look to the horse's 2nd (profit from the horse). The horse is 12th house, so its 2nd is the radical 1st. Ignore the querent for a moment, giving Lord 1 to the profit from the horse. Ideally, it would be a strong benefic, benefitting either the 1st or 2nd house (1st now seen as the querent) by placement. Otherwise, an aspect between Lord 1 and either the Moon or Lord 2 will show a profit.

I once asked a horary about a bet on a football match. The chart showed Lord 2 applying to Lord 1 by opposition. This made no sense. How could my money come to me? Either my money would disappear or the bookie's money would come to me. Consumed with curiosity, I placed the bet. The match was abandoned at half-time and all bets refunded. My money did come to me – by opposition, as I had the nuisance of having to make the journey to collect it.

The partner's money

A favourite question in Lilly's day was 'Has my prospective spouse got any money, and can I get my hands on it?' The spouse's money is shown by the 8th house. To find how much money there is, look at the condition of Lord 8 and any afflictions or benefits to the 8th house. To see if the querent will get the cash, look for an aspect to Lord 1, the Moon or Lord 2. Judge aspects according to their nature: e.g. by trine it comes easily, by opposition it comes with such effort that it isn't worth the fight.

Example: suppose Lord 1 is in the exaltation of Lord 8. Querent thinks there is lots of money, and badly wants it. Suppose Lord 8 is in its detriment. There is little money. Querent makes a trine to Lord 8. There may not be much money, but the querent is welcome to what there is.

This can be an important consideration when weighing up prospective business partners.

The government's money

If the querent is asking about a tax rebate, pension, social security or any other payment from the government, the money is shown by Lord 11 (2nd from the 10th: the government's money). Look for an aspect to the querent or Lord 2 to show receipt; the strength of Lord 11 and the 11th house to show how much.

The 11th also shows 'the gift of the king': whatever favour we require from the person in power. For a social security payment to which the person is entitled, the receptions of Lord 10 (the government) can be ignored: the process does not depend on who likes whom. But for e.g. 'Will I get the Arts Council grant?' the attitude of the awarding body (Lord 10) is important. Ideally, we would hope to find its significator exalting our querent. Kings are busy people, and so may not have time to exalt everyone who qualifies for their gift, but negative reception (by detriment or fall) would be unpromising. The more unique the gift (the Victoria Cross or just a campaign medal?) the stronger the reception that we would expect to see.

Legacies

Legacies are 8th house only in general terms: money from the dead. For any specific enquiry, take the 2nd house of whomever may be leaving the money. The money is considered as still belonging to the deceased. As usual, look for an aspect to show it is coming and strength to show how much. Look out for aspects from the significator of the money to other planets, or untoward mutual receptions: these can show someone else having a finger in the pie. Identify this invasive planet by the house it rules. For example, the aspect from the money to Lord 1 is prohibited by Lord 6: the money goes to the cats' home.

It does, of course, help if the person who is leaving the money likes – or at least does not hate – the querent, so consider the receptions of that person's planet and what these reveal about the deceased's attitude towards the querent.

Example on making money (chart on page 162)

Using techniques other than horary, I had made an astrological assessment of a sports match. I was tempted to bet on my choice of victor, so asked the question, 'Will I win by backing X?'

The bookie's money, which I hope to win, is Lord 8: Mercury. Is there an applying aspect between Mercury and Lord 1 (Saturn)? No.

Is there an applying aspect between Mercury and the Moon? Yes, although the Moon's square to Jupiter might be a prohibition.

Is there an applying aspect between Mercury and Lord 2 (Jupiter)? No, although the Moon does aspect first Jupiter, then Mercury, so translating light from Jupiter to Mercury.

Note also that Mercury and Jupiter are very close by antiscion (antiscion of

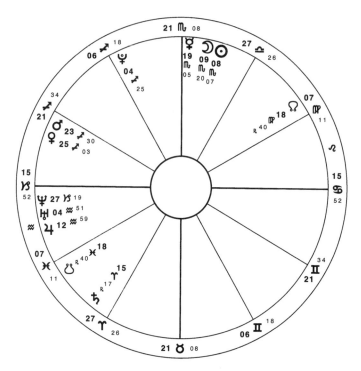

Should I buy silver? October 31st 1997, 12.36 pm GMT, London.

Mercury at 10.55 Aquarius; of Jupiter at 17.01 Scorpio). But each planet is separating from the antiscion of the other.

So: there are two positive testimonies. First, the Moon goes to Mercury, and, because aspects often don't prohibit conjunctions, that will bring me and the money together. Second, the Moon picks up Jupiter (my money) and carries it to Mercury (the money I want).

This looks promising. BUT: both these testimonies depend on the Moon, and the Moon is combust. It has no power to act. Insofar as it is possible to be weaker than totally destroyed, the Moon combust is weaker than any other planet combust, because the Moon's power to act is always dependent upon its having light, and when conjunct the Sun it has none.

Will I win? No. The extreme weakness of the Moon cannot make the positive testimonies work.

Such a judgement was, and will be for you, given a little practice, the matter of a few moments: a quick glance around the chart. I still had this chart on my computer screen when a client phoned. He was a regular client, asking simple questions directly, so no significant time elapsed between my setting my own chart and my hearing his question. The chart was the same.

His question was, 'Should I buy silver?' We can judge such questions by looking at Lord 2, construing the question as 'Should I convert my money into silver?' But the word 'silver' directs our attention to the Moon.

How is the Moon? Yuk! It is in the sign of its fall; it is combust, so close to the Sun that it has no light. It could hardly be weaker.

The Moon *is* silver; so is this a good time to buy silver? Yes! It is so weak that it cannot get weaker: this is, at the very least, a no-lose bet.

That the Moon is beginning to separate from the Sun is important. Though it has almost no light, it is starting its upward swing, beginning to pick up light.

This testimony is sufficient for judgement. It is confirmed by Lord 2, which is heading towards Pisces, its own sign.

'Yes, buy silver.' The price of silver increased dramatically in the months that followed.

This chart is of particular interest as it shows two questions which are overtly the same – 'Will I make a profit?' – judged from the same chart, yet giving opposing answers. For all its simplicity, the method is unendingly subtle.

17

Third House Questions

TRUE OR FALSE?

Is this information, gossip, rumour true?

We are looking here for testimonies that it is true. If we have few or none of these, it will, by default, be false. A void of course Moon indicates that nothing will come of it, true or false.

To be true:

* the angles of the chart should be in fixed signs
* Lord 1, Lord 3, the Moon and the Moon's dispositor should be in fixed signs and angular houses, or at least fixed signs and succedent houses.

Look at the condition of the third house: an affliction there (such as debilitated Saturn on the cusp) could show falsehood; but be cautious: it could also show that the querent will be harmed by this information. The context will usually make clear which is the more likely.

With so many testimonies we will rarely get a unanimous verdict. A majority decision will do.

Angularity and fixity both carry a sense of solidity, so what we are doing here is banging the information against the chart to see if it is real or illusion.

Is this prediction or dream true?

Take the same testimonies as above, but look at the 9th house and Lord 9 instead of the 3rd and Lord 3.

Caution

These questions are rare; keep them rare! You can say 'Is it true that I will marry Jane?' 'Is it true that I will get the job?' Fall into this trap and you will soon be judging every question as a 3rd house matter. You can fall into the same trap with the 11th, the house of hopes and wishes: 'Will I get my wish of marrying Jane/getting the job?' Always take the shortest route: what appears to be an 'Is it true?' question can usually be relocated. If the querent asks, 'I've heard a rumour that my boyfriend is two-timing me. Is it true?' cut to the chase: this is a 7th house question about her boyfriend, not a 3rd house question about truth or falsehood. Even if you have had a dream about marrying your sweetheart, rather than asking 'Is my dream true?' ask 'Will I marry her?'

Throughout my career I have not judged more than a handful of questions as 'Is it true?' The ones that come to mind are a querent who was hoping to claim the reward for finding a missing boy, asking if rumours of his whereabouts were accurate, and my own question about an unlikely prediction made by a media astrologer on a New Year's Eve TV show.

Can I trust him?

Look at that person's significator, chosen by house as usual. The more essential dignity it has, the more honourable he is. Fixity here is not necessarily a good thing: if his planet is in detriment and fixed he will be stubborn in his dishonesty.

Mercury is always tricky, even if dignified. Mercury is by nature amoral, so even if it is strong or another planet has plenty of essential dignity by being in a Mercury sign, it is likely to show someone who is honest only as long as it suits him. If in Gemini he may have a playful disregard for truth, a joy in sleight of hand; if in Virgo he will bring out the small print to prove that his dishonesty is honest after all, and more fool you for believing him.

LETTERS, PHONE-CALLS, VISITORS

The radical 3rd is rarely of relevance here. If the question were, 'Did she get my letter?' we could look for a separating aspect (showing something that has already happened) between her and Lord 3, the letter. Lord 3 in either her 1st or her 2nd house would be testimony of its arrival: the letter is with her or in her possession.

Usually, the question is about someone else's letter: 'When will I hear from him?' 'When will the book I ordered arrive?' Take the ruler of the sender's 3rd house to show that person's letter. This usually brings us to the 9th, as such questions are usually asked about either sweethearts or those with whom the querent has a business deal (such as ordering the book). All such people are shown by the 7th house, the 3rd from which is the radical 9th. Once you have located the correct significator, look for an applying aspect with Lord 1, the Moon or Lord 2. An aspect with Lord 2 shows the letter coming into the querent's possession. Then time the arrival by degrees in the usual way. No aspect: no arrival.

If you have ordered a book, the point at issue is the arrival of the book: the seller's parcel, 3rd from the 7th. With your sweetheart or the phone-call from Mum, the point at issue is the contact with that person. As such, an aspect from that person (Lord 7 or Lord 10) to the querent will give a 'Yes': there is no need to particularise the phone-call as the turned 3rd house. Once we've ordered the book, we don't want any further contact with the seller, so an applying aspect with Lord 7 in that case will not do.

Remember that once you have the letter it is no longer the sender's 3rd, but your 2nd: your possession.

If the question is 'When will this person arrive?' take the ruler of that person's house (11th if it is the querent's friend; 6th if it is the plumber) and look for an aspect to – in order of preference – the Ascendant, Lord 1, the Moon, the 4th cusp (being the querent's home). No aspect, no arrival. If there is an aspect, time it in the usual way. Such questions typically have a limited time-scale, assuming, for instance, that the arrival will be sometime that afternoon. This makes timing much easier. Anything less than a degree can usually be taken as 'immediately', although we can time to the minute. In such questions minutes of arc can often be taken as minutes of time, so if the significator is 35' from the Ascendant, arrival will be in 35 minutes.

It doesn't matter which planet applies to which. If Lord 1 applies to the visitor instead of the visitor applying to Lord 1, it doesn't mean that the querent needs to set out to collect her. Who goes to whom is given by the question.

Aspects to the Ascendant show arrival *only* if that person's arrival is assumed by the question (as in my examples here) or confirmed by other testimony in the chart. If the question is 'Will I ever see my long-lost friend again?' the friend's significator applying to the Ascendant shows that he is weighing on my mind; it doesn't show that he will be knocking on my door at any moment.

18

Fourth House Questions

PROPERTY DEALS

Will I buy/sell the house?

These questions are both judged in the same way. The querent, whether buyer or seller, is, as ever, given the 1st house; the other party is given the 7th. What we want to see is an applying aspect between Lord 1 and Lord 7. This question is really, 'Will we do the deal?' hence our concern being with Lords 1 and 7 rather than with the property itself, which is Lord 4.

If the other party has a specific house in the chart, use that instead of the 7th. If the question is 'Will my brother buy my house?' or 'Can I buy my friend's house?' use the 3rd or the 11th.

It doesn't matter what the aspect between buyer and seller is: few charts on these questions have anything more optimistic than a square. Oppositions seem to be the norm, but without their usual connotations of regret. This probably reflects the inordinate effort usually needed to force these deals to a conclusion. Note the receptions. A mutual reception between Lords 1 and 7 is most encouraging: they both want to do the deal. The absence of reception is not usually a problem; negative reception (by detriment or fall) is. A seller whose significator is in the fall of the buyer's will be reluctant to sell to him, although need may force his hand.

The positions of the significators and their strength show who has the upper hand in the negotiations. In this context there is a vital distinction between being on or inside a house cusp. **The planet on the cusp has power over that house, like the enemy battering at your castle gate; the planet inside the cusp is in the power of that house, like the enemy trapped within.** So: Lord 7 on the Asc shows the other party is keen to do the deal (in sign of Lord 1) and may be forcing the pace (the planet on Asc can often be seen as something weighing down on the querent). Lord 7 just inside the 1st house shows the querent has the other party in the palm of his hand. More often, we find Lord 1 just inside the 7th house: the querent is desperate and the other party knows it.

While it might seem logical that Lord 4 applying to aspect with the buyer's significator will show the property being sold, this is a much less convincing testimony than Lords 1 and 7 coming together. Lord 10 shows the price of the property. Having this going to the seller is so minor a testimony it can usually be ignored: don't be tempted to hang a judgement on that alone. Without the deal, as shown by Lords 1 and 7, neither property nor money will change hands.

A common scenario: Lords 1 and 7 are applying to aspect, showing that the seller (our querent, Lord 1) will sell his property. But before the aspect perfects, there is a prohibition. What is this planet that gets in the way? Lord 8: the buyer's money (2nd from 7th: the other person's money). It is in its detriment. What is it that stops the deal being done? The buyer can't raise the money.

Any unidentified planet aspecting the seller before the buyer's significator perfects an aspect can be taken as some other person coming in to buy the property.

You do not need to go looking for the estate agent. If there is an aspect between Lords 1 and 7, the involvement of an agent is irrelevant; we do not need that character on stage. If, however, there is a planet translating or collecting light to bring this aspect about, this can be taken as showing the agent.

The condition of the house

Lord 4 is the house, so its condition will show the state of the property. Lord 4 in its own sign: very good – the property is sound. In its exaltation, remembering the sense of exaggerated good that this dignity carries, the house is in good condition, but perhaps not quite as good as it seems: watch out for a cosmetic coat of paint hiding minor problems. Lesser dignities show lesser degrees of good condition. If Lord 4 is peregrine, the house is not so good, and – peregrine planets inclining more to evil – may be deteriorating. Unless it is a mobile home, when the significator being peregrine can be taken as describing the nature of the property without any such malign implications.

If Lord 4 is in its detriment or fall, there are problems. The nature of the sign will indicate what these problems are:

* air signs: check the roof and the windows
* water signs: check the plumbing and the damp-course

* fire signs: check the heating, walls and plastering
* earth signs: check the foundations.

Look out for other afflictions to the significator. Opposed by Saturn, for instance: the house might be lovely, but that factory opposite will make life there a misery. Debilitated planets in the 4th will show other problems, identified by the nature of the sign.

Lord 10 is the price. Its condition will tell whether the price is high or low. If the querent is the buyer, it can be significant that the price is in a fixed sign: it is no use making a lower offer. At the end of a fixed sign: an offer is worth a try. Be aware here too of the nature of exaltation: it suggests the price is inflated. In a seller's market this may be inescapable, but there may be other reasons for this exaggeration – rumours that the railroad is coming to town, or that a film star has bought a house locally.

What we hope for is a balance between the condition of the property and the condition of the price. Ideally, any imbalance would be in the querent's favour. There may be a strong imbalance against him, yet even so there are reasons for him to buy: the house may be falling down, but granny used to live there, or he is desperate to be near his favourite team's stadium. The chart will provide a clear analysis so the querent can decide whether the imbalance is acceptable or not.

Examples:

* Lord 4 in its own sign; Lord 10 in its own sign: the house is expensive, but you will get what you pay for
* Lord 4 in its term; Lord 10 in its exaltation: the house is OK, but the price is inflated
* Lord 4 in its detriment; Lord 10 in its detriment: the place is a dump, but the low price means it could still be worth buying.

Note receptions between Lords 1 and 4. Lord 1 in the exaltation of Lord 4: the querent has, as it were, a crush on the house. No matter how good the house might be, it is unlikely to live up to expectations. If the querent is buying the house where his favourite poet lived, the exaltation would be understandable: he values the house more highly than it really deserves. Lord 4 in the detriment of Lord 1: the house hates the querent, and so will not make him happy.

Most purchasers would like to see scope for future improvement in the price: consider the condition of Lord 10 now, its condition as it moves forward through the zodiac and the nature of its present sign – fixed signs showing lack of change.

If the house is being bought primarily for profit, whether to improve and sell on or to let out, the profit is shown by Lord 5 (2nd from the 4th: the house's money).

If the querent is asking about a property he is thinking of buying, have a look at the neighbours. We are concerned with the neighbours of the house that is being bought, not the querent's neighbours now, so the neighbours will be shown by the 6th house, which is the 3rd from the 4th: the house's neighbours. A querent asked if she should relocate permanently to her holiday home. Lord 4 was the Sun in Libra, so the house was in a bad way (in its fall). It was ruled by, or dominated by, Venus, which was itself in detriment. Venus ruled the 6th. The house was in its fall (in Libra) because it was dominated by the neighbours (Venus), who were themselves horrible (in detriment). The querent later told me hair-raising stories about the neighbours terrorising the village.

Letting property

Questions about letting or renting property should be judged in the same way as questions about buying or selling it. It is the same question: 'Can I do the deal?' These questions are judged from the 1st and 7th houses. Modern writers follow Lilly in assigning tenants to the 6th house, but this is wrong. In Lilly's day, your tenant was subservient to you: he would probably have worked on your land; he would certainly, if he had a vote, have cast it as you instructed him. This is no longer the case: a tenancy agreement is made between two parties on equal footing. Note that it is not the astrology that has changed; it is the meaning of the word.

The only difference between a selling and a letting question comes if Lords 1 and 7 join by opposition. While this is acceptable with a selling/buying question, it promises regret in the long-term relationship that will exist between tenant and landlord.

'Should I let to these people?' Consider the nature and condition of Lord 7: the better its condition, the more they can be trusted. Suppose Lord 7 is Jupiter in fall: a debilitated benefic. They look OK, but are rotten within. Be careful that Lord 7 is not afflicting Lord 4 or 5 (tenants harm the property or the profit from it).

If the question is 'Should I sell my house, or rent it out?' finding Lord 7 in a cardinal or fixed sign would suggest selling; the duality implicit in a double-bodied sign would suggest renting. If Lord 7 shows renting, and that this will be harmful, advise the querent to sell, and vice versa. Perhaps Lord 10 (the price) in a sale question is weak now, but will soon gain in strength: we might advise the querent to let the property for a while, then sell when the market rises.

Should I take the farm, or the business?

If the querent is thinking of buying or renting a place to work on or in, treat the chart slightly differently from an ordinary house purchase. These questions assume that the property is available if the querent decides to take it, so we are not looking for an aspect between Lords 1 and 7. They also assume that the place will be put to work in some way: 'Should I buy this farm?' 'Should I rent this recording-studio?' 'Should I buy this shop?'

The querent is 1st house; the seller or lessor is 7th. The 10th shows the profit that the querent will make from taking the place. The 4th shows the final outcome.

Finding Lord 1 in the first, or in a sign that aspects the sign on the Ascendant by trine or sextile is a good indication that the querent is making a beneficial deal. The closer Lord 1 is to the Ascendant or its aspect, and the more essential dignity it has, the better. Similarly, a fortune (once again: this is *any* planet with good essential dignity) in the 1st house is a positive sign. Any debilitated planet is a bad sign, unless this debilitated planet is Lord 7. If Lord 7 is in the sign on the Ascendant, it will always be in its detriment. If Lord 7 is sitting on the Ascendant, it shows that the other party is pushing to get the deal done; if Lord 7 is just inside the Ascendant, it shows that the querent has the other party in his power, and so has considerable strength from which to dictate terms.

Consider the trustworthiness of the seller. If Lord 7 is in its detriment and in the 12th house, caveat emptor! Lord 7 badly debilitated or the 7th house afflicted by the presence of a debilitated planet warns the querent to check the small-print in the contract: the terms could be disadvantageous.

Judge the condition of the 10th house and its Lord in the usual way. The 4th shows 'the end of the matter': will the querent look back on this as a good deal done, or look back with regret? Judge from the usual considerations, e.g. Lord 4 is dignified Jupiter, it is a good deal; debilitated Saturn, it is a bad one; strong Venus in the 4th house, it is a good deal; debilitated Mars, it is a bad one.

OTHER SALE QUESTIONS

If the question is whether or not the deal will be done, these can be judged exactly as house purchase questions above: we want an applying aspect between Lords 1 and 7. For non-property sales, this aspect being an opposition would tell us that the deal will bring regret. If the other party has a specific house in the chart ('Will my uncle sell me his car?'), use that instead of the 7th.

More often the question is not whether the deal can be done, but whether it should be done: 'Should I buy this car/boat/antique?' The object is shown by the 2nd house. Although it is not yet the querent's possession, it is the querent's potential possession, so we can judge from the 2nd in the same way that we can judge the querent's romantic prospects with a potential partner by giving the potential partner the 7th. The question is all about the querent's movable possessions (2nd house); it boils down to 'Should I exchange some of my 2nd-house stuff (money) for this other 2nd-house thing (object desired)?' What the chart shows us is the quality of the object desired.

What is its condition? Suppose the second-hand car I am thinking of buying is shown by Venus at 28 Pisces. It is currently in its exaltation (nice, but overrated) and is about to enter its detriment. Don't buy it! As always, if the testimony can be read as descriptive, debilities can usually be ignored. If I plan to soup up this car and take it racing, its significator's entry into cardinal fire Aries would be entirely appropriate.

If the seller's trustworthiness is in doubt, look at Lord 7. The more essential dignity, the more the seller can be trusted.

19

Fifth House Questions

Am I pregnant?

With pregnancy testing so readily available across the chemist's counter, this question is asked more rarely than once it was. More common is 'Is my dog pregnant?' The method is the same, turning the chart if the enquiry is about the dog.

The clearest and strongest testimony is finding Lord 5 in the 1st house, close to the Ascendant. This gives a clear picture of the baby (Lord 5) inside the mother, and is a definite Yes. With so clear a picture of the situation, we do not need an aspect linking mother and baby. Lord 1 or the Moon in the 5th shows only that the querent is thinking about pregnancy; this needs supporting testimony to allow a Yes. Its being closely aspected by a strong benefic, or there being a strong benefic close to the 5th cusp, would be sufficient.

Lord 1, Lord 5 or the Moon aspecting and in strong mutual reception with a planet in an angular house is testimony for Yes. Lord 1 in close trine or sextile to the Ascendant is helpful.

A malefic close to the 5th cusp or the Ascendant is testimony for No, unless the malefic in question is Lord 1 or 5. Lord 5 combust is a strong No.

Pregnancy and death are the places where antiscia will not do the job of a bodily aspect: do not judge Yes to any question on pregnancy on the strength of an antiscion alone.

NB: while these testimonies being in fertile signs is encouraging, their being in barren signs does not preclude a positive result. The barren signs are more significant in general questions of the 'will I ever...?' variety (see below).

N even more B: finding Lord 5 in the 8th is *not* a problem. It does not mean that the querent is carrying a dead baby! But the ruler of the 5th entering the 8th can be testimony that the querent is pregnant and will miscarry.

In any question on pregnancy, if other testimonies show that the woman is pregnant, finding the South Node or a debilitated malefic in her 5th house gives the potential for miscarriage. This potential needs supporting testimony if it is to be realised: do not judge on that alone. Miscarriage is an event, not a potential, and as such needs action in the chart to show it happening.

Is she pregnant?

This is judged much as above, except that Lord 5 in the 1st will not, of course, give a Yes: it is not the querent's pregnancy that concerns us. This question is usually asked by a man of a woman with whom he has slept at least once, which makes her (in this context) a 7th-house person. So Lord 5 in the 7th would show a Yes, as would also Lord 11 (5th from the 7th, so her baby) in the 7th. In one such chart, Lords 5 and 11 were conjunct in the 7th: this did underline the Yes; it did not promise twins. Had they been in a double-bodied sign, it might have.

If the question is not about a 7th-house person, but, for instance, the querent's sister or mother, we would look to that house and the 5th from there. The only circumstance in which we can have two houses showing the baby is when a male querent is asking if a woman is carrying his child: the radical 5th is 'my baby', the turned 5th is 'her baby' (with no suggestion of this meaning it was not fathered by the querent). Do not involve the turned 11th house in questions asked by someone other than the father.

When considering those testimonies that involve angularity, it is the radical angular houses that matter: **houses do not become angular by being turned** (e.g. the 4th from the 3rd is not angular in a chart about my sister).

Will I conceive?

My experience is that this question is usually asked by those contemplating fertility treatment, occasionally as 'Will I conceive on this holiday?' or similar.

In principle, nothing is simpler: we look for an aspect linking mother (Lord 1 and the Moon) and baby (Lord 5) in the usual way. Lord 5 and one or both of the querent's significators being in a fertile sign (Cancer, Scorpio, Pisces) makes the judgement more confident. Even if all three of these significators are in barren signs (Gemini, Leo, Virgo), a clear aspect between strong planets will still give conception. As supporting testimonies, a benefic planet in the 5th house, especially Jupiter in Cancer or Pisces, is helpful. So is the North Node.

Watch for afflictions to the significators or the 5th house, especially from Saturn. Saturn in the 5th, especially if close to the cusp, is a strong negative testimony (unless it is Lord 1, when this placement would reflect the querent's interest in the subject). Lord 5 combust is a definite No, unless the Sun is Lord 1.

Do remember the basic point that Jupiter and Venus are not necessarily helpful. How benefic they can be depends on their condition. A client asked about her inability to conceive. Jupiter was just inside the 7th house, in Gemini. Being in its detriment, it afflicts the house it is in: the husband. Jupiter is natural ruler of sperm. In its detriment and in a barren sign: the husband has a low sperm count. Or Venus in Virgo: dignity by triplicity, debility by fall, in a barren sign; fun, but no conception. It is well to remind the querent that, even the best of astrologers being fallible, prediction is not a reliable form of contraception.

Charts for questions about fertility treatment are often finely balanced, and tact is required in dealing with the querent. The charts are finely balanced because the situation is finely balanced: if the couple was brimming over with fertility, the question would not be asked. Often the judgement is either, 'It really doesn't look like it; but do remember that the astrologer is fallible', or 'I can't give a definite Yes, but there is sufficient potential here that you may think it worth proceeding'.

First look for potential fertility: check Lords 1, 5, 7 and 11, the Moon, the Moon's dispositor. We consider Lords 5 and 11 as significators of the husband and his baby-potential (though for straight 'Will I conceive?' questions joining Lord 11 to Lord 1 will *not* give conception).

Are they in fertile or barren signs? The other signs are neutral. Fertile signs are positive, but the absence of barren signs is enough to give hope. Do not consider the signs on the cusps of these houses: with so many houses in play, we are most likely to find a scattering of fertile and barren there, but the house rulers can be anywhere.

Then consider benefits or afflictions to houses 1, 5, 7, 11 and their rulers. By now you may have a clear No, in which case you can stop. As long as testimony of barrenness is not overwhelming, carry on to look for an aspect to show that what potential there is will be realised. Do not look to the 10th house for the fertility treatment: the 10th is the treatment in sickness charts, but is not relevant here. If conception is to be by fertility treatment, a connection between mother and baby by either collection or translation of light is typical. It doesn't matter which planet is making this connection, or which house it rules: it still gives conception. The involvement of a third planet in translation and collection of light mirrors the third-party involvement in fertility treatment.

Once you have a planet connecting Mum and baby, consider its nature (nice planet or nasty planet?), its receptions with Lords 1 and 5 (is it in Mum's sign, so wanting to help her, or is it in her fall, harming her?), and whatever other testimonies there may be around the 5th house. The aspect is enough to show conception; these other factors will tell what happens next – particularly whether the baby will be carried full term.

Then the most important step: engage your brain and, more important still, your heart before speaking to the querent. You cannot lie; but all that is seen does not need to be told.

Will I ever conceive?

As with 'Will I ever marry?' we must consider the default option here. If the querent is 20, we must judge Yes unless the chart shows a clear No. If the querent is 50, we must judge No unless there is a very clear Yes.

For the 'will I ever' part we need only to consider the potential, as above: check Lords 1, 5, 7 and 11, the Moon, the Moon's dispositor. Are they in fertile or barren signs? The other signs are neutral. Fertile signs are positive, but just the absence of barren signs gives hope. Do not consider the signs on the cusps of these houses: it is the signs the house rulers are in that concern us. If there is an aspect between Lords 1 and 5, so much the better, but for a querent of 20, some sign of fertility and the absence of major afflictions to the 5th house or its ruler is sufficient to judge Yes.

If our querent is 50, we would need to see all or most of our key planets in fertile signs and a strong aspect linking Lords 1 and 5, with no serious afflictions.

This question is often accompanied by a 'when', or indeed is phrased as 'when' with the 'will I' assumed. In the latter case, unless the Yes leaps out of the chart in the form of an aspect, we must determine the 'if' before tackling the 'when'. Once we have decided that the querent will conceive, we know that the timing must be in the chart somewhere. Well-behaved charts give us a clear aspect to work from; but not all charts are so well-behaved. This can demand a stretch of the astrological muscles. But with a long-term issue like this we can push planets through the usual prohibitions, such as other aspects or changes of sign. The only pass-nots are station and conjunction with the Sun. With this freedom, you will find a way of linking querent and Lord 5. NB: you can do this *only* because you have already found that the main answer to the question is 'Yes'. Once you have connected Mum and baby, calculate the timing in the usual way.

Number and gender

Do not strive for precision in predicting the number of children the querent will have. This is, as Lilly would say, 'too scrupulous a quere'. Our choices are: 1, 1 or 2, a few, lots. This is quite accurate enough.

Consider Lords 1, 5, 7 and 11, the Moon, the Moon's dispositor. Once you have decided that there will be at least one child, how strong are the testimonies of fertility? All these planets in fertile signs would be testimony for 'lots'; only one fertile would suggest only one child. The planets showing fertility being accidentally strong (seriously strong – there is no need to quibble here) increases the number they are likely to give. Angularity is particularly important here; but vary your idea of 'accidentally strong' to fit the question. For example, suppose Lord 1 is Jupiter in Cancer – about as fertile an indication as can be – and is close to the 5th cusp: this would be a powerful testimony for many children, even though it is not angular.

Note that although Gemini and Virgo are barren signs, they are also double-bodied. If the overall judgement is that the querent will have children, they can give more than one.

For gender, consider the same planets: are they masculine or feminine? Are the signs they are in masculine or feminine? Although it is tempting to ignore the fact that the Moon is feminine, because the Moon is present in every such assessment, I suggest that including this – giving feminine a head start – helps reduce the imbalance in favour of masculine. Give added weight to any of these planets with good accidental strength.

The majority verdict gives the sex of the first child. If there is a significant dissenting opinion, this can be taken to show the sex of the second – if you have judged that there will be a second. Further than that we need not go.

ADOPTION

The child that the querent is hoping to adopt is 11th house: 5th from the 7th – someone else's child (unless it is the child of someone specific: e.g. the sister's child would be 5th from the 3rd). The usual question is 'Will I get this child?' for which we hope to find an aspect between the querent's significators and Lord 11.

Once the child has been adopted, it is the querent's. All questions about it should be judged from the 5th house, exactly as if it were a natural child.

20

Sixth and Eighth House Questions

MEDICAL QUESTIONS

The judgement of medical questions is a huge subject, to deal with which in full would demand in itself a book longer than this one. I can do no more here than give an overview of the method, which will suffice for many simple enquiries, and to point the reader requiring a more exhaustive treatment of this topic in the right direction.

The vital first point is that **although the 6th is the house of illness, it does *not* signify the illness in a medical question**. Suppose the question were 'Will I win the gold medal?' and Lord 1 was applying to aspect with Lord 10 (success, victory: the medal), when the aspect was prohibited by Lord 6. Judgement would be, 'You would; but you're going to get ill'. A question such as this has illness as one issue among many. In the chart for a medical question, however, the whole chart is concerned with this sick person suffering from this illness: the subject of illness is not confined to one house. Do not, then, leap to Lord 6 as significator of the illness.

Prognosis or diagnosis?

Medical questions fall into two groups: 'What is wrong?' and 'What will happen?' It is the diagnosis question that is too complex to be handled here; but I can give the method. Following this will enable you to identify the planet that signifies the illness. You can then refer to Richard Saunders' *Astrological Judgement and Practice of Physic* for the diagnosis.[38]

---

[38] London, 1677. There is a good modern edition in the Astrology Classics series from The Astrology Center of America.

Saunders was a contemporary of Lilly, who held him in high esteem. His book contains a breakdown of each planet in each part of each sign, describing the ailments that this placement shows, their immediate cause (the bodily imbalance of which the symptoms are a manifestation), and what can be done to treat them. He also gives a method of approaching the horary question on illness, but ignore this: follow it and you will be consistently wrong. Use the method I give here, then go to Saunders for the diagnosis.

Warning: Saunders, as is usual in traditional medicine, divides ailments into four categories, from those of the first degree, which are the mildest, to those of the fourth degree, which are 'beyond nature' and often fatal. You will no doubt remember the films where the cops give someone 'the third degree': a serious beating, but not fatal. These degrees must be taken within the context given by the illness itself: if the querent's cold is described as being 'in the fourth degree', this means that it is a bad cold; it does not mean the querent will die from it.

The methods given in the texts, including Saunders' *Astrological Judgement*, are confused and often faulty, largely because the authors mix horary method with the method of judging a *decumbiture* chart, with no distinction between the two. A decumbiture is the chart set for the moment at which the patient takes to his bed, or when a sample of his urine is delivered to the astrologer/physician. Decumbiture is far more cumbersome than horary, and is to be used only if you are the treating physician and if you will be visiting the patient every couple of days to revise your treatment.

The starting-point: am I ill?

This is occasionally the question asked: 'Are these snuffles going to turn into a cold that will ruin my holiday?' 'Should I call off my world record attempt?' More often, this question is redundant: if the person were not ill, the question would not have been asked. Either way, this is our point of entry to the medical horary.

Look at Lord 1, if the querent is asking about himself, or the ruler of whichever house signifies the person. I shall call it Lord 1 throughout this section; adjust as necessary if the querent is asking about someone else. What is its nature: hot/dry, cold/dry, hot/moist or cold/moist? Then look at the sign it is in: what is its nature? If the planet is in a sign that does not exactly match its nature, this is an indication that the person is indeed unwell. So also if the planet is debilitated, retrograde, combust or otherwise afflicted. Note that a planet can be in a sign of contrary nature and yet rule that sign, e.g. hot/dry Mars in cold/moist Scorpio.

The significator of the illness will be whichever planet is harming Lord 1. If Lord 1 is in a sign of different nature to its own, this will be the ruler of that sign. So also if Lord 1 is in its detriment or fall. If Lord 1 is combust, take the Sun, which is the afflicting planet; it is also worth having a look at the ruler of whichever sign the two planets are in. If Lord 1 is suffering from an adverse aspect, take the aspecting planet. Look also at planets in tight aspect to the Ascendant, especially if the problem is located in the head or face.

Lord 1 can itself signify the illness, most commonly if it is in a sign that it rules but which is of contrary nature, or if it is retrograde. If retrograde, look also at the ruler of the sign it is in.

There can be more than one significator for the illness. Sometimes this shows different levels of causation ('You are suffering from palpitations of the heart, but this is exacerbated by your financial worries'); sometimes there is more than one problem. Note that any planet in any condition can be a significator of illness: it's not only the bad guys. When Jupiter was passing through Cancer, I saw many charts where he was significator and the illness was marked by an excess of moisture.

Now that you have the significator(s) of the illness, refer to Saunders for the diagnosis. Writing in the Seventeenth century, Saunders does not use the same medical model as a modern doctor, but his diagnostic is none the less accurate for that.

What will happen?

If the significator of the illness is in a fixed sign, the illness will be long-lasting; if in a cardinal sign, it will be short; if in a mutable sign it will come and go, or give better days and worse days. Qualify this by the sign that the person's own significator is in, according to the same criteria.

Look at whatever it is that is afflicting the person's significator. Is the significator moving away from it or moving towards it? For example, if illness is shown by the significator being in an incompatible sign, has it recently entered that sign, or is it about to leave it? If it leaves, will its condition get better or worse? If the affliction is an aspect, is the aspect applying (getting worse) or separating (getting better)?

Is the significator changing direction? A planet in first station (turning retrograde) is likened to a man taking to his sickbed: he is ill and will get worse. A planet in second station is likened to a man rising from his sickbed: he feels shaky now, but is recovering.

Mars afflictions are usually acute, Saturn afflictions long-lasting. But do factor in the nature of the problem: the breaking of a leg is a quick, Mars-type action, but recovery is slow.

These general indications apply to run-of-the-mill, non-threatening illnesses. My experience is that people with run-of-the-mill, non-threatening illnesses are less likely to consult a horary astrologer than those with illnesses that may prove fatal. With the majority of medical enquiries we must begin by working out if the patient will live or die. So:

QUESTIONS ON DEATH

I will consider here all questions about death, those that involve illness and those that do not.

You may well decide that you do not wish to handle questions on death, but it is as well that you should know how they are judged. Questions do not have to be overtly about death for it to be involved: in many circumstances we need to look at testimonies of death to assure ourselves that it is not going to happen (e.g. a political exile asking 'Is it safe for me to go home?'). Although the idea of predicting death may seem off-putting, there are many reasons for people sincerely wanting to know. The most common are when the querent has to make financial provision for the care of an elderly relative ('Do I extend the overdraft, or do I need to remortgage the house?') and when the patient is receiving treatment for a potentially fatal illness.

Although the techniques of predicting death from a horary are reliable, do remember that you are not. Except in cases of serious illness, I most strongly advise that you do not predict death unless, if at all possible, you have checked with the birthchart. This is not a fail-safe, but it does mean you must get it wrong twice to be in error with your judgement. "So why bother with the horary if I'm going to refer to the nativity anyway?" Because it will give you a valuable short-cut: instead of searching through years of progressions, it will take you straight to a likely date.

As always, be realistic with the precision you provide. If death will occur next week, it is reasonable that you should give the day, or at least whether it will be early or late in the week. If the death will occur in twenty years' time, giving the year is accuracy enough. Achieving greater precision is very clever, but our purpose is not to demonstrate how clever we are.

There are two main enquiries on this subject: the general 'When will I die?' and the more particular 'Will I die?' referring to death from this illness that the querent has now.

When will I die?

The great thing with this question is that the event is certain, so we know that there must be a timing in the chart somewhere. This means we can set aside many of the usual rules. We can ignore prohibitions: they can be taken to show events along the way. We can push our significators as far as we need through sign after sign. There are only two barriers that we cannot allow our significators to pass:

* conjunction with the Sun
* station.

Conjunction with the Sun is a pass-not. At station a planet's speed slows to nothing. As, when timing, we must adjust the time if the planet is significantly faster or slower than usual, a planet at zero speed would give us infinite time. This might please the querent, but is unlikely to prove accurate.

Well-behaved charts have an applying aspect between Lords 1 and 8. As ever, it does not matter which applies to which. Any aspect can kill: there is no difference between trines and oppositions. Any planet can kill: even if Lord 8 is a strongly dignified benefic, the person will still die. I would be most reluctant to judge death from an antiscion. Death cannot have the sense of the covert or hidden that antiscia carry: even if the death is unknown to others, it is clear enough to the person who dies.

Lord 1 on the 8th cusp is *not* a testimony in this question: it shows only that the querent is thinking about death. Similarly with Lord 8 applying to conjunct the Ascendant: it shows the idea of death weighing down on the querent, but it does not show Death himself paying a call. But these can be taken as testimony of death, and as such give us the timing, in questions where death within a short period of time is regarded as certain ('I've been told I have only weeks to live; when will the end come?'). But while in such circumstances Lord 1 entering the 8th can show death, Lord 1 already in the 8th does not: the querent is not already dead.

In those charts where there is no applying aspect between Lords 1 and 8 (remember: the aspect must perfect) we must find another significator for one or the other. As there can be only two reasons for the lack of aspect – as above – find a replacement significator for whichever planet is either conjuncting the Sun or passing through station. This is the significator that is being uncooperative, so change this one and keep the other. So if Lord 1 turns retrograde before aspecting Lord 8, keep Lord 8 as significator of death and find an alternative for Lord 1.

If the Moon, as is usual, is cosignificator of the querent, it can be used instead. If that too is ruled out, the Sun is a good alternative, in its role as Lord of Life. If it is Lord 8 that is ruled out, use either Saturn, as natural ruler of death, or the dispositor of the Part of Death.

There are several versions of the Part of Death. I use Asc + 8th cusp – Moon and 8th cusp + Saturn – Moon. Neither reverses by night. Don't get carried away with these Parts, though! They are useful in emergencies, when the planets are not cooperating and we know there must be a death. In any question where death is not certain, do not take the Parts as providing it: if death is not shown by the planets, the person is most unlikely to die.

If you are turning the chart, because the querent is asking about someone else's death, you must consider the ruler of both the radical and the turned 8th house. You will usually find that one or other of them is in play; sometimes both.

When you have found the aspect showing death, time it in the usual way, bearing in mind the querent's age. This is a time when the astrologer crosses his fingers and hopes for the best result: predicting early death is not pleasant. If, however, you are not prepared to do it, you should not be judging such questions.

Will I die?

Odd though some horaries are, I have yet to be asked 'Will I die?' as a general, long-term question. I deal here with death from a particular illness or a particular situation ('Is it safe for me to go back to my country?'). I will treat this as if the querent is asking about himself and refer to Lord 1; if the querent is asking about somebody else, use the ruler of the appropriate house instead. Remember that **the Moon does not become cosignificator of the person the querent is asking about.**

An applying aspect between Lords 1 and 8 is the prime testimony of death. Time it in the usual way. A separating aspect must be judged according to the situation. Death has presumably not already happened, or the question should not be asked, so it is usually a positive testimony: the person has come into contact with death; he is still alive; he will survive. Unless there is other killing testimony coming up. If, however, the person is in a coma this separating aspect usually means that death, in any meaningful sense of the word, has already occurred: see the chart below for an example.

Keep your eyes open for translations or collections of light.

Remember that if the querent is asking about someone else, you must consider the Lords of both the radical and the turned 8th houses: either can kill.

Entering combustion or being combust and still applying to the Sun is testimony of death. Being combust and separating from the Sun is testimony that the worst has passed. With the usual rider of 'all things being equal' this can be taken as testimony of survival.

If the situation is serious enough, any major deterioration in the condition of the main significator can be taken as fatal. In one chart, the person asked about was in a coma, his significator the Moon in Cancer. All might seem fine: lots of essential dignity and a cold/moist planet in a cold/moist sign. But the testimonies must be judged within the context of the question. The Moon was in the 30th degree of Cancer, on the point of leaving the sign, on which it would enter hot/dry Leo and lose all its dignity. The person's condition was about to deteriorate dramatically. He was in a coma: how much worse could he get? This was testimony of death.

Most important: mutual reception between the significator of the person and the significator of death saves. As Lilly says, 'after desperation, there will be recovery'.[39] Yes, this works, even with a clear applying aspect between Lords 1 and 8 – although it works only with reception by major dignity. Be aware of what is happening in the chart, though: in the example in the last paragraph death was signified by Jupiter in Cancer. With the person's significator being the Moon in Cancer, there was powerful mutual reception between person and death. But with the person's significator changing sign and losing that mutual reception, death was certain.

"Surely if Death and person love each other (mutual reception) they will want to be together, so the person will die?" No. The idea here is that Death and the person are friends, so Death leaves the keys on the table and turns his back, letting the person escape from his clutches.

Death is an event of some significance: you will not find it shown by a minor testimony in some dark corner of the chart. If there is no clear testimony for death, the person will live.

---

[39] *Lilly* p. 254.

A close aspect, especially conjunction, between Lord 1 and either Venus or Jupiter in major dignity is a positive sign – unless this helpful planet rules the 8th house or is significator of the illness.

The person's significator close to the 7th cusp is testimony of death. Although being angular is strengthening, by primary motion (the apparent movement of the planets around the Earth) a planet on the Descendant is setting, which is an obvious indication of dying. This is all the more true if this significator is the Sun.

The person's cusp or significator falling on Antares, with its sense of the ending of cycles, is a bad sign.

Will my friend live?

The querent said, 'My friend has been taken to hospital. She is in a coma. The doctors don't know what's wrong with her, but think she may have had a brain haemorrhage. What is the problem? What is going to happen?'

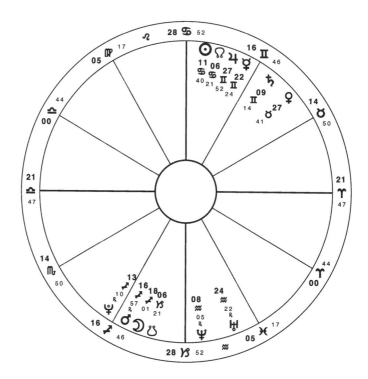

Will my friend live? July 3rd 2001, 2.18 pm BST, London.

The querent is not involved in this question, so we go straight to the 11th, the house of friends. Its ruler, Mercury, signifies the friend. Seeing Mercury in Gemini, we might think that the friend is doing fine. But no: although Mercury is in a sign that it rules, in a medical question it is in a very bad condition. Mercury is a cold/dry planet. It is in a hot/moist sign, a sign contrary to its nature. It is dis-eased. The friend is not well. This much we know, of course: the woman is in a coma.

Which planet is causing Mercury problems? We can look to the ruler of the sign Mercury is in. This brings us back to Mercury. There is no reason that the significator of the illness should not be the same as that of the patient. But here we have a more likely culprit, especially considering the sudden onset of the illness. Mercury is just separating from opposition to Mars. Mars is peregrine and retrograde, so it is a nasty sort of Mars.

The Moon's most recent aspect can also be taken into account. Its last aspect was to this nasty Mars. Mars is confirmed as significator of the illness.

Mars in this part of Sagittarius, Saunders says,[40] 'is hot and dry above nature, consuming and drying up the radical moisture and humidity of the body, and utterly extinguishing the life of man'. It does this by infecting 'the body and blood with much thick, red choler that is hot and very dry'. Choler is the fiery humour, the fiery part of the human constitution. The doctors suspected a brain haemorrhage; had this fatal Mars been in the friend's 1st house (the 1st being the house of the head), it could well have shown this: a kind of fiery explosion in the brain. It isn't; it is in her 5th (the 5th house from the 11th), which is the house of the heart. She has had a heart attack. This was confirmed at the post mortem.

What will happen to her? She is in a coma, so our first question must be, 'Will she live or will she die?' Looking into the death of somebody other than the querent, we must consider both the turned and the radical 8th house. Here, the turned 8th house (8th from the 11th: the radical 6th) is ruled by Mars. Mercury (the friend) is separating from opposition to it. If the sick person is sitting up in bed and chatting, this is a most positive sign: she has come into contact with death; she is still alive; she is going to survive. In the context of someone in a coma it can be taken that death, in the real sense, has already happened.

The Moon separates from Mars and applies to Mercury, translating light between them and so remaking the aspect: the friend will die. The number of degrees the Moon must travel to perfect the opposition gives the timing: she will

[40] Saunders, op. cit., p.152.

be pronounced dead at the end of that afternoon. In the blessedly small number of horaries I have been asked to judge on death in comas, this remaking of a separated aspect by translation of light is typical for showing the doctors' recognition that hope has gone.

DOCTORS, MEDICINE AND SURGERY

'Is this doctor any good?' 'Is this treatment working?' 'Should I have this operation?' When judging such questions, do be cautious. The astrology may be eloquent, but unless you have a sound knowledge of medicine you are unlikely to fully understand what it says. But we can, even without such a knowledge, make the suggestion that 'These pills seem to be doing you more harm than good; maybe there's an alternative', or 'This doctor seems to be out of his depth; can you insist on seeing a specialist?'

Doctors in general, seen as learned people, are 9th house ('Was that the doctor's cat who chased mine down the street?'), but the doctor that is dealing with this illness, or who is potentially dealing with it, is 7th house. If the querent is asking about someone else's illness, the doctor will be that person's 7th house. People often ask about their spouse's treatment: spouse is 7th, so the spouse's doctor will be 7th from the 7th, which is the 1st. That's fine: we don't need to have the querent in the chart, so we can give Lord 1 to the doctor.

In this context, take the treatment as Lord 10. This is only in this context: the 10th is the treatment that is being given, not the treatment that should be given. In some cases, surgery will be seen as part of the range of treatment prescribed and so can be taken as 10th house. In itself, however, surgery is a 6th-house matter. There is an idea that it is 8th-house, but this is wrong: the aim of surgery is to keep us out of the 8th house. In practice, we can usually go straight to Mars, natural ruler of surgery. If you need to distinguish between doctor and surgeon ('My doctor says this but my surgeon says that.') keep the 7th house for the doctor and use the dispositor of the planet signifying the surgery (usually Mars) for the surgeon. There is no problem with this planet dispositing itself: read the same indications for the surgeon and the surgery.

Once you have identified the relevant planet, consider its strength and its receptions with the patient and the illness. Essential debility is not necessarily a problem, if it is descriptive. Example: if Mars is the surgery, Mars in a Venus sign would well describe gynaecological or cosmetic surgery. If that were the nature of the operation, the essential debility could be ignored. More important than dignity – though strength is of course helpful – is reception. We would hope to see the significator of the illness in strong dignities of either the doctor, the treatment or the surgery. If the illness is disposited by the doctor, he has power over it. Finding doctor, treatment or surgery in strong dignity of the illness is negative testimony: the illness is boss. Doctor, treatment or surgery in dignity of the patient's significator is helpful, although less so than testimony showing power over the illness; but it is most important that doctor, treatment or surgery is not in the detriment or fall of the patient's significator.

Examples: suppose the patient is Jupiter, the illness is Mars and the treatment Saturn. Mars is in Aquarius: good – the treatment has power over the illness. Saturn is in Sagittarius: good – the treatment loves the patient, and so will want to help him. But Saturn in Capricorn would be bad news: despite its essential strength, it exalts Mars, showing that the illness has power over the treatment, and is in the fall of Jupiter, showing it harming the patient.

Certain fixed stars can be important in questions about eye surgery. See page 114.

Don't expect charts for questions on surgery to look pretty. No matter how beneficial the surgery might be, it remains a drastic intervention.

You will sometimes be asked to compare two doctors. They cannot both be shown by the patient's 7th house. Asking for a brief description of the two will enable you to identify them in the chart. For instance, a querent thought her son would need an operation, and asked if this should be carried out by a National Health Service surgeon, or if she should go private. Her son was receiving NHS treatment, and his 7th house (the doctor treating him) was ruled by the Moon (the people). The ruler of the querent's 7th (which we could read as the doctor the mother was considering) was Jupiter, natural ruler of rich folks. The Moon, at 29 Scorpio, was immediately leaving Mars dignities: the NHS surgeon decided that he did not need the operation after all.

HIRING STAFF

If you are hiring someone at work, taking on a new downstairs maid or calling a plumber, the prospective employee is shown by the 6th house. Ideally, Lord 6 will be essentially strong (the person is honest and has the necessary skills), accidentally unafflicted (no impediment to using those skills) and in dignities of

Lord 1. The latter is important because the servant must accept orders. Too often the chart shows the reverse: Lord 1 is in major dignities of Lord 6, showing that the querent likes the prospective servant. This is not the best reason for hiring someone. Lord 6 in the detriment or fall of Lord 1 would be a definite No.

Watch out for afflictions to the 6th house. The South Node, for instance, in the 6th would be a definite No. Always be cautious with Mercury and the signs that it rules: even at its best, its concept of honesty can be flexible. A client phoned to ask if she could trust her cleaner, who was shown by Jupiter in Gemini. Debilitated planet in a Mercury sign: definitely not! She called back a few minutes later to say she had gone upstairs to find the cleaner packing her best clothes into a suitcase.

If you are asked 'Should I employ A, B or C?' give the 6th house to the favoured candidate and find other significators for the rivals. Keep it to A, B or C: the querent who can't come up with a shortlist is not treating the matter seriously, so why should you? Ask the querent for a brief description of each candidate. As long as it is kept brief, the description will contain whatever clues you need to pin the candidate to a planet. 'One of them is a redhead (Mars) and the other is really solemn (Saturn).' You can trust that each querent will give the appropriate identifying words, because the chart is a picture of that querent's reality. Once you found a planet for each candidate, compare them by the criteria above.

We are not looking for aspects in this question, as it assumes that the querent can hire that person if they decide to do so. But querent and candidate applying by opposition is a strong warning that employing that one will lead to regret.

When will the plumber arrive?

Casting such a chart, I would expect to find Lord 6 applying to conjunct the Ascendant (coming to the querent's house). Failing that, an aspect between Lords 1 and 6 or, at a pinch, Lord 6 applying to the 4th cusp will do. Take the timing in the usual way. No aspect, no arrival.

21

Seventh House Questions

When I first started in horary practice, I expected questions on relationships to make up the greater proportion of my trade. This did not prove so – I could never have imagined the range of questions that do get asked – but there have been substantially more questions on relationships than on any other single issue. These fall broadly into two groups: 'Will it start?' and 'Will it end?' Lest you wonder why I pay such attention here to marital disharmony, remember that people in happy relationships are rarely impelled to consult astrologers about them.

The significators

In questions about love and marriage, the querent is signified, as ever, by Lord 1 and the Moon (unless the Moon is ruler of the house enquired about, in this case the 7th) and the quesited, the person asked about, is shown by Lord 7. The quesited is shown by Lord 7 even if the relationship exists as yet only as a desire or a possibility. For instance, if the question is 'When will I meet the man I will marry?' we look to the 7th even if there is no candidate on the horizon at the moment. If the querent is thinking of promoting a friend to 7th-house duties, we would look to the 7th, not the 11th: the question is really 'Is so-and-so a suitable partner?' That so-and-so happens to be a friend now is irrelevant. If the question is about some specific person's feelings for the querent, however, we may need to look at a different house. For example, to judge 'Has my neighbour got a crush on me?' we would look at Lord 3.

The man, whether querent or quesited, will be given the Sun as cosignificator and the woman, Venus. This is *only* in relationship questions. If the Sun or Venus rules the 1st or 7th house, it cannot be assigned in this way: the person shown by that house has first claim on its services. Do *not* use Mars instead of the Sun, even if the Sun is already in use. If the question concerns a man/man or woman/woman relationship, the Sun and Venus cannot be used in this way, because we have no reason for assigning them to one person rather than to the other.

So:

1. Querent gets Lord 1 and the Moon.
2. Person asked about gets Lord 7.
3. Whether they are querent or quesited, the man gets the Sun and the woman gets Venus – UNLESS they have already been claimed under points 1 and 2.

In many relationship questions there is more than one 7th-house person involved: 'I'm married, but do I have a future with my lover?' Always give Lord 7 to the person specifically asked about, which in this example is the lover. We can, if necessary, then find another planet to signify the other one. It is usually safe to take Saturn as significator of the unwanted spouse. If in doubt, the receptions will make the choice of planet clear, or confirm that we have chosen correctly: see below for more detail on this.

Some questions with more than one 7th-house person do not involve cheated spouses: 'I've been dating Tom for a few weeks, but, Wow! there's this new guy at work!' In many cases this question boils down to 'What are the prospects of a relationship with the new guy?' so, as the person directly asked about, he would be given the 7th. In others, the situation is more ambivalent. Be open to what the chart is showing you. For example, a planet recently aspected by one of the querent's significators could show the new guy; so could a planet recently arrived in the 10th house (just come into the workplace).

Receptions will often guide us to the correct significator in those charts where someone other than Lord 7 is involved. If this person is in some way an issue there will be receptions confirming this. For example: a woman asks 'Is my marriage going to survive?' Venus is Lord 1 and Mars is Lord 7. The querent has the Moon as her cosignificator, and would also have Venus, because she is a woman, were it not that she already has Venus as Lord 1. Her husband has the Sun as his cosignificator, because he is a man. Suppose Mars and the Sun are both in Cancer while the Moon is in Pisces: one of our querent's significators and both of her husband's are in strong Jupiter dignities. Whatever Jupiter signifies must be important to them both. The husband exalts Jupiter, with all that this dignity tells us of exaggerated regard, while the Moon is ruled by it. Jupiter, then, may well signify the husband's mistress: he is crazy about her, while she, by virtue of the role she has assumed in her life, has power over the querent.

Lilly tells us to take the planet from which the Moon has most recently separated as another significator for the querent, and that to which it next applies as another significator for the quesited. Don't! These extra significators do nothing but clutter the picture to no purpose.

Another significator which is often of the greatest importance is the dispositor of the Part of Marriage. If our main significators share a strong interest, as shown by reception, in a planet which as yet has no role in the chart, four times out of five you will find that this planet is the dispositor of the Part of Marriage. Refer back to pages 120-123 for a discussion of this and related Parts.

In some questions the Part of Divorce is useful (see page 123). Mars itself can also be a significator of divorce, if it's not already in use signifying one of the people involved. If, and only if, it is very close to the action, Uranus too can show divorce or separation. For instance, if the question is 'Will this relationship last?' finding Uranus on the 7th cusp is testimony that it will not. Finding it on the Ascendant, however, may show only that the idea of divorce is weighing on the querent.

Receptions

Look back at chapter 8, on receptions.

We now have up to three significators (Lord 1, Moon and either Sun or Venus) for our querent and either one or two (Lord 7 and either Sun or Venus) for the quesited. Each of the different significators shows a different facet of that person:
* Lord 1 and Lord 7 show that person as thinking being, as personality, as 'head'
* the Moon shows the querent, but specifically the querent's emotions: the heart
* the Sun and Venus, *if in use as natural significator of man or woman,* show the animal. This has much to do with sexual attraction, and you will rarely go far wrong by using this to give a simple division of the person into head, heart and lust. There is, though, more to it than that. It shows the biological imperative to unite with someone of the opposite sex. Forget all about political correctness when considering this: it is pure Tarzan and Jane – 'You good woman. Come back to my cave and bear me strong children'. It is the man in his Man-stuff; the woman in her Woman-stuff. My experience is that the problems behind many questions asked on relationships revolve around a failure to recognise how great a role this side of the nature plays in the formation of attitude.

Receptions show the motives and values of the people involved. In many relationship questions an analysis of this is all that is required: 'Does he really love me?' or 'What is going on in our relationship?' Even in those questions that are oriented towards an event ('Will she marry me?') the receptions are of the utmost importance: the other person will not marry (or date, or continue a relationship) without a motive for doing so. This motive does not need to be love. Example: the querent's significators are not in any dignity of the quesited's, but they do exalt Lord 8. 'You don't love this guy; you're after his money (8th house is 2nd from 7th: the partner's money). Unfortunately, (Lord 8 in its detriment) he hasn't got any.'

As that example suggests, in these questions we are often clarifying the querent's own feelings as much as analysing the other person's. Suppose the question is 'Does my relationship with X have a future?' and the querent's significators show little interest in X's significators, but are all disposited by the ruler of the Part of Marriage: 'You don't have any real feelings for this guy; you just want a relationship and he happened along'. This is not the full answer to such a question, but it will have a great bearing on it. Often the answer to 'Is there a future with him?' is not Yes or No, but 'Are you quite sure you want a future with him?'

That we are given different significators to show different parts of the person's being is important. It is a rare chart in which the querent's significators all agree with each other. People probably don't ask horary questions if they are completely unified in their view of the other person, but only when they feel an uncomfortable ambivalence.

Example: the querent is a man and:

Lord Asc (querent as head) is in the fall of Lord 7;
the Moon (querent's heart) is in Leo
the Sun (querent as Man) is in the exaltation of Lord 7.

'You are very attracted to her (Sun exalts Lord 7); this extreme (exaltation) attraction is dominating your feelings and no doubt making you think that you love her (Moon is ruled by the Sun, which is querent as Man, but has itself no interest in lord 7); but you can't stand her personality (Lord Asc in fall of Lord 7).'

Miscellaneous notes

Reception by exaltation is very powerful, but is not built to last. Remember that exaltation, like all receptions, doesn't tell us anything about the other person's feelings: we must look at the receptions of the other person's significators to find out about that. It is not uncommon for 'Is there a future in our relationship?' to show one of the querent's significators nearing the end of the sign in which it exalts Lord 7. If other testimonies agree, this shows 'No, your relationship is coming to an end – because soon you will not want it to continue'. As the querent is still in the thrall of this exaltation, such a judgement is invariably met with disbelief.

A woman's significator is combust in a chart where the Sun signifies the man as Man: she is overwhelmed by his masculine attraction. This can happen even if receptions are negative. Combustion too doesn't last.

A female querent's significators are weak, show little interest in the man she's asking about, and are ruled by Venus, Venus signifying her as Woman. She feels that she as Woman is in need of some attention. Similarly with a man whose significators are weak and in major Sun dignities.

Don't be unrealistic in what you expect to find! People do manage to have satisfactory relationships without all their significators being strong and in powerful mutual reception.

Lord 1 in the sign on the 7th cusp will automatically be in its detriment. This shows that querent loves the person asked about, and, because of that love, is vulnerable. In this case the detriment can be disregarded. If Lord 1 is in the other sign ruled by Lord 7, it will still be in its detriment and, again, the reception shows that the querent loves that person. But this shows a quite different dynamic: the querent is miserable, and therefore loves that person ('Oh wonderful person, who will stop me being unhappy'). With the obvious implication that if the querent stops being miserable, the love too will stop. The same distinction is true of Lord 7 in the sign on the Ascendant or in the other sign ruled by Lord 1.

Conjunction: in a question about relationships, if one of the main significators is conjunct a planet that is not one of the main significators, it is a certain sign that the person signified is with someone else. Remember that Lilly and his contemporaries used 'copulation' as a synonym for conjunction – which it is: that is what conjunction means. A woman asked 'When will I meet a man?' and the chart showed her main significator conjunct two other planets. 'What do you mean? You're with two men now.' 'Yes. But they don't count.'

Mars: if receptions show Mars as important in the situation, but it is not significator of either person or dispositor of the Part of Marriage, it may well be acting as natural ruler of either lust or divorce. Or, as with any unassigned planet, it may signify 'some other person'.

Do not introduce extra characters without good evidence for doing so. You are not writing soap opera!

When will I?

Identify the significators, then look for an aspect between any of the querent's and any of the quesited's, timing it in the usual way. Application to the 7th cusp will *not* do. Nor will application to the Part of Marriage or its dispositor. Consider the receptions: without some suitable reception the aspect will not produce the event.

If the question is 'When will I marry?' the timing shown is for the decision: the timing of the event itself – when the church is booked and when the caterers are available – is up to the people involved. I know of no way to distinguish between marriage and commitment without marriage, although if the relationship already exists an applying aspect can be taken to show its formalisation in marriage.

The chart will usually show the next significant relationship rather than the 'soul mate' that is sometimes requested.

"What if there is no aspect?" Querents commonly ignore the preliminary question of 'Will I?' and jump straight to 'When?' If the chart shows an aspect, we can do the same; if it does not, we may need to investigate if there will ever be such a relationship: see below. Usually, however, in such cases the querent's significators are weak and there is more reception between the querent's own significators than there is between them and the significators of the prospective mate. You will usually find that the querent's significators are heading towards places where they are less weak. Often the next sign they enter will be their own. In such cases we don't need to address the 'Will I ever?' but can suggest that the querent is unhappy at the moment, and is too busy licking past wounds to be ready for a relationship, but after whatever length of time (timing the gain of strength as usual) will be once again – so let's take another look at the situation then. Such charts often show the break-up of a recent relationship by separating aspects, especially oppositions.

If a description of the quesited is required, take it from Lord 7, not from any cosignificator. Qualify the indications of Lord 7 by its dispositor, other major dignities and tight aspects to it. Judge the quesited's wealth from the 8th house (2nd from the 7th) and job from the 4th (10th from the 7th).

To decide where they will meet, we need to decide who is going to whom. This is *not* shown by which significator applies to which. Whose significators have more accidental strength? It will be that person who goes to where the other one is. BUT: although being in an angular house gives accidental strength, if the quesited's significator is close to the 7th cusp *and* in the same sign as that cusp, this is powerful testimony that this person is not coming out to play, no matter what aspects there might be. Similarly, if the querent's planets are in the 1st house the querent will not stir much to make things happen. It might seem odd that the querent has asked this question with such an attitude, but it is by no means rare. Other testimonies usually show that the querent feels she ought to be in a relationship, even though she does not really want one – or doesn't want one that involves another person.

Having decided which person is going to which – person A is going to person B – take the house occupied by person B's aspected significator to show where the meeting happens. This will usually be the 10th (at work), 11th (through friends) or 9th house. The 9th covers most of the other usual meeting-places: evening-class, church, holidays. For a querent from a culture where an arranged or introduced match is anticipated, it will show the marriage bureau. This fills the role once taken by the local wise man (9th) in arranging a match, and so is itself shown by the 9th house.

Will I ever?

This is one of the questions with which we must be aware of the default option. If the querent is 20, we must judge Yes unless the chart shouts No; if the querent is 80, we must judge No unless the chart shouts Yes.

Testimonies for marriage:

* Lord 1, Moon or Venus/Sun (depending on querent's sex) in a fertile sign
* Lord 1 in the 7th, or Lord 7 in the 1st
* Moon beholding Sun or Venus (regardless of querent's sex). See page 98 for a definition of 'beholding'.

If the querent is 80, I would be reluctant to judge Yes without a direct aspect between main significators.

Major negative testimonies would be:

* debilitated Saturn on the 7th cusp – unless Saturn is Lord 1
* debilitated Saturn on Ascendant – unless Saturn is Lord 7
* Lord 7 combust and applying to the Sun – unless the querent is male or the Sun is Lord 1.

If the question is, 'Will I ever, and when?' and these testimonies and the default option are enough to allow a Yes, you can be very flexible with the usual rules when finding the timing. Once you know that the event will happen, you know that the timing must be in the chart somewhere – and sometimes this timing is not so obvious. With the usual limitations of not taking a planet through either its station or conjunction with the Sun, you can ignore the other prohibitions, which can instead be read as events along the way. Prohibiting aspects will not prohibit and you can take a planet into its next sign. But do use your common sense: if you have to take the significator forward by three signs to find an aspect, you have probably missed another option.

Regardless of what signifies whom, an applying Sun/Moon conjunction is an excellent indicator of marriage.

Will it last?

If the question is about a marriage, or about the starting of a relationship, the nature of the aspect showing the event does *not* tell us anything about how the marriage will proceed. Whether the aspect is, for example, a sextile or a square shows how easily the couple gets to the altar; it shows nothing about what happens afterwards. A square aspect could bring the happiest of marriages, but it will show that there are some snags on the way to the wedding. Maybe he has to ask her more than once. Maybe the wedding has to wait until her mother can attend. The only aspect that affects what happens afterwards is the opposition. This brings the two parties together with regret, which, in our society, usually results in divorce.

To judge 'Will we be happy?' look at the receptions between the two people's significators. Don't expect too much, and don't be put off by some major negatives amid positives: we are dealing with real life, not fairy tale. Do be wary of strong receptions which a change of sign is about to end. Look also at the Part of Marriage and, especially, its dispositor. Consider its essential strength (showing happiness) and the nature of the sign it is in. Fixed shows permanence, cardinal a quick flame that burns and dies, mutable a coming and going. But read this, as always, in the light of other testimonies.

You will often be asked 'Is there a future in this relationship?' when the couple has barely met. Some charts show a clear No; the occasional one shows a strong long-term bond; most show sufficient to keep the relationship alive for a while, but not beyond that. Unless a decision must be made on whether to commit in some way – perhaps by taking a joint mortgage – or if the other person is a serial killer, the purpose of asking such a question quite escapes me. If the querent were to drop every man when the astrologer says No, she would never acquire the emotional education needed to embark on that relationship for which the astrologer might say Yes.

You will also often be asked the same question at moments of crisis in an established relationship. It is always wise to enquire if there is anyone else involved when the question is first asked; if you do so when delivering your judgement later the querent may assume that you have seen this in the chart, when in fact you are only seeking to clarify a planet's role that you're not sure about. Judgement on such questions will be largely by receptions, and as such can identify stresses and potentials – which is surely more useful than making a flat prediction. Even if there is little positive reception between the spouses, remember that the status quo will continue unless someone decides to end it. Even if they loathe each other, is anyone going to act? Look for oppositions and for planets changing house or sign. Such changes may be positive, especially if they involve an increase in reception, or they may show nothing of significance; but, for instance, Lord 7 leaving the 1st house can show 'Your wife's about to leave you', or Lord 1 leaving a sign ruled by the dispositor of the Part of Marriage can show 'It looks as if you are on the point of walking out'.

Such charts will often suggest possibilities for improving the relationship, or spotlight behaviours that exacerbate the situation, so the judgement is often 'If you carry on doing xyz, he'll leave' or 'Unless you do abc she'll divorce you'. Examples: suppose with a male querent Lord 1 is keen on Lord 7, but the Sun hates her, and Lord 7 and Venus show major interest in the Sun: 'Unless you show her some physical attention...' Or if the Moon loves Lord 7, but is in a mute sign, 'Unless you tell her you love her...'

Be wary of announcing affairs on any evidence other than that of conjunction. And even then, be wary of announcing affairs: you may be able to see it; this does not necessarily mean that the querent needs to hear it. Mutual reception, no matter how strong, may show a high mutual regard between two people, but is not in itself evidence of infidelity. Although if the receptions show all the spouse's attention directed towards someone else, the situation is hardly satisfactory. But be careful: are you sure that it is someone else? Perhaps there is powerful mutual reception between Lord 7 and another planet – but maybe that planet rules the turned 10th, showing hubby wrapped up in his work. If you have a conjunction, there need not be any reception at all between the two planets: the people may be happily conjuncting without their emotions being involved. Do not underestimate the power of flattery: if the suspect planet is in the sign or exaltation of Lord 7, Lord 7 may have his head turned without reciprocating the feelings. Especially if the suspect planet is just inside the 7th house. Similarly if a woman is asking and an unidentified planet is combust (Sun being husband as animal man): he has someone throwing herself at him. But without close conjunction, there is no firm evidence that he is responding. The more essential dignity the suspected spouse's planets have (showing him/her honourable) and the more reception they have with the querent's planets (showing love for the querent), the less likely he/she will be to stray.

Querents sometimes ask if the partner is homosexual. If the suspicion is of an affair with some particular person, treat this exactly as affair questions above. More often, it is a general enquiry. If the partner is male, look for his significators in strong Sun dignities, or in the detriment or fall of Venus, showing a liking for men or a hatred of women. Yes, if the Sun is in strong Sun dignities it could show that he is full of the usual sexual feelings, but the question is presumably not asked if the querent is receiving these. Remember that the question asked determines the reality of the chart. The Sun in the turned 12th house (the radical 6th) gives cause for suspicion: he seems to be hiding something about his sexuality, though this may not be that he is homosexual. The Sun in the radical 12th could show that he is up to something he would prefer the querent not to know about, but this too may be unconnected to homosexuality. If the querent is a man asking about his female partner, look for her significators in strong Venus dignities or in the detriment or fall of the Sun, or Venus in the turned 12th. Important: do not import these testimonies into questions where this is not the issue addressed! If you find, for instance, the Sun in Scorpio in the chart for any other relationship question, this does not mean that the man is homosexual.

Will he take me back?

We have here an aberration. If a woman has been thrown out of her husband's home and asks if he will forgive her, Lilly gives the woman the 7th house, even though she is the querent.[41] At first I thought this was a historical oddity, but from the tiny number of charts I have judged on this matter, at least one seems to make better sense judged like this. I can see no sound reason for departing from

---

[41] *Lilly*, p. 318.

usual practice here, and so suggest that you approach such questions in the usual way, but you should be aware of this point. If there is clear evidence in the chart encouraging you to take Lord 7 as the querent (perhaps the querent admits to having had an affair, and Lord 7 is separating from conjunction with a planet that is not Lord 1), you may, with all due caution, decide to follow Lilly.

Writing in the Seventeenth century, he would have regarded the idea of a woman throwing her husband out of the house as ludicrous, and so gave no instructions for that.

Example charts on relationship questions
See the charts on pages 78 and 106.

SHOULD I STAY OR SHOULD I GO?

'Am I better off in London, or should I move away?' 'Maybe I should go home?' 'Should I move to France?' 'Should I stay at work, or go back to college?' Although these questions are usually phrased as 'Should I do X or Y?' they are rarely such an even choice, i.e. which of two roads to take. The question is usually 'Should I make this change or should I leave things as they are?' What the chart shows us is the view forward, as if the querent were standing at the top of a hill, looking at the road stretching into the distance, and thinking either 'Oo-er, I don't like the look of that', or 'Wow, that looks inviting!'

As such, the 1st house and Lord 1 show things as they are; the 7th house and Lord 7 show things as they will become if the change is made. So:

* 7th house better than 1st: go. If not, stay.
* Lord 7 stronger than Lord 1: go. If not, stay.
* Moon or Lord 1 separating (by any aspect) from a benefic and going to a malefic: stay.
* Moon or Lord 1 separating from a malefic and going to a benefic: go.

NB: when considering the planet to and from which the Moon and Lord 1 are moving, do remember that ANY planet in strong essential dignity is good, and ANY planet in essential debility is bad.
Examples:

* Planet in detriment in 7th house, Lord 1 in its exaltation: stay put.

* Dignified planet in 1st house, Moon separates from dignified planet and applies to one that is peregrine: stay put.
* South Node in 1st house, North Node in 7th: go.

"But what if there is conflicting testimony?" There often will be: few such situations are clear-cut. Weigh the number and strength of the various testimonies. In many such charts staying and going are equally good, equally bad: if that is what the chart shows, that is the judgement. Don't feel that you must produce an unequivocal answer. The answer is often, 'It doesn't make much difference'.

Such questions are about change, so the prospective change is often shown in the chart by an imminent change of sign. Lord 1 and/or the Moon will be at the end of a sign, about to enter a new one. Do we let them make this change, or do we keep things as they are? Perhaps they both gain in dignity as they make the change: go! Or perhaps they conjunct debilitated Saturn or enter combustion as soon as they change sign: stay! Or perhaps the change makes no significant difference: stay or go as you please. In such cases the chart is saying 'This is your prospective future. Do you want to accept this, by moving your planets forward into it, or do you want to stay as you are?'

If the question gives a specific place for 'there', you can pick up the querent's planets and drop them into that house. So if the querent asks, 'Should I get a job or go to university?' imagine that you can pick up Lord 1 and place it just inside the 10th cusp. How is it there, by essential and accidental dignity? Then imagine it just inside the 9th cusp. How is it there? This will give a comparison of work and university. If the querent is especially concerned about emotional happiness, do this with the Moon as well as or instead of Lord 1. NB: if you are 'sending the querent to work' like this, you cannot, of course, think 'Lord 1 is in the 10th, therefore it is strong', because this would always be the case, whatever the work. You can think, 'If I put Lord 1 in the 10th it is conjunct the South Node and in its detriment. Yuk!'

You CANNOT do this with the general 'Stay or go?' 1st versus 7th house question, because putting Lord 1 just inside the 7th cusp will automatically put it in its detriment.

Be aware of changes. Suppose the question is 'How will I get on at college?' and putting Lord 1 just inside the 9th cusp puts it into its detriment. But the 9th cusp is at 27 degrees of its sign, and putting Lord 1 into that next sign gives it strong essential dignity, or brings it conjunct a strongly dignified Jupiter: 'You'll get off to a slow start, but once you've found your feet you'll do wonderfully'.

You can do this if the querent is an immigrant and is asking, 'Should I go back to X?' The 1st house will show where he is now, the 4th will show 'home' (even if this is an ancestral homeland where the querent has never set foot) and the 9th will show a foreign country. You need to ask the querent, 'Which do you call home: the country where you live now or the land of your roots?' This will tell you if the proposed destination is 4th house (my homeland) or 9th (a foreign country).

In general 'stay or go' questions, be careful with Lord 4: sometimes it shows the present house, sometimes the potential one. It is best to leave it out of judgement unless you can see which. For instance, if Lord 1 is applying to Lord 4, Lord 4 must be the potential house.

SPORTS AND CONTESTS

Will we win?

Whether this question is asked by a supporter or by someone who is taking part in the match, it is Us against Them. The team the querent supports is given the 1st house, as an extension of the self, in the same way that the querent would say 'We won', despite not himself playing. The unspeakable ruffians his team is competing against are the open enemies: 7th house.

Be careful: if the querent's main concern is with betting on the match, treat this as a question of profit (chapter 16).

For us to be able to judge this question, the querent must have some interest in the outcome of the match for its own sake. His support for the good guys may be only lukewarm, but he must have some preference for one of the teams over the other. If his own team is not playing, it is possible that he might have a hearty dislike of one of the teams involved – perhaps it is his favourite's local rival. In that case the question is really, 'Will my enemy be defeated?' so the enemy is given the 7th house and its opponents – the enemy's enemy – the 1st. If the querent is indifferent to both teams, we have no criterion for deciding which gets the 1st house and which the 7th, so we cannot judge the chart. Do not be tempted to give the 1st house to the home team, or to the team the querent names first: whatever that might be, it is not horary. Nor can we give it the 7th, as 'any old person', because the querent's indifference makes both teams 'any old person'.

This method can be used for questions on individual sports, provided the querent supports or dislikes one or other of the players. It is still Us against Them, as in 'Will the heroic Brit win this tennis-match?' The answer to which is 'No'.

Although we are regarding the team favoured as an extension of the querent, the Moon does not have its usual role as the querent's cosignificator. At least, it does only in moments of dire emergency when nothing else is happening in the chart. Its role in these questions is usually a minor one, occasionally having a function as 'the flow of events'.

Neither should you concern yourself with houses other than the 1st and the 7th. Too many sports horaries disappear in a fog of confusion as the astrologer seeks to locate the team's fans, its players and its bank balance in the chart. Keep It Simple! All that concerns us is who will win. This will be shown by the first and seventh houses. While the manager of every losing team may blame defeat on the referee, the horary chart is far more sporting and has no role for Lord 10.

Lilly tells us to take the planet from which the Moon has most recently separated as another significator for the querent in a contest horary, and that to which it next applies as another significator for the enemy. Don't! These extra significators do nothing but clutter the picture.

Begin by assessing the condition of the houses themselves. What, if anything, is in them? If there is something there, does it strengthen the house or afflict it? Remember that the closer a planet is to the house cusp, the greater its effect on that house. The effect of a planet that is in the house, but in a different sign to the house cusp, will be much diminished. This is so no matter how close the planet might be to the cusp (e.g. cusp at 29 Aries; planet at 0 Taurus: effect still much reduced). Example: suppose the Ascendant is at 15 Pisces, with Saturn in the 1st at 2 Aries. The presence of this debilitated Saturn (in its fall) is a serious affliction to the good guys. Jupiter is at 17 Pisces, so the presence of this strongly dignified Jupiter is highly beneficial to the good guys. Jupiter being much closer to the Ascendant and, most importantly, being in the same sign as the Ascendant, the benefic influence of Jupiter is much stronger than the malign influence of Saturn.

The houses that concern us oppose each other, so ignore planets casting aspects to them. If a planet aspects one house, it will also aspect the house opposite with an aspect of similar quality.

The Moon's Nodes can be treated very simply in these charts: North good,

South bad. They come as a pair, so if one is in the good guys' house, the other will be in the bad guys'. This means that we must consider only one of them – it doesn't matter which. If the North Node is in the 1st, we can judge that house to be strengthened, or we can judge the 7th house to be weakened by the presence of the South Node. Don't count these as two separate testimonies. In all astrological judgement we must be wary of anything that follows automatically.

Now consider Lords 1 and 7. Which is the stronger? The major accidental dignities are much more important than essential dignity in these questions. Essential dignity might tell us who deserves to win; accidental dignity will tell us who does win. But if all other testimonies are more or less equal, a strong discrepancy in essential dignity can be crucial. The exception to this general downplaying of essential dignity is the exaltation. The team whose significator is in its own exaltation will take the field believing it is a team of gods playing mere mortals. Such an attitude makes it more likely to win. In contest horaries, exaltation is stronger than sign rulership.

Receptions between Lords 1 and 7 are important. Not, of course, for showing who likes whom, but for showing who is in whose power. Again, exaltation is stronger than sign-rulership: if Lord 1 is ruled by Lord 7 and Lord 7 is in the exaltation of Lord 1, it is Lord 1 who benefits. The enemy is overawed by our team. Mutual reception with other planets is not strengthening. Mutual reception is like friendship. No matter what good friends the querent or his team might have, they are not going to run onto the pitch to score the winning goal.

House placement and combustion are the most important accidental dignities in these charts. A planet in an angular house has a great advantage over one in a succedent or cadent house. The closer to the cusp, the greater the advantage. A planet in a house but not in the sign of the cusp is strengthened, but much less. A significator in its own house is especially strengthened; a significator in its opponent's house is usually a conclusive sign of defeat: it is in the hands of the enemy. A significator on the cusp of, rather than inside, the enemy's house, however, is in an exceptionally powerful position. Planet in a house is controlled by that house; planet on a house controls that house.

Combustion being the most grievous of all afflictions, a significator combust shows that team will lose. It would be a rare combination of horrors that could outweigh that.

Close aspect with a benefic will help that planet; close aspect with a malefic will harm it, remembering, as always, that any essentially strong planet will be helpful, any essentially debilitated planet malign. Five degrees of separation is the absolute maximum with which we need concern ourselves; the closer the stronger.

In a chart cast to find the outcome of a match, disregard sign changes. A significator might be about to enter its own sign, bringing a massive increase in essential strength, but however close to that change it might be, this will not be relevant to the result of a single game. If the question were on a longer-term issue, such as 'Will my team do better than team X this season?' such a change would be most relevant: 'You'll start off badly, but will soon hit your stride'.

As the Moon shows the flow of events, its application to one or other of the significators will be a minor testimony in favour of that team. It can swing an even balance, but will not outweigh any strong indications.

I have found little use for the Arabian Parts in these charts. Even Fortuna and the Part of Victory disdain to get involved.

If we want reliable judgements, we must be thorough, but there is no virtue in splitting hairs. In most charts, the balance of power will be clear-cut. If arguments for each team are equally persuasive, we are unlikely to choose the victor by microscopic analysis of testimony. In some sports, this even balance will be a judgement in itself: the match will be drawn. In games that must produce a winner, check that you haven't missed something – antiscia, for instance. Then follow William Lilly's advice, 'When the testimonies of Fortunes and Infortunes are equal, defer judgement, it's not possible to know which way the balance will turn'.[42] Regard for the limitations of knowledge, whether individual or collective, is no failure.

The exception to the 1st house versus 7th house rule is in contests where kingship is significant, such as boxing title fights. Here the question is 'Will the king retain his crown?' This approach must not be taken in other sports: that team A happened to win the championship last season does not make any difference to today's match, for at the beginning of each new season all teams begin as equals. In a boxing title fight, the sole reason for the contest is that the challenger has the opportunity to depose the champion.

Give the champion the 10th house, the challenger the 4th (7th from the 10th). If they do not rule either of these houses, the Sun can also stand for the champion, as natural ruler of kings, and the Moon – natural ruler of the common people – for the challenger. Judgement is much as above, with three variations:

---

[42] *Lilly*, p. 123.

* The Arabian Part of Resignation and Dismissal (Saturn + Jupiter – Sun) is worth noting.
* Changes of dignity can show the outcome on their own. If the significator of the champion is about to enter the sign of its fall, or that of the challenger its exaltation, we have a clear testimony of victory for one or the other.
* A void of course Moon, which can be ignored in most contest charts, because we know that something will happen – there will be a match, which will have some outcome – is a strong testimony that the status quo will be preserved. Nothing will happen, so the champion will retain his crown.

The long-term forecast

'How will my team do this season?', 'Will my team win the championship?', 'Will it be relegated?'

In distinction to the one-against-one contest horaries above, this can be asked about a team or individual player to which the querent is indifferent: 'How will team X do this season?' 'Will Venus Williams win this tournament?' This is possible because the enquiry concerns only one team, so we do not encounter the problem of deciding which team should be assigned to which house. If the querent is indifferent to it, the team or player named is 'any old person' and so is given the 7th.

Judgement is usually simple, as long as we shun the temptation to force the spectacular answer. Ego tells us it is a far better thing to predict the unlikely. It is not: it is a far better thing to predict what will happen. Most of the time, the unlikely does not happen. 'How will my team do this season?' – in most cases the answer to this will be 'Indifferently'. Few teams win things; few are relegated. While 'Will my team win the championship?' 'No', is not the most satisfying of client/consultant exchanges, if that is what will happen, that is what will happen.

The querent's team will be signified by the ruler of the 1st. Do not take the Moon as cosignificator. Look for significant changes in essential dignity and connections to appropriate houses. In practice, anything that will merit an answer other than 'Indifferently' is usually fairly obvious. A planet entering its own term, for instance, is nothing to get excited about. A planet entering the sign of its exaltation is.

Examples: 'How will my team do?' Significator enters its own sign or exaltation: it will win promotion. Significator enters its fall: it will – literally enough –

go down. Significator conjuncts 10th cusp or Lord 10: it will win the championship. It enters the 12th or 8th house, or conjuncts one of their rulers: the team will be relegated. 'Will we win the championship?' with querent's planet applying to conjunct Lord 10: Yes. If this conjunction happens in the next sign: 'Not this season, but you will next'.

A querent asked if her team would win anything that season; the chart showed a conjunction with Lord 10, but not until the next sign. That conjunction was in a double-bodied sign: her team won both major competitions the next season.

The 8th, the house of death, can show the extinction of the club; but we must be cautious. It is more likely that its meaning will be found within the assumptions of the question, which will usually relate only to on-field matters. Even in a context where the club's survival could not be taken for granted, there would need to be serious 2nd-house (financial) problems apparent in the chart before we predicted so dire a fate.

Combustion and cazimi are important. 'Will Venus Williams win Wimbledon?' Her planet combust: no chance. Her planet cazimi: no one else has a chance. Contacts with planets other than the Sun or the rulers of the relevant houses are usually insignificant. No matter how fortunate that trine from a benefic might be, it will not bring the championship; no matter how hard that Saturn opposition, it will not bring relegation. Such testimonies can add precision to a judgement. Suppose the significator is very weak, but favoured by a trine from strong Jupiter: 'Your team will struggle all season, but will not go down'. But this is just decoration.

Answering the general enquiry, 'Who will win the league?' would be easy – if the teams in that league were called Jupiter, Mars and Venus. I have not found any method of linking planets to a full field of teams. At least, no method that works. But if the chart shows a void of course Moon, this question can still be answered. Void of course Moon: nothing changes. The team that won last year will win again.

TRIALS

I deal here with civil trials, which are the subject of questions more often than criminal cases. Criminal trials are discussed in chapter 25.

The difference between a trial and a contest is that the outcome of a contest is decided by clear external criteria: you score more points, you get me in checkmate, you force my arm down onto the table. In a trial the decision is given by a judge, based on what he thinks best. Yes, in our society the decision is usually made by a jury, but I find it simpler to follow Lilly in referring to the decision-maker as 'the judge'. This clarifies the thought process when we approach the chart: 'Good judge? Bad judge?' Keep it simple! But remember that when we refer to 'the judge' we mean 'the legal process'. It is not necessary to distinguish between judge and jury: we are concerned with the outcome, not with giving a running commentary on the events of the trial.

There are four key players in a trial chart: the querent (Lord 1); the enemy (Lord 7); the judge, or the 'the legal process' if you wish to be long-winded (Lord 10); the verdict, which, as 'the end of the matter', is Lord 4. The Moon is, as usual, cosignificator of the querent, although with three other houses in play she will often be the ruler of one of those instead. The 2nd house of the querent and that of the enemy show their money and/or their lawyers and witnesses. If the lawyer is asking the question, treat it as Us against Them, giving the 1st house to both the lawyer and the lawyer's client, and the 7th to both the enemy and the enemy's lawyer. Even if the lawyer is the querent, priority will always be with the person directly involved in the action: it is as if the lawyer were asking as that person's mouthpiece.

First consider the condition of Lords 1 and 7. Essential dignity tends to show the justice of the case, and has lamentably little to do with the matter of who wins. Reception can be important, though, especially if aspects show the possibility of settling out of court. Suppose Lord 7 is in the exaltation of Lord 1: great news! Our querent is in a fine position to push for a settlement. Suppose Lord 1 exalts Lord 7, but further examination shows that our querent will win in court: we must caution him to resist his feelings that he cannot win, refuse any proffered settlement and let justice take its course.

Accidental dignity says more about who will win or lose than essential dignity. The accidentally stronger protagonist will win – *if* contact with the judge or the verdict does not determine otherwise. Contacts with the judge or verdict usually do determine otherwise.

Consider the condition of Lord 10. Lots of essential dignity: good judge. In detriment or fall: bad judge. But remember that the judge could sleep through the whole trial and decide the verdict by tossing a coin, yet still arrive at a just outcome. PLEASE do not say 'Lord 10 is accidentally strong, so the judge has a major say in the outcome'. Of course he does: he's the judge.

Consider the receptions between the judge and Lords 1 and 7. Does the judge

like one party and dislike the other? This can be crucial, especially with an applying aspect between the judge and either the liked or the disliked party. Such a
contact will override any balance of strength between Lords 1 and 7, giving the
verdict to whichever the judge prefers. Again, do not say 'Lord 7 is ruled by Lord
10: the judge has power over him'. Of course the judge has power over him: he is
in court.

Lord 10, then, is of great importance. But even more important than Lord 10
is Lord 4: the verdict. In life both parties get the verdict: one likes it; one doesn't.
In the horary chart Lord 4 is like a prize: who gets there first wins. So look for an
applying aspect between Lord 1 or Lord 7 and Lord 4.

Are Lords 1 and 7 themselves applying to aspect? If to conjunction, the parties
will reach an agreement before the case comes to court. To any other aspect, they
will agree after the case opens, but before the verdict is handed down. This is an
occasion for the astrologer to offer useful advice: should the querent accept a
settlement, or is he better to fight it out? Should he take a paltry settlement,
because if he doesn't he will lose everything? Remember the qualities of the signs:
if the enemy is in a fixed sign, he will not budge; if cardinal, he will soon give up;
if mutable, he will be flexible.

Will we win?

This question was asked by the lawyer, so Lord 1 shows Us and Lord 7 Them.

How are the good guys? Lord 1 is in its own term, suggesting that she has a
certain amount of right on her side; but is in the 9th, so not so strong. "But the
9th is the house of law." No: the 9th house covers law only as an abstract subject
– higher learning. It has nothing whatever to do with law in action, as in a court
case.

How are the bad guys? Lord 7 is in its fall: boo!! I find it helpful to think in
such pantomime terms, as it keeps the main lines of the argument so clear. He's
in his fall: yes, he really is a baddie. But he is also in his triplicity and term. And
he is powerfully placed on the MC. This accords with what the querent said
about him: that he was a well known villain who was adept at twisting the law in
his favour. If there were no other significant testimony, this placement would be
enough to give him the victory.

How is the judge? Lord 10 is in its detriment: bad judge. There is a powerful
mutual reception between Lords 7 and 10. Lord 7 is ruled by the Moon, the judge.
Big deal: we know that, as he is in court. But the judge exalts him: this is not good.

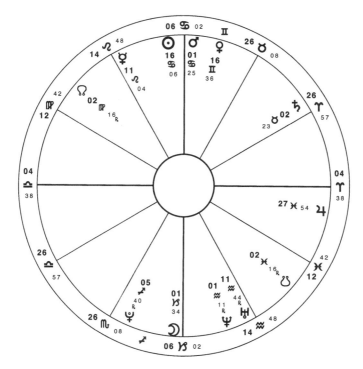

Will we win? July 8th 1998, 12.22 pm BST, London.

Lord 10 separates from its aspect to Lord 7. This is a puzzle. What are we to make of this? Yes, it could show past contact between baddie and judge. Lilly gives a long list of testimonies that show the judge has been bribed:[43] follow this list and you will find it so comprehensive that you will never see a legitimate court case. I strongly suggest that you disregard such possibilities unless the querent raises them in the question, in which case such past contact, especially with so heavy a mutual reception and Lord 10 so debilitated, would be evidence.

This separating contact with such mutual reception could show that the judge's mind is already made up. Perhaps the case has already opened, the verdict has been decided and all that awaits now is an announcement of the decision. But that was not the situation here: the trial had not yet started. So what does this separating aspect mean?

Look at what Lord 10 is doing.

---

[43] *Lilly*, pp. 374-5.

It separates from aspect to Lord 7 and applies to aspect with Saturn. What is Saturn? Lord 4: the verdict.

This is a translation of light. The Moon picks up Lord 7 and carries its light to Lord 4, effectively connecting Lord 7 with Lord 4, so taking the bad guy to the verdict. Because the verdict is seen as a prize, the first one there gets it: this means that the bad guy wins. The translation shows this perfectly: the (bad) judge carries the (evil) enemy to the verdict.

He wins. But let's look further. There is a weak malefic afflicting the 8th house (enemy's money) by its presence. What is this weak malefic? It is Lord 4: the verdict. Even though he wins, the verdict harms his pocket. Look at the reception between verdict and baddie. Mars is in the detriment of Saturn: the baddie hates the verdict. Saturn is in the detriment of Mars: the verdict hates or harms the baddie.

How come? Look at Lord 10. The judge exalts the bad guy. But, in this case, he can do that only by being in his detriment (Moon, which is Lord 10, can exalt Mars, which is Lord 7, only by being in Capricorn, which is its detriment). The judge can exalt this bad guy only by being a bad judge. Lord 10 is also in the triplicity and term of Venus, Lord 1. The judge likes our querent; but this liking is weaker than the exaggerated infatuation that is exaltation. We have seen that the enemy really is a baddie, but has points of law on his side.

So what do we have? The judge (= the court system) has to rule in favour of the enemy on point of law. But (Lord 10 in significant dignities of Lord 1) he can still see the virtues of our querent's case. So although the law demands that judgement is given in favour of the baddie, the verdict (Lord 4 afflicts baddie's 2nd) is framed in such a way that it still harms his pocket.

POLITICS

I deal here with elections, but these principles will enable you to judge any other common political question.

In a horary about an election, which candidate is given which house depends on who is asking the question. As I write this, George Bush has recently been re-elected, defeating John Kerry. Consider the various questions that might have been asked before the election:

* Bush asks 'Will I win?' He is 1st; his opponent 7th.

* Mrs Bush asks 'Will George win?' Technically, this should give George the 7th house, because she is asking about her husband. The question could probably be read as 'Will we win?' however, giving Bush the 1st, his opponent the 7th.
* A Republican asks, 'Will we win?' Us against Them: 1st versus 7th.
* John Kerry asks 'Will I win?' Read this as 'Can I beat the king?' giving Kerry the 1st and Bush the 10th. Similarly if a Democrat asks, 'Will we win?'
* If Bush were not already in power and Kerry asked 'Will I win?' there would be no king involved. Kerry would be 1st; Bush 7th.
* A impartial American asks, 'Who will win?' Give Bush the 10th, because he is king, Kerry the 4th, because he is the king's enemy.
* I ask, 'Who will win?' Bush is the king of a foreign country: 10th from the 9th = 6th. His enemy is the 7th from the 6th = 12th.

The exact situation will vary depending on the constitution of the country, but following the basic rules of house meaning will enable you to select the correct houses. Ignore the fact that in most countries the theory is that no one is in power when the election is held: most elections can be seen as the king against someone, whether the 'king' is an individual or a party. In an open election, with various candidates running for a vacant office, 'Will Cedric win?' will give Cedric the 1st house (I think he's wonderful), the 7th house (either I think he's dreadful or I couldn't care less) or the 3rd house (he's my brother).

The Moon is of extreme importance in horaries about elections. It is natural ruler of the people, and so signifies the electorate. If the Moon goes to aspect the significator of one of the candidates, that candidate will win. This is so *despite* its receptions. Even if the Moon is in the fall of Cedric's significator, if it applies to aspect that significator Cedric will win. The Moon's receptions become important if it makes no aspect to either significator: look to see which candidate the Moon favours. The receptions, however, may not be decisive. A void of course Moon is testimony of the status quo being preserved.

If the Moon is not making the electorate's feelings clear, consider the condition of the main significators. Essential dignity is not so important: being a bad guy will not stop a candidate being elected. Imminent changes of dignity, however, for better or for worse, can be crucial. Look especially at house placement (significator entering the 10th is positive; significator in the opponent's house is strongly negative), sign placement (the king in the middle of a fixed sign is likely to stay in power; leaving a fixed sign, his reign may be over) and the major accidental qualities, especially combustion. Be more cautious than usual with cazimi: the candidate wants to be the king, so being 'in the bosom of the king' will not be enough; but if other testimonies are lacking cazimi can still prevail.

Be cautious too when a significator is entering its own house, whether this is its mundane house (= house) or its celestial house (= the sign that it rules). While this makes the planet stronger, it can often be taken literally, showing the candidate going home. In many situations this will be testimony of defeat.

If neither candidate is king, leaving the 10th house unengaged, a significator applying to aspect Lord 10 will be strong testimony that that candidate will become king.

If one candidate is king, it is worth casting the Part of Resignation & Dismissal. Contact (mainly conjunction or opposition; other aspects only as minor testimony) with that or its dispositor will help unseat him.

When will she fall?

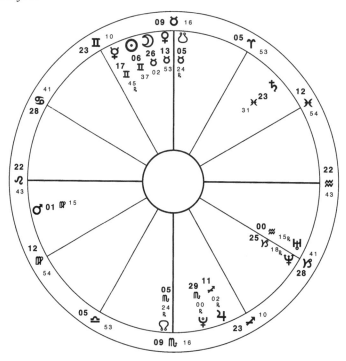

When will she fall? May 28th 1995, 11.06 am BST, London.

The querent, who was well placed to know, expected Benazir Bhutto to lose power at any moment. He asked, 'When will she fall?'

The querent is Pakistani, so she is his 'king': 10th house. Lord 10, Venus, is sitting most comfortably in the middle of its own, fixed sign, just inside the 10th house. Whatever expectations the querent might have, Mrs Bhutto's position is secure.

The Moon losing what little light it has, however, is indication that the situation is coming to an end. Venus must travel 17 degrees to leave its sign. It is fixed and angular, giving long + long for the timing. With the event anticipated within days and the Moon so late in its cycle, confirming that the event would happen, months seemed to be the longest reasonable time-unit. Allowing a few days grace for action to follow astrology, the prediction was for the next November.

The querent assured me that this was impossible, as she could not hold onto power for so long. The event followed as predicted.

22

Nineth House Questions

KNOWLEDGE, JOURNEYS AND DREAMS

Will I profit from my knowledge?

This is the method for those frequent questions on 'Can I earn a living as an astrologer/tarot-reader/psychic?' as well as queries on less arcane forms of knowledge, all usually occasioned by the urgent need to turn a penny. The knowledge itself is shown by the 9th house. Potential profit from it is seen as the knowledge's money: 2nd from the 9th, which is the 10th house.

Although in the abstract the distinction between this and certain 10th-house questions on career might seem blurred, in practice it is always clear enough. Even though the knowledge involved is astrological, my question 'Will I get paid well if I go to work for Astrologers Inc.?' is not a 9th-house matter: that would be 10th for the position and 11th for the wages. There is a distinction between a job (10th house) and the utilisation of my knowledge (9th house).

It is, I suppose, feasible that someone might ask 'Will I profit from my ability to read and write?' in which case the knowledge, being elementary, would be 3rd house and the profit from it 4th.

First, consider the condition of the querent's knowledge. There is no direct connection – as the earnings of so many astrologers so clearly show – between the soundness of the knowledge and the profits that can be made from it. It is nonetheless helpful to see if the querent has any knowledge or not. Look at Lord 9 and the 9th house itself.

The more essential dignity Lord 9 has, the better the knowledge. Generally, accidental strength or weakness will strengthen or weaken the knowledge, but, as ever, we must read the testimonies within the context. For example, finding Lord 9 in an angular house would strengthen the knowledge, in a cadent would weaken it. Yet if the knowledge is connected with large animals, finding Lord 9 in the 12th would be only appropriate and could not be taken as a debility. Or:

being in an angular house would be an indication that the knowledge can be expressed easily, can manifest in the world. Yet if Lord 9 is in the 1st, especially if in a fixed sign, the knowledge could be stuck inside the querent, incapable of expression.

Note other accidental features, such as the nature of the sign Lord 9 is in. A mute sign, for instance, does not bode well for any expression of this knowledge. Maybe Lord 9 has recently increased in dignity by entering a sign which is fixed: there has been a recent improvement in the querent's knowledge, but (fixed signs moving slowly) it won't improve further for a long time. Again, be aware of what the points you are considering might mean in context. Lord 9 retrograde, for example, which would usually be a debility, can be taken as a fitting description of the knowledge, and hence as no debility, if the knowledge involves looking back to the past.

Consider any aspects to Lord 9: do these show help or hindrance? As ever, you must consider the receptions to fully understand the effect of the aspect. Example: Lord 9 is squared by Lord 5. With a positive mutual reception between them, perhaps the querent's children, although their demands apparently hinder the querent's knowledge, in fact further it by what he learns in his interactions with them. With Lord 5 receiving Lord 9 into its detriment, the same square might show the querent's love of alehouses and taverns harming his knowledge.

Planets in the 9th house will help or hinder the knowledge according to their nature: essentially dignified planets will help it; essentially debilitated ones will hinder it. The nearer the cusp, the more powerful the effect.

We do not need to find an aspect between Lord 9 and Lord 1, but if there is an aspect we must consider its nature. Suppose Lord 1 is conjunct Lord 9, which is in its fall: the querent is afflicted by his lack of knowledge.

The profit from the knowledge is judged by considering the 10th house and its ruler, in the same way as we have assessed the state of the querent's knowledge by looking at the 9th and its ruler.

NB: we do not need to find an aspect between Lord 10 and either Lord 1 (querent) or Lord 9 (querent's knowledge) to show the profit coming to the querent. That it is profit from the knowledge assumes that it is coming to the querent: it would not be profit otherwise. But if there is an aspect, we must consider its nature. Examples:

* Lord 10 in its detriment, applying to Lord 1 by trine. There is very little profit, but what there is comes easily.
* Lord 10 in its exaltation, squaring Lord 1. Big profit, but you'll have to struggle for it.
* Lord 10 opposing Lord 1. No matter how much profit there might be, it will not be worth the effort expended to gain it.

Being adjacent houses, the 9th and 10th often have the same planet as ruler. This is not a problem, because we do not need to find an aspect between their rulers. It tells us that the knowledge and its rewards are of the same quality (as long as nothing is happening to the houses themselves to show otherwise).

We must also consider the 8th house. Being 2nd from the 7th it is 'other people's money', the other people in this context being the customers. Restrictions in the amount of money the customers have will limit the potential profits.

Consider this as with the 9th and 10th houses above, with one exception: if Lord 8 is in its own sign it shows that the customers have plenty of money; if it is also in the 8th house, even though they have plenty of money, it is staying in their pockets. This is no good to our querent! If Lord 8 is also in a fixed sign, the money is staying all the more resolutely in their pockets.

Once the 9th, 10th and 8th houses have been judged, take a look at the querent. If the judgement so far has shown difficulties, is the querent capable of taking action to overcome them? If, on the other hand, Lord 1 is badly debilitated, the querent might be unable to stir himself to take advantage of even the most glowing financial prospects.

Examinations

'Will I pass the exam?' is a specific form of profit from knowledge question. The exam is the profit, so is shown by the 10th house. An aspect between querent and exam is helpful, but given enough reception we can manage without. A square will give a pass, unless the receptions are bad; an opposition will fail, unless the receptions are especially good, when it can show a pass at a disappointing grade.

Do remind the querent that however positive your prediction might be, it is still necessary to do some work.

Will I profit from the voyage?

This is judged in the same way as the knowledge questions above: the 9th house shows the voyage and the 10th its profit. So if Saturn squares Lord 9 there are delays to the voyage; if it squares Lord 10, there are restrictions to the profit. Venus trines Lord 9 but opposes Lord 10: the voyage is lots of fun, but doesn't pay for itself.

This also covers questions such as:

* Will this course boost my earning power?
* Is going to this trade-show a good idea?

Dream analysis

If the dream is prophetic and the question is about its veracity, use the method for determining truth or falsehood described in chapter 17. If the question is 'What was that all about?' set the chart as usual for the time this question is asked. Don't try to establish the time of the dream. Find the significators for the characters in the dream from their usual houses: the querent, dreaming the dream, will be the 1st, even if he's dreamed he's Elvis; his farm will be the 4th; his dog the 6th. In essence, treat the dream exactly as if it were an event in daily life. The aspects and receptions between the significators will enable you to tease out the meaning of the dream.

You do not need to pay any special attention to the 9th house when doing this. The whole chart is about the dream, not only the 9th house. The 9th would be used if the dream featured, for instance, a priest or teacher or voyage, or there were a dream within the dream. The situation is the same as in a medical horary: there, the whole chart is about the illness, so the illness is not confined to the 6th house.

Choosing a school

Parents ask about their children's schools. Elementary school is 3rd house; anything above that level is 9th. If there is a distinction between higher and lower levels of education, the lower can always be given to the 3rd, the higher to the 9th ('Will she enjoy university better than high school?'). Even though the child is not usually the querent in these questions, do not turn the chart to locate the school: use the radical 9th or 3rd houses, not the 9th or 3rd from the 5th.

Although we speak of 'my school', the school does not belong to the child.

'How will she do at her new school?' is straightforward: look at the receptions and any applying aspects between Lord 5 (the child) and Lord 9 (the school). In a question like this we do not need to have an aspect, because we are not asking if something will happen; we are enquiring about a state of affairs. But if there is an aspect, we must take notice of it.

Look at the condition of Lord 9 to see how good a school it is. No matter how good the school might be, however, it does not necessarily suit this particular child, hence the importance of the receptions. Lord 9 in the exaltation of Lord 5: the school thinks the child is wonderful and will favour her. Lord 9 in the fall of Lord 5: the school thinks she is dreadful and will harm her.

Mentally pick up the child's significator and drop it just inside the 9th house. How is it there? Consider both essential and accidental testimony. Lord 5 finds itself in its exaltation: she'll do well. In combustion: she'll do badly. Perhaps the sign changes a few degrees into the 9th house. Dropping Lord 5 just inside the house leaves it weak, but in that next sign it will be strong: she'll get off to a shaky start, but will quickly find her feet.

As always, benefics or malefics in the 9th house will affect the quality of that house, with direct reference to the context of the question – which in this case is how the child will fare. Jupiter in Pisces in the 9th is most fortunate. Saturn in Aries is to be avoided. As always, it is the amount of essential dignity a planet has that makes it benefic. Saturn in its own sign or exaltation in the 9th would be strongly fortunate. Not as much fun as Jupiter or Venus in dignity, but fortunate nonetheless.

If the question is about the choice of this school or that school, the querent's favoured option is given the 9th (or 3rd) house. We must then find a significator for the alternative or alternatives. Do make the querent do some of the work: you have every right to demand that they narrow the options to a short-list. If you are presented with half-a-dozen or more alternatives, send the querent away to think about it some more.

There are various theories on how to find significators for the other schools. A popular one suggests taking the 3rd from the 9th. Don't! This is a false extrapolation from the technique of using the 3rd from the 3rd to show my brother's brother (i.e. my younger brother). The alternative school is not the first school's brother.

Holding slightly more water is the idea of taking the 7th from the 9th (the 3rd) to show the rival school. But the alternative schools are not really rivals, in the sense that candidates for a job or contestants in a game are. While if there is more than one alternative, this still leaves the problem of locating the others.

I recommend that you ask the querent to describe the different schools. Stress that this description should be brief: no more than a few words. If the descriptions are kept short, the querent will concentrate on the salient distinguishing features. You can then choose significators by planetary nature. 'That school is very arty; the other is much more old-fashioned': the first is Venus, the second Saturn.

Once you have chosen the significators, compare their strength and consider their receptions with Lord 5. Again, remember that the best school (most dignity) may not be the one best suited to this individual, so weight the receptions when making judgement.

23

Tenth House Questions

JOB QUESTIONS

Will I get the job?

The querent is Lord 1 and the Moon; the job is Lord 10. If there is an applying aspect between them, all things being equal, the querent will get the job. The nature of the aspect must be judged in the usual way: if it is a trine, he gets the job easily; if an opposition, he gets it, but wishes he hadn't, or doesn't keep it for long. As always, look out for collections or translations of light, especially if an intermediary, such as an agent or head-hunter, is involved.

Lilly says that an aspect to the Sun will work instead of one to Lord 10, but this is on the assumption that the querent is seeking a royal appointment.

Finding the querent's significator in the 10th house is only a minor testimony of success. It shows that the querent wants the job (or, if not in the same sign as the 10th cusp, that he wants a job), and the querent who wants it is more likely to get it than the one who does not. But it shows no more than that. If other testimony confirms that the job will be given, application of the querent's significator to the 10th cusp can show the timing.

Finding Lord 10 in the 1st house is much more positive: the job is in the querent's pocket. The closer Lord 10 is to the cusp, the stronger is the testimony. But if Lord 10 is on the cusp rather than inside the house it usually shows nothing more than that the idea of getting a job is weighing on the querent.

Even if there is an aspect, pay attention to the strength of the querent's significator: would you employ Saturn retrograde in its detriment? Chances are, no one else will either. The more strength the querent's planet has, the more sought-after the querent is likely to be. In certain cases, especially if the querent is making a speculative application rather than one for a known vacancy, the job (which can be taken as synonymous with the company: Lord 10) may be too weak to offer employment, even if reception shows that it would like to do so.

If the querent's planets are in dignities of Lord 10, the querent wants the job to whatever extent the dignities suggest: if in the sign of Lord 10, he wants it a lot; if in the face, he has a small interest in it; if in the exaltation of Lord 10, he exaggerates its qualities. Exaltation does not tell us anything about the job itself, but it does show that the querent overrates it, so no matter how good the job might be it is unlikely to live up to expectations.

Of course, people who apply for jobs are not always driven by enthusiasm for the job itself. You will often find the querent's planets showing a strong interest in Lord 2, the querent's bank balance. In such cases, Lord 2 is usually weak: 'I'm broke – I need a job!' Sometimes they will show a strong interest in Lord 11, the 2nd from the 10th: the job's money. Check the condition of Lord 11 to see if the pay will be good. Suppose Lord 11 applies to the querent by trine, is itself strong, and is in the sign of the querent's exaltation: he'll be paid well and without delays, and (exalts him) can expect bonuses. Suppose Lord 11 is in fall and applies to the querent by square: the pay is dreadful, less than expected, and he will have to fight for it. It is also worth checking the relationship between Lord 11 and Lord 2: the querent's bank balance and the wages loving each other (mutual reception) is a positive sign. An aspect between querent and wages is *not* testimony of getting the job.

With all but a few jobs we cannot expect to see Lord 10 in any dignity of our querent. With all but a few jobs, it is a matter of indifference to the job whether it is done by Tom, Dick or Harry. It is only with jobs requiring rare skills or having a high profile, the type of job for which one might be headhunted, that we would expect to see Lord 10 showing a strong interest in the querent. So with most charts on this subject, finding Lord 10 in even the term or face of Lord 1 is a positive testimony: the job likes the querent. We still need an aspect, though. Lord 10 in the detriment or fall of Lord 1 shows a strong dislike, so the querent would be unlikely to get the job. If the querent were particularly strong the job might overlook its dislike in view of his qualifications.

The North Node or a strongly dignified planet in the 10th, especially if close to the cusp, shows fortune in 10th house matters; the South Node or a debilitated planet there shows loss. These do not necessarily relate directly to the Yes or No of 'Will I get the job?' For example, with the South Node in the 10th other testimonies may show that the querent gets the job, but it's a horrible job.

As in any question where change is required, a void of course Moon is a strong negative indicator, suggesting that the issue is going nowhere. As always, it can be overruled by more compelling testimony.

Lord 7 shows the querent's open enemies: the rivals for the position. If Lord 10 aspects Lord 7 before it reaches Lord 1, the other applicant gets the job. If Lord 12 were involved in the action, this could show a secret enemy: the one who writes the anonymous letter that rubbishes the querent's application.

If the querent is asking about someone else – usually a spouse or a child – applying for a job, use the radical 10th for the job. The job is something external to the person, so we take the radical 10th in the same way that 'Will my daughter get into university?' would be shown by the radical 9th. Use the turned 10th to judge a question about that person's career, boss or a job they already have. If the question is about a 10th-house person ('Will Mum get the job?') we have to use the turned 10th for the job.

People at work

In a question directly about the boss ('Will I get along with my new boss?') the boss is shown by the tenth house and Lord 10. Any of my superiors, even the most minor of them, will be 10th house if that person is the subject of the question. If we need to distinguish between different levels of authority over me, we can take the rulers of the various dignities my significator is in. Example: suppose the question is 'To which level of management should I take my complaint?' and my significator is Saturn at 12 Sagittarius in a daytime chart. It is disposited by Jupiter, in the triplicity of the Sun, the term of Venus and the face of the Moon. Jupiter is in Leo, the detriment of Saturn, so I won't get any sympathy from the big boss. The Sun is in Taurus, so the next level of management will be indifferent. The Moon, my face-ruler, is in Cancer, so my immediate superior doesn't like me either. But Venus is in Capricorn: if I go to the next level up, I will receive a sympathetic hearing. If Venus were accidentally strong, so much the better: this superior can do something about my problem.

If we need to identify the boss in a question about the job ('Will I get this job and how will I get along with the boss?'), we cannot give the boss the 10th because that is already being used to show the job. Sometimes we can turn the chart, taking the 10th from the 10th (radical 7th) as 'the boss of the job'. But in many questions the 7th is already busy, signifying either the rivals for the position or the co-workers. In that case, we can use the dispositor of Lord 10, which is literally the ruler of the job.

If the question were 'Will I get along with my new boss?' the prime consideration would be the receptions between the significators. We do not need to find an aspect, because we are analysing a situation, not looking for an event; but if there is an aspect between the significators, we must take notice of what it is. Look also at which planets have influence over the boss by disposition. Example: suppose my significator is Saturn and the boss's is Venus. Venus is in Capricorn: so far, so good – the boss likes me a lot. But in Capricorn it also exalts Mars, and when I look at Mars I find it is in Leo, the sign where Saturn (me) is in detriment. This is not so good: although he likes me, the boss has an inflated regard (exaltation) for someone else (Mars), who hates me (in the sign where my planet is in detriment).

My co-workers are 7th house. They are my equals, people on the same level as me. My colleagues are not 11th house: they are colleagues, not friends. If I happen to befriend one among them, that person would become 11th house, although remaining 7th in the context of most questions I might ask about my job. It is as if we were members of a troupe of actors. That I enjoy the company of this actor when we are off-stage is irrelevant to the roles we play in the drama.

My subordinates, those below me in the pecking-order, are 6th house: my servants.

Will I keep the job?

The first thing to look for here is fixity. The angles, Lord 1 or Lord 10 in a fixed sign is a strong argument for the situation staying as it is, so the querent keeps the job. The Moon void of course says the same.

Lord 1 or Lord 10 about to leave a sign is a strong argument that there will be change, so the job will not be kept. This is so even if the sign it is leaving is fixed. If it also loses dignity or enters debility as it moves, this is an even stronger testimony. I would not put much significance on the Moon, if it is the querent's cosignificator, leaving its sign: this is more likely to show the worry that has precipitated the question.

We do not need an aspect to see either the querent keeping the job or losing it. If there is an aspect, it may well be significant. Look too at any past aspect between Lords 1 and 10: if they came together by opposition, the querent will not stay in the job. This does not tell us that the querent is leaving now, though: we would need to find another indicator to show us when. Example: perhaps Lords 1 and 10 came together by opposition with mutual reception by sign. The opposition says that the job will not last. Lord 1 or Lord 10 changing sign, and hence breaking the mutual reception, would be a likely indicator of the timing.

Receptions between the job and the querent can be significant testimony: if the job likes the querent, it is more likely to keep him on. But this can be overruled by the considerations above. If it is a 'me or him' situation, the other candidate for dismissal will be Lord 7, and no matter how bad the querent's position, if Lord 7 is in a worse it is the querent who will survive. But be alive to the possibility that the company may change its mind, laying off neither or both.

It is worth casting the Part of Resignation & Dismissal, to see if that has anything to contribute. Lord 1 applying immediately to conjunct or oppose it would be strong testimony of losing the job. The Ascendant, 10th cusp or Lords 1 or 10 on Antares, star of cycles ending, suggests the same.

Do not regard what the company has told the querent as truth! The truth is in the chart.

Will I get my job back?

A common testimony here is Lord 1 or Lord 10 either retrograde or moving forward having recently been retrograde. Either way, it is travelling in the opposite direction to its recent direction, so if that recent direction has taken it out of the job, the return will bring it back in. Lord 1 re-entering either the 10th house, the sign on the 10th cusp or the other sign ruled by Lord 10 would be a conclusive testimony of recovery. Note that in 'Will I get the job?' Lord 1 entering the 10th house will not give a Yes; in 'Will I get the job back?' its re-entry will, because in this case there is a concrete context for its having been in the 10th: it was in the job (10th house), left it (moved out) and now is going to be in it again (re-entry).

Lord 10 in the 1st is a strong positive testimony, as is an applying aspect between Lords 1 and 10.

What will the job be like?

'Should I take the job?' and 'Will I get the job?' are not the same question. The first assumes that the job is, at least potentially, gettable. We do not need to look for an aspect, although if there is an aspect between job and querent its nature must be considered. If it is an opposition, for instance, the querent will regret taking the job or will not hold it for long.

Look at Lord 10, considering its strength, both essentially and accidentally. An essentially strong Lord 10 that is accidentally afflicted may show what is in essence a good job being less able to be the nice number that it truly is because of external constraints. The nature of any affliction can often help us identify what the problem is. Perhaps Lord 10 is in 1st station: business is about to decline. Lords 7 and 10 are each in the other's detriment: there is strife between the company and the querent's putative co-workers. Applying opposition between Lord 10 and Lord 5 (which is the 8th from the 10th): the company is about to go bust (meet its death). Consider also the effects of any planets in the 10th house, especially those close to the cusp: the South Node or a malefic are warnings of trouble; a strong Jupiter would promise benefit.

Do not be unrealistic in what you expect to find: it can still be a nice job without the company being a market leader, and 'good enough' is the answer here more often than 'wonderful'. Neither should you expect to find Lord 10 showing any liking for the querent by reception (see above). If it does, this is a bonus.

Pay special attention to the condition of Lord 11, the pay. Try to identify any afflictions to Lord 1 from the list of office-staff above, e.g. opposition from Lord 7: 'You won't get along with your workmates'.

You can mentally pick up the querent's significator and place it just inside the 10th cusp, thus sending it to work. How is it there? If in strong essential dignity, it is happy; if debilitated, it is not. Accidental dignity or debility may be important too. Perhaps it is cazimi there: 'You'll be the boss's blue-eyed boy' (cazimi: 'like a man raised up to sit beside the king'). Perhaps it is conjunct a weak Saturn: there will be problems, which looking at what Saturn signifies in that chart may enable you to identify. As 'Should I take the job?' is often as much an emotional as a rational decision, it is often more important to drop the Moon into the 10th, sending the querent's emotions to work. Be careful: if you are doing this you cannot say, 'It's in the 10th, so it's strong'. That would be the case with any job.

The next job

'Should I pack this job in and go to work for so-and-so?' With this and similar questions we need to distinguish between the present and the possible future job. In most cases we can take the sign on the 10th cusp and its ruler to show the present job and the next sign round in the order of the zodiac (anticlockwise) and its ruler to show the next job. Consider them as in 'What will the job be like?' above.

Be flexible! Suppose the MC is at 2 Gemini and the querent has held the present job for years. The long time spent in that job does not fit with only 2 degrees of that sign having passed the MC. In this case it would make sense to regard Taurus as the present job and Gemini as the next one, as if the querent were mentally already in it. Always be open to what the chart is trying to tell you.

If Lord 1 is about to change sign this will show the proposed change of job, even if neither its present nor its next sign has any connection with the 10th house. The chart is showing change; the change under discussion is a change of job: this must be the change shown by the chart. Is the planet stronger in the next sign, or weaker? This will usually be judged by essential dignity, but sometimes accidentals are in play. Suppose that as soon as the significator enters the new sign it becomes combust: 'Stay where you are!'

Is the company I work for going bust?

This translates as 'Is the company going to die?' and should be judged accordingly. Treat it exactly as if the company were a person, following the method described in chapter 20.

Vocational questions

I strongly advise that you do not accept such questions without requiring the querent to come up with some options. So great is the variety of jobs that unless you do this whatever answer you produce will say more about the limits of your imagination than about the querent's vocational aptitude. Sometimes the question will be phrased as 'I want to be a movie-star, but maybe I should stick to accountancy'; even if it is not, provided that the querent gives us some clues, we can feed possibilities into the chart to see which holds the best prospects.

Once you have some options, look at the chart and find the planets that signify them, working from house rulerships and the planets' natural rulerships. For example, the acting career would be shown by Lord 5 and accountancy by Mercury. "But what if Lord 5 is Mercury?" The chart is tailored to the question, so Lord 5 will probably not be Mercury. If it is, the chart will provide another obvious indicator. Trust; it works.

Once you have the significators, compare them, considering their own dignities (essential and accidental) and their receptions with Lord 1 and the Moon (taking the Moon as cosignificator of the querent, with particular reference to the querent's emotions). Be careful when considering dignities: if a testimony is descriptive, treat it as such and do not regard it as debilitating. Suppose the querent wants to be a blacksmith: Saturn in Aries would be an ideal astrological job description, so we would ignore Saturn's being in fall there. But Saturn being retrograde would be a problem – unless the querent were intent on reviving lost smithing skills, or had some other aim (resurrecting an ancestral business, perhaps) that rendered the retrogradation entirely suitable.

Pay great attention to the receptions between the significator of the job and those of the querent. If the question is about earning a wage with no concern for how congenial the job might be, we do not need to concern ourselves with querent/job compatibility. This question is usually about job suitability, so the greater the level of mutual reception between querent and job, the better.

"Where's the money in this?" If you are choosing a significator for the job because it is the appropriate house ruler (e.g. Lord 5 for acting), use the 2nd house from that house to show the wages. If you are choosing a planet for its own indications (Mercury for accountancy, Saturn for grave-digging) take the 2nd sign from the sign that planet is in. So if the querent wants to be a couturier (Venus) and Venus is in Sagittarius, you would take the 2nd sign from there (1st from Sagittarius is Sagittarius; 2nd is Capricorn) and its ruler to show the wages.

For a general question with no possible vocations suggested by the querent, consider Mercury, Venus and Mars, taking the strongest of them to signify the vocation. Broadly, Mercury shows brainwork, Mars works with muscle, Venus works by charm or aesthetics. Take further description from sign, house and close aspects. Accidental debilities often show description rather than disadvantage. For example, strong Mars in the 7th (open enemies): go and be a soldier. In the 6th (illness): be a surgeon. In the 12th (large animals): join the cavalry. Mars opposing Saturn (buildings): be a demolition worker.

Especially if you have no clear answer from the above, it can be worth casting the Part of Vocation. Consider the Part itself and, especially, its dispositor.

Do bear in mind the obvious: many careers that are open at 20 are not open at 50. Read the chart in that light.

We are sometimes asked about someone else's career. This is usually as a subsidiary question to 'When will I meet the man I will marry?' In this case, take the turned 10th house and its ruler.

We cannot use that person's main significator to describe the job, because the main significator will describe that person. This would imply that, for instance, everyone who's built like a soldier becomes a soldier. Nor can we take the strongest of Mercury, Venus and Mars, because this would be the same for both the other person and the querent. Note that we did not consider Lord 10 when finding the querent's vocation. This is because the 10th house shows what the person does do, rather than what they should do. With 'What will my future husband do for a living?' it is what he does do that concerns us.

Follow the usual clues for linking planet to job. Keep your judgements broad: precision has its place in horary, but that place is not here. 'Something artistic' is a better answer to this question than 'Second viola in the London Symphony Orchestra'.

Although we cannot take the profession from the person's main significator, the main significator can rule out possibilities. If we have decided, from Lord 7, that the future husband is a skinny little guy, he will not be working as a black-smith. If his Lord 10 suggests that he is, we will have to think of another job that it might describe.

24

Eleventh House Questions

WILL I GET MY WISH?

Our forebears devoted much ink to the problem of what we should do when the querent refuses to specify the question, insisting instead on 'Will I get this thing that I'm not going to tell you about?' I strongly suggest that the response must be 'If you won't tell me the question, I'll do the chart, but won't tell you the answer'. Always remember that it's easier for you to find another client than it is for the client to find another good astrologer.

Once you have a certain number of horaries under your belt, you will begin to recognise what charts on certain subjects look like. Most notably, you will be able to spot the love question that masquerades as something else. It is not unusual for questions about moving home or job advancement to have their real theme as, in simple terms, 'Does he love me?' If the querent doesn't ask, my opinion is that we should not answer; but we can gently nudge the querent to see if she wishes to open this issue.

HOW MUCH IS MY TAX BILL?

The government is 10th house, its coffers are 11th. These charts will usually show an applying aspect between Lord 2 (querent's money) and either Lord 10 or Lord 11. Consider the receptions, checking to see what Lords 10 and 11 – with special emphasis on whichever of them is making the aspect to Lord 2 – think of the querent's money. The more the taxman loves it, the more of it he will want. If he exalts Lord 2, it is a sign that he overestimates how much the querent has, or, at least, how much is owed.

If finding the government or its coffers love the querent's money (in the sign of Lord 2) is bad news, finding this love is reciprocated is encouraging. A strong mutual reception between them will reduce the bill. It is like the movies where the hero loves her, but gallantly sends her back to someone else: the mutual reception shows that even though the taxman wants the money, he will reduce his demands.

Consider also any other forthcoming afflictions to Lord 2, and Lord 2's strength, which will show how capable the querent's purse is of surviving the taxman's predations (such questions are usually asked *in extremis*!).

25

Twelfth House Questions

WITCHCRAFT AND IMPRISONMENT

Am I bewitched?

For all that this might seem a question occurring only in dusty texts from days long past, it is asked, and not infrequently. Sometimes by querents whose culture has a different view of witchcraft than our own; sometimes by those who have dabbled beyond their depth; most often in modern guise: 'Am I under psychic attack?' or 'Is he controlling my thoughts?' being the usual contemporary framing of what is essentially the same question.

We must always be open to the querent's world-view, no matter how bizarre it might seem to us. While the astrologer who does not recognise that 'there are more things in Heaven and Earth' than his preconceptions allow will be a poor astrologer, there is yet a dividing line between those of different views and those who are crazy, looking only for someone to latch on to. It is well to develop a nose for these, as once admitted into your working life it can take a disproportionate amount of time and effort to usher them through the exit.

It is the nature of the assault that makes this a 12th house issue, not whether the querent knows the supposed assailant's name. If the question is 'Is Albert psychically attacking me?' it is a 12th-house matter. Remember: in the past when querents would ask 'Am I bewitched?' they would usually know the identity of the village witch who was supposedly hexing their cattle. In certain specific circumstances, if the accused has a particular relationship to the querent, you will need to check that house ('Has my ex-lover put a spell on me?'). Usually, however, we can go straight to the 12th.

The major testimonies of bewitchment are:

* the same planet rules both 1st and 12th houses
* close contact between Lords 1 and 12.

Look at the receptions: as ever, these will hold the key. If Lord 12 is ruled by Lord 1, the querent is not bewitched: the querent has power over the supposed witch. If Lord 1 is ruled by Lord 12, remember that the supposition of witchcraft can be enough to give that person power over the native, without the suspect having done anything. A contact with Lord 12 is much more convincing. An applying aspect between Lords 1 and 12 is not evidence. An applying aspect shows something in the future, and the question is not 'Will I be bewitched?'

Am I harming myself?

The 12th is the house of self-undoing, and so is the relevant house in questions about addictions and other harmful practices. If the querent asks, for example, 'Is my drinking harming me, and how?' it is a 12th-house matter. Any idea that it might be 5th-house (pleasure) is dispelled by the nature of the question. Look to Lord 12: is it nice or nasty? Remember that even benefic planets in detriment or fall are nasty. What is its relationship to Lord 1? A weak planet with power over Lord 1 (e.g. Lord 1 in sign of Lord 12) is testimony that the vice has power over the querent. The stronger the reception, the more the power (e.g. Lord 1 in a face ruled by Lord 12: the power is small).

The mode of the sign will show how stubborn will be the problem: a fixed sign shows it is a long-term issue; mutable, that it will come and go; cardinal, that it may be a problem now, but won't be for long. Where is Lord 1 going? Leaving a fixed sign where it is ruled by Lord 12 for a mutable where it is not: the querent is finding a way out of this problem. Leaving a cardinal sign where it is under minor rulership of Lord 12 (term or face, maybe) for a fixed sign where it is in major dignity of Lord 12: the querent thinks the problem is under control, but is falling more seriously into its grasp.

Imprisonment

Questions of whether someone will be sent to or get out of prison are usually straightforward. Remember that if the querent is asking about someone else, we must consider both the turned and radical 12th houses. It is important that you know whether the person is already in prison or not.

Imprisonment is often shown simply: the person's significator on the cusp of the 12th (or turned 12th) house. The planet about to enter the house of imprisonment is a compelling testimony that the person will follow suit. If the planet turns retrograde before entering the house, it shows that no matter how certain imprisonment might seem the person will go free.

When the person is on remand, it is usual to find his significator already in the 12th: he is already in prison. If its condition is about to worsen, perhaps by aspecting a malefic planet or by losing essential dignity, he will be committed. The chart is showing that the person's condition is worsening, in a way fitting the context of the question. We might judge the same if the significator, in the 12th, were moving from a cardinal to a fixed sign.

An applying aspect with Lord 12 or Lord of the turned 12th would show the same. Another common indicator is the significator entering the sign of its fall: it is, literally, going down.

The greater the essential dignity the planet has, the more likely the person is to be innocent.

If the question is about somebody being released, the desired testimonies will be the reverse of the above.

Will Deirdre be sent down?

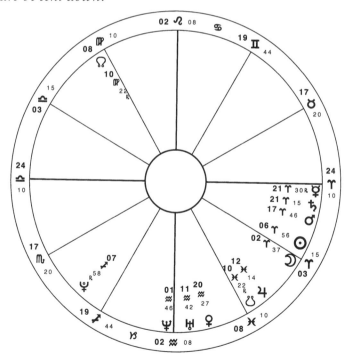

Will Deirdre be sent down? March 27th 1998, 7.58 pm GMT, London.

To while away long evenings, William Lilly would 'in merriment' ask a servant to hide something and then cast a chart to find it. I have never developed his affection for lost object questions; my preferred horary merriment comes in predicting the story line in soap operas.

In *Coronation Street,* Deirdre was in the dock, facing charges of fraud after falling for a charming but unscrupulous con-man. As the foreman of the jury stood up to give the verdict, the credits began to roll. Rather than wait three days to find out, I set the chart.

I had no particular interest in Deirdre, so she is 'any old person': 7th house. Had I strongly identified with her, perhaps having experienced something similar myself, she would be given the 1st house, as if the question were 'Will we be sent down?' If I were strongly smitten with her, she would still be 7th, this time as the object of my affections.

Deirdre was already in prison, as she had been refused bail. Lord 7, Mars, shows this: it is in the turned 12th house (12 from 7th = radical 6th). It is in its own sign: lots of essential dignity, so Deirdre is innocent. But it is about to conjunct Saturn, which is in its fall and so is very nasty. It is also the natural ruler of imprisonment. Something horrible is going to happen to her: she will be convicted and sentenced to jail.

This is all happening in a cardinal sign, however, suggesting things that are quickly over. Once past Saturn, Mars hasn't far to travel before it enters Deirdre's 1st. She is entering her own house. This, as so often in horary, can be taken literally: she will soon be coming home. Before Mars gets home it meets Mercury, which is retrograde: what has been said (Mercury) will change (retrograde). Someone's story will change, as a result of which Deirdre will be freed.

The South Node close to the cusp of the turned 11th (11 from 7th = radical 5th) shows where Deirdre will be hurt: through her friends. Although there is a moderately strong mutual reception between Mars and Jupiter, ruler of this house (each in the other's triplicity), they oppose each other by antiscion. It was the testimony of a friend that was crucial to her conviction. But the friends (Jupiter is in a double-bodied sign, so there is more than one) are honest (strong essential dignity), so the false testimony must have been given in error. Jupiter being a strongly dignified benefic, they will want to act for the best, and the mutual reception shows them helping.

Note here an example of that important point about mutual reception: it can work only to the extent that both planets are strong. Here both planets are strong, so the friends are capable of helping and Deirdre is capable of being helped.

To smooth the feathers of those horrified at the asking of so 'trivial' a question – merriment being forbidden in some outposts of contemporary horary – I should add that Deirdre's imprisonment brought front-page headlines in the national press and questions in parliament. Not, perhaps, quite so trivial! The story unfolded as the chart shows.

26

The Weather

Questions about the weather are among the simplest of horaries. Judgement is made using some of the fundamental building-blocks of astrology: hot, cold, moist and dry. Given these and some wind, we have all that we need for accurate weather-forecasting. So don't complicate it!

If it is a general question about the weather in this area, use the 1st house: 'Will we have a hot summer this year?' 'When will this rainy spell end?' If the question relates to a specific event, use the house that shows that event: 'I'm playing golf tomorrow: what will the weather be like?' (5th house); 'I'm going to stay with my friend; do I need to take warm clothes?' (11th house: 'What is the weather at my friend's house?'). Such questions are often asked about sailing trips: if it is a long voyage, look to the 9th house; if it is 'messing about in boats', or sailing around without a destination, look to the 5th; if it is the ferry that you catch to go to work each day, it is a routine journey and so 3rd.

Although you can ask general questions about the weather in the place where you are, you cannot ask them routinely with the expectation of getting an accurate answer. You cannot mechanically repeat 'What's the weather going to be today?' when you wake each morning.

Once you have chosen the appropriate house, the ruler of that house shows the event in question (the party, the voyage), even if it is a 1st house matter and the event is only the vague 'here'. The house ruler itself *is* the event: it is not the weather at that event. If the house is ruled by Saturn, this does not mean that the weather will be cold and dry; we have to look at what is happening to Saturn.

Planets are things; signs describe them. Planets are nouns; signs are adjectives. The sign will describe the planet within the context determined by the question; in a weather question, the sign will describe the house ruler in terms of the weather: it will be hot, cold, moist or dry. If the house-ruler is in an earth sign, which is cold and dry, the weather at that event will be cold and dry; if in an air sign (hot and moist), it will be hot and moist. Yes, it is this simple.

For more detail on exactly how cold and dry this earth sign shows it will be, look to the ruler of that sign. The example chart below will make this clearer. Then note any close aspects to the significator. An aspect from a moist planet in a moist sign will bring rain; a sextile might show a light shower; an opposition, a destructive downpour. Qualify your judgement by the season: 'hot' in the middle of winter is not going to be the same as 'hot' in the middle of summer. Cold moisture in winter may be snow, depending on where you are.

Jupiter, the Great Benefic, is natural ruler of rain. Astrology shares the farmer's rather than the holiday-maker's idea of what is good weather. Mercury rules wind, so aspects from Mercury will show whether the wind is helpful or a hindrance for your voyage. The condition of Mercury will show how strong the wind will be. On a grander scale, Mercury is also natural ruler of earthquakes, which are seen as wind within the earth.

What will the weather be at my party?

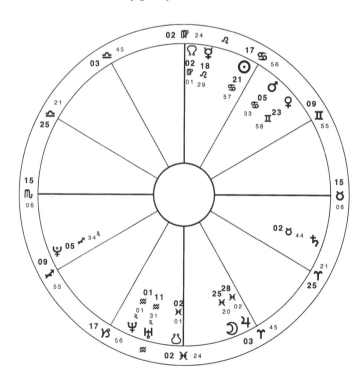

What will the weather be? July 14th 1998, 3.49 pm BST, London.

The querent held an annual barbecue party with a huge crowd of guests, so the weather on the chosen day was of some importance.

It is a party, so look to the 5th house. The sign on the cusp of the 5th well describes the party: it is a hot and dry sort of party – a barbecue. This describes the party; it does not describe the weather. Nor does Mars, ruling this house, have any effect upon the weather. Mars *is* the party; we are looking at what affects Mars.

Mars signifies the barbecue. What sort of barbecue? It is in a cold/moist sign: a wet sort of barbecue.

What sort of wet? The Moon (ruler of the sign that told us it was wet) signifies the wet. It is in Pisces, another water sign: it will be a wet sort of wet. It is conjunct Jupiter: a big wet sort of wet. Conjunct Jupiter in Pisces: a very big wet sort of wet.

It rained torrentially from morning till night.

27

Electing with Horary

Electional astrology is choosing the optimum moment at which to act. It is a time-consuming business, and so if done by a professional is expensive. It cannot be done without the study of the birthchart. For those querents who, whether for lack of known birth-data or financial reasons, a full election is not possible, or for those who do not need precision of time in their election, we can choose the time to act with horary.

This will not give us a timing to the minute, as can be done with a full election, but it does provide what is for many purposes all the accuracy that is needed.

Once again, this is very simple. Don't complicate it! All you need do is to identify the relevant planet, which will be the ruler of the house in question. 'When is the best day to have my party?': Lord 5. 'When is the best day to launch this work project?': Lord 10. In many cases the question boils down to 'When is the best day for me?': take Lord 1.

Having identified the planet, look at its movement. What is it going to do? What is going to happen to it? No matter how dire its position now might be, sooner or later it will be in a stronger position. Ask yourself, 'What is the best situation for this planet in the near future?' Once you have identified this, take the distance from where the planet is now to where it will be when it gets there and judge the timing in the usual way.

In many questions of this kind there are severe time restraints: 'Should I do the deal on Monday or Thursday?'

In such cases the transits to the horary chart on the specified days can be eloquent. Suppose, for example, the question is, 'I have a choice of June 20th or June 30th for my interview to get into college; which is best?' and the ephemeris shows that on the 20th Lord 1 (the querent) conjuncts the 9th cusp of the horary chart (the college), where it is exalted. 'Go on the 20th: they'll think the world of you!' Or maybe between the 20th and 30th the ruler of the 9th (the college) changes sign and enters some dignity of Lord 1 (the querent): 'Go on the 30th, because they will like you more then'.

Usually, however, we can concentrate on the task of getting our one significator as strong as possible. Example: suppose the question is 'When is the best day to submit my masterpiece to a publisher?' Your masterpiece is your baby: 5th house. Suppose Mars rules the 5th and will conjunct the North Node in 3 degrees. This will make it stronger, which is what we want, and the 3 degrees will give us the timing: 3 days, weeks or months, depending on the sign and house it is in. These questions usually carry their own time-limits, which makes the choice of time-unit easy ('When within the next fortnight should I do this?'). Or suppose that Mars is at 26 Sagittarius. In 4 degrees it will enter Capricorn, where it is exalted. So the answer might be, 'Wait four days, then do it any time you like'.

Most important: do not do anything that implies the setting of a new chart for the elected time. To do this is to begin to do a full election, and this cannot be done without the study of the birthchart. With a horary, you do not have the necessary information – so don't try to do it. Examples of this would be, 'Mars gets strong in 4 days, and on that day the Moon is in the 10th,' or 'And on that day Venus trines Saturn.' Neither should you aim for precision with a horary election. It is rare for the answer to be more specific than, at most, a particular day. You cannot get a time from an election like this, so don't try. Often the answer will be 'After such a date' or 'As soon as possible'.

28

Astrologer and Client

Working in the Seventeenth century, William Lilly did the occasional postal consultation, but most of his clients were sitting in front of him while he judged the charts for their questions. Many would have been in a distressed state, whether about their medical problems, their marital prospects or the lost cow on whose recovery their financial future depended. The modern horary astrologer will probably do most consultations by phone, post or email. With such a distance between astrologer and client, it is easy to forget that these charts are not abstract mental exercises, but people's lives. We are dealing with flesh, blood and tender hearts, not a collection of symbols on a page.

There are advantages and disadvantages to the querent being present while the chart is judged. The main advantage, other than reminding us that we are dealing with a human being, is that we can easily ask for information about points that puzzle us in the chart. But in practice this is necessary more rarely than might be expected. If it is needed, we can contact the querent.

The main disadvantage is that the querent's presence is distracting. I prefer to have my total attention on the astrology while I judge the chart, then have my total attention on the client while giving the judgement. Lilly's contemporaries would customarily accuse each other of twisting judgements to get the client's cash. The awareness of the financial transaction is a problem, but more serious is the awareness of the client's emotional state. There is a natural human desire to please, in which even horary astrologers share; having the client's hopes and fears hanging over you as you judge can lead you astray. It is far more likely to do so if the client is sitting in front of you at the time. I suspect that this caused more distortion of judgement in Lilly's day than deliberate financial chicanery.

Assuming that the astrologer has made the financial arrangement with the client clear, so that there is no 'Cross my palm with silver and I'll tell you more', the money problem arises only with such questions as 'Should I invest in...?' and 'Should I employ...?' There, the astrologer will be aware that the answer 'No' may well bring another question about the next prospective investment or employee, and therefore another fee. And the astrologer will be aware that the client knows this too. This can start a game of 'I think that he thinks that I think...' There is no answer to this other than striving to give each judgement with a clear conscience, and pointing out whatever errors in attitude the chart might suggest: 'You're seeking to change your investments because you feel that you ought to be acting, but they're fine where they are'; 'Try choosing an employee because she knows her job, not because you fancy her'.

Even if you prefer to deal with clients in person, modern reality will usually not allow it. No matter how good at horary you may become, you are unlikely to find querents queuing at your door. Many horary questions have one word answers; this is fully satisfactory in a telephone call, less so if the client has travelled for some hours to reach you – no matter how valuable that one word might be.

A one word answer is often all that is needed. If that is all, that is all; do not turn it into a counselling session because you feel you need to fill up some time. You have done your work.

Resist the temptation to turn every judgement into a choice of black or white. In many situations, mediocrity is all that is on offer, so if mediocrity is what the chart shows, that is the answer. Questions are often phrased in the hope of the marvellous – the perfect mate, the ideal job – but the judgement to such questions is often 'You could do a lot worse', 'It's OK', or 'It doesn't much matter which you choose'. This is a valid answer.

Sometimes you will feel confident in your judgement; sometimes you will not. There is no need to pretend otherwise. It is acceptable to say, 'This chart's really clear. I am fallible, but I'm pretty confident that xyz will happen', or 'This chart's really a puzzle. I *think* I'm reading it right, in which case...'

You will get questions wrong, and you will continue to do so no matter how much knowledge and experience you gain. Some questions allow you a second shot: if, for instance, the lost object isn't where you judged it to be, you can go back to the chart to find another interpretation of the testimonies. Some questions do not allow a second shot, because the time for it has passed. This is unfortunate, and hearing 'You told me such-and-such, but...' hurts to the same extent that 'I told you your prediction was impossible, but...' pleases. It does not mean you need to don sackcloth and ashes. Study the chart so you learn from your mistakes, but do not demean yourself before the client: your being perfect is not part of the contract.

You will become familiar with the words 'What if?' You have just answered your client's question by telling her that the object of her affection does not love her. 'But what if I were Julia Roberts?' she asks, 'You might have given me a different answer'.

'But you're not Julia Roberts.'

'But what if I were?'

I have never had that conversation with a client, but I have often had the conversation that begins, 'But what if I'd asked you the question at a different time? You might have given a different answer.'

'But you didn't.'

'But what if I had?'

Perhaps the greatest lesson of horary is that there is no such thing as 'What if?' What is, is; what is not, is not. The assumption of horary is that the question is a product of that person in the reality of that person's life. It is asked when it is asked because the querent is who the querent is. Only when the querent can become someone else can the question be asked at a different time.

In dealing with querents, there are many pits into which the unwary may fall. It is well be aware of the more common ones, as avoiding them is a lot easier than clambering out of them. You will need to decide a policy on various issues with which querents will confront you. Don't worry: this policy need not be set in stone. If situations show you've got it wrong, you'll change it, while you'll find there are exceptions to most of the rules you may make. You may, for example, decide to accept a certain question from a friend or long-standing client that you would not take from a first-time querent. Remember: once you have accepted the question you can rarely go back. If you do, no matter what explanation you give, the querent will usually assume that you have looked at the chart and seen something so horrible that you cannot bear to tell it. So it is worth deciding what you will do in difficult situations before these situations arise.

Most questions involve someone other than the querent, so where will you set the barrier between legitimate enquiry and unwarranted intrusion?

Will you accept questions on death? Or serious illness? Fear not, if you have a sensitive spot, your querents will find it! What about questions that touch on your deeply held beliefs? Perhaps you are a Catholic, for instance, and are asked 'Should I have an abortion?' It may be tempting to side-step these issues by not accepting questions of such import. But even what appear the most innocuous of questions can carry a huge emotional cargo: avoid questions of import and you will avoid all questions.

I strongly suggest that the basis for any consultation must be that we are adults dealing with adults. Many of the reservations commonly voiced to answering certain questions are patronising in the extreme, their basic theme being 'I can't say that in case I upset the poor little client'. Unless you intend hanging a sign outside your booth, 'Horary Astrologer: pleasing answers only', we must play by grown-ups' rules: you ask the question, you get the answer. But you have the right to refuse questions, and you have the right to refuse clients.

For all that we play by grown-ups' rules, there are judgements that are not easy to give. Here follows my reply to a student who asked how to handle these, and William Lilly's own letter to the Student in Astrology:

'I can't say it better than Lilly, where he advises us to 'afflict not the querent with harsh judgement'. We must tell the truth, and if they have asked the question they must get the answer to it, no matter how unpleasant: the biggest danger is that we put so much sugar on it that the answer itself gets lost. But we can be judicious with what we say: we don't need to tell all that we see, just because we can see it – that makes us feel clever, but doesn't benefit the client.

'We must make it clear that we are not infallible: this leaves room for hope, which must never be destroyed. Especially when predicting death, reminding the client that all is in the hands of God is important. Prayer is always helpful. Or when saying that there is no future with Prince Charming, 'by all means prove me wrong, but I really can't see it'.

'Strive to find a positive – but only if there is one. A common scenario is 'No, there is no future with X, but it seems that you're only in this relationship because you're at such a low spot. By the autumn you should be feeling more confident in yourself and will be ready for the quality of relationship that you deserve'. Or things about not being ready at the moment, as if your capacity for finding a loving relationship isn't quite ripe yet. These may sound anodyne, but such things are often shown in the chart.

'You will be surprised how easily people take what you might think to be the worst possible news: it often comes as a relief, or as a confirmation of what they sensed would happen. Just say what you have to say quickly, simply and clearly. There is an Arab saying that we must always be kind – but sometimes being kind means chopping the limb off with one stroke. Sawing away at it only prolongs the pain.

'And as Polonius said: to thine own self be true. Say things as you would say them: if you try to adopt a style that isn't you, the falsehood in that will grate.

The judgements I regret are not the ones I've got wrong – which is always allow-able – but those where the tone in which I've delivered the judgement has been inappropriate. That is not allowable!'

To The Student In Astrology.[44]

My Friend, whoever thou art, that with so much ease shall receive the benefit of my hard studies, and dost intend to proceed in this heavenly knowledge of the stars, wherein the great and admirable works of the invisible and all-glorious God are so manifestly apparent. In the first place, consider and admire thy Creator, and be thankful unto him. Be thou humble, and let no natural knowledge, how profound and transcendent soever it be, elate thy mind to neglect that divine Providence, by whose all-seeing order and appointment all things heavenly and earthly have their constant motion; but the more thy knowledge is enlarged, the more do thou magnify the power and wisdom of Almighty God, and strive to preserve thyself in his favour, being confident, the more holy thou art, and more near to God, the purer Judgment thou shalt give. Beware of pride and self-conceit, and remember how that long ago no irrational creature durst offend man, the microcosm, but did faithfully serve and obey him, so long as he was master of his own reason and passions, or until he subjected his will to the unrea-sonable part. But alas! when iniquity abounded, and man gave the reins to his own affection, and deferred reason, then every beast, creature and outward harmful thing became rebellious and unserviceable to his command. Stand fast, oh man! to thy God, and assured principles. Then consider thy own nobleness, how all created things, both present and to come, were for thy sake created; nay, for thy sake God became man. Thou art that creature, who being conversant with Christ, livest and reignest above the heavens, and sits above all power and author-ity. How many preeminences, privileges, advantages hath God bestowed on thee? Thou rangest above the heavens by contemplation, conceivest the motion and magnitude of the stars; thou talkest with angels, yea with God himself; thou hast all creatures within thy dominion, and keepest the devils in subjection. Do not then, for shame, deface thy Nature, or make thyself unworthy of such gifts, or deprive thyself of that great power, glory and blessedness God hath allotted thee, by casting from thee his fear, for possession of a few imperfect pleasures.

---

44 *Lilly*, introductory pages. Punctuation modernised.

Having considered thy God, and what thyself art, during thy being God's servant, now receive instruction how in thy practice I would have thee carry thyself. As thou daily conversest with the heavens, so instruct and form thy mind according to the image of Divinity. Learn all the ornaments of virtue; be sufficiently instructed therein. Be humane, courteous, familiar to all, easy of access. Afflict not the miserable with terror of a harsh judgment. In such cases, let them know their hard fate by degrees; direct them to call on God to divert his judgements impending over them. Be modest; conversant with the learned, civil, sober man; covet not an estate; give freely to the poor, both money and judgment. Let no worldly wealth procure an erroneous judgment from thee, or such as may dishonour the Art, or this divine Science. Love good men; cherish those honest men that cordially study this Art. Be sparing in delivering judgment against the Commonwealth thou livest in. Give not judgment of the death of thy Prince; yet I know experimentally, that *Reges subjacent legibus stellarum.*[45] Marry a wife of thy own; rejoice in the number of thy friends; avoid law and controversy. In thy Study, be *totus in illis*[46] that thou mayest be *singulus in arte.* Be not extravagant or desirous to learn every science; be not *aliquid in omnibus.*[47] Be faithful, tenacious, betray no one's secrets; no, no, I charge thee – never divulge either friend or enemy's trust committed to thy faith. Instruct all men to live well; be a good example thyself; avoid the fashion of the times; love thy own native country; exprobrate no man, no not an enemy; be not dismayed if ill spoken of, *Conscientia mille testes;*[48] God suffers no sin unpunished, no lie unrevenged.

William Lilly

[45] Kings are subject to the law of the stars.
[46] Be dedicated, that thou mayest be without peer.
[47] A jack of all trades.
[48] A good conscience is a thousand witnesses.

APPENDIX 1

Chart Calculation

You need: the time of the question; latitude and longitude of the place. An ephemeris. A Table of Houses.

Tables for Regiomontanus houses are, as far as I know, unavailable, so use Placidus houses. Although I recommend Regiomontanus, if you use another valid system with sincerity, you will find it will work: you will be asked the right questions at the right times to fit with the house system you are using.

There is a table of Placidus houses in *Raphael's Ephemeris*. If you are using an ephemeris that does not contain such a table, buy a copy of *Raphael's*. You will only need one annual edition, because the table remains the same year after year.

Reduce local time to GMT.
A: Work out how many hours & minutes since previous noon GMT.
B: Add 4 minutes per degree east of Greenwich; subtract 4 minutes/degree west.
C: Add 10 seconds per hour of GMT since previous noon.
D: Add A+B+C.

Look in ephemeris for Sidereal Time for previous noon.
Add your total at D to this.
You now have local sidereal time. (You may need to subtract 24 hours to get a number less than 24)

Look at the Table of Houses for your latitude.
Locate the local sidereal time you have calculated in this table.
Read off the house-cusps. Six are given: the other six are their opposites.
You now have located the signs in your chart.

Look in the ephemeris to locate the planets at that time on that day.
The ephemeris will give you the positions of the planets each noon: you will need to work out their exact positions by proportion. Don't be too fussy about this!

Whatever other books might claim, you do not need logarithms. Logarithms are a comparatively recent discovery: throughout most of astrology's long history astrologers happily managed without them. So can you.

You will not usually need to calculate the planets' positions precisely. The only times you need exactitude are:

* when you need to know if this aspect happens before that aspect
* when you need to know if this aspect happens before or after the planets change sign.

If you are using *Raphael's*, you will find this information in the back of the ephemeris, so you don't need to work it out yourself.

Practice this by calculating the charts given in this book. Remember that you are using a different house system, so the house cusps may be a few degrees out. As long as they roughly agree, your calculation is probably right.

House Meanings

Your son's pet rabbit

Your son is 5th; rabbits are animals smaller than goats, so 6th. 6th from the 5th is the 10th. Count this round on the chart to make sure that when you count 6th from the 5th you get the 10th, not the 11th. Always count the house you start with as the 1st, so the 1st from the 5th is the 5th, 2nd from the 5th is the 6th, etc.

Your father's house

Your father is 4th; houses are 4th: 4th from 4th, which is the 7th. BUT: although this is true in theory, in practice someone else's house is usually shown by their 1st. This is literally 'their house'. Exactly as in the cat chart on page 4: the cat is in the cat's 1st: he is in the cat's house.

We need take the person's 4th (in this example, the 4th from the 4th) only if we need to distinguish between person and property, as in 'Will my father sell his house this year?'

Your pregnant sister

Your sister is 3rd. Pregnant or not pregnant, she is still your sister; she is still 3rd.

Your new car

Your movable possession: 2nd house.

Your journey to work

Routine journey: 3rd house. Even if you make this journey in your car, the car is not the journey, so the car is never your 3rd house.

Your boss

10th house.

The guy who shares your office
A colleague: 7th house.

The dream your friend is telling you about
Your friend is 11th; dreams are 9th. His dream is 9th from the 11th, which is the radical 7th.

Your brothers
3rd house.

Your younger brother, in contrast to your elder brother
All your brothers and any of your brothers may be signified by the 3rd. If you need to distinguish between different brothers, you can turn the chart. The elder brother would be shown by the 3rd; a younger would be regarded as his brother, hence 3rd from the 3rd, which is the radical 5th.

If you specifically asked the question about your younger brother, he would be given the 3rd. If you then needed to include your elder brother in the judgement, he would be shown by the 3rd from the 3rd.

This taking of 3rd from the 3rd to show another brother has given birth to a brood of errors. Your first wife may be 7th, but your second wife is not 3rd from the 7th, unless you intend marrying your first wife's sister. Nor is your next job 3rd from the 10th (your job's brother). The 3rd house from something does not show 'another thing of that kind'. It shows that thing's sibling.

That the 3rd from the 3rd shows my brother's brother has led many to find other representatives of a house by repeating the number of that house, claiming for instance that if your present job is 10th your next job will be 10th from the 10th, or that your second spouse will be 7th from the 7th. 10th from the 10th would be your job's job, or your job's boss (this is one way of locating the boss in a question about a job). 7th from the 7th would be your spouse's spouse (you). Unless you marry yourself, it is not your second spouse.

Your children
5th house.

Your younger child, in contrast to your elder child
In this case, taking the 3rd house is valid: your younger child is seen as the elder's sibling. 3rd from the 5th = 7th. The same would be true if you asked specifically

about your younger child: the elder would be seen as the younger's sibling. 3rd from the 5th again.

   It is not 5th from the 5th. That is your child's child, your grandchild.

Your ex-spouse
If you are asking specifically about this person ('Will my ex turn up at the party?'), use the 7th. If you are asking about your present spouse, the present spouse is 7th and you can find another significator for the ex. See chapter 21 for details of how to do this.

The local priest
9th. Whether you follow his faith or not, even if he bought his ordination on the internet, he is still 9th house.

The priest's brother
3rd from the 9th = 11th.

The priest's sister-in-law
The priest's brother is 11th. His wife is 7th from 11th = 5th.

The priest's sister-in-law's neighbour
The sister-in-law is 5th, so the neighbour is 3rd from the 5th = 7th.

The king of Spain
If you live in Spain, he is your king: 10th. If you don't, he is the king of a foreign country: 10th from the 9th = 6th. With expatriates, use your common sense to decide which to use, depending on the context of the question.

Your father's liver
The liver is 5th house. 5th from the 4th = 8th.

That packet of rice you bought this morning
Your movable possession: 2nd.

That wrap of cocaine you bought this morning
Your movable possession: 2nd. It is not 12th house: the cocaine is not your self-undoing; your taking it is your self-undoing. It is that vital distinction between function and object again.

The book you borrowed from the library
2nd house. It is, albeit temporarily, yours. In the same way, the money you have lent to other people is not your 2nd house, but theirs.

The book you have written
Your baby: 5th house.

The person who told the cops about your secret life as a criminal mastermind
Informer: 12th house. Whether you are a criminal mastermind or not, he still informed against you, so is still 12th house.

Your butler
6th. Jeeves' relationship to Wooster is 2nd house: he is less a servant than an advisor; but this is unusual. My butler's duties are limited to supervising other staff and decanting the port: he is my servant, so 6th house.

Your job as a butler
10th. As your job always is. If we didn't serve somebody, somehow, while we worked, we would never get paid.

Mines
4th house. Bottom of the chart.

The man who's come to repair your plumbing
Your servant: 6th house.

The man who's just whispered a hot tip for the next race into your ear
Your advisor: 2nd house. Or, if he knows you've been attending Gamblers Anonymous and is seeking to lead you astray, 12th house (your secret enemy).

Your university
9th house.

Your daughter's university
9th house. Although we say it is hers, it isn't: she just goes there. Unless we need to distinguish, as in 'Is my university better than hers?' in which case we would give hers the 9th from the 5th = 1st.

Your teacher's university
Now we must distinguish, because the teacher himself is 9th, so we cannot take the 9th for his university. 9th from the 9th = 5th.

Astrology
Higher knowledge: 9th house.

Particle physics
Higher knowledge: 9th house.

Your mistress's brother's Great Dane
Your mistress is 7th house. Her brother is 3rd from 7th = 9th. Great Danes may be larger than most goats, but dogs are generically smaller than goats, so he is 6th house. 6th from 9th = 2nd.

The cruise you're thinking of taking
Special journey: 9th house.

The ship on which you'll be taking it
The ship you sail in: 1st house.

Your dog's ball
Her possession: 2nd from 6th = 7th. It is not her 5th. The game she plays with it might be her 5th, but not the ball itself. Function and object again.

Your mother's friend's child
Your mother is 10th, so her friend is 11th from 10th = 8th. Her child is 5th from 8th = 12th.

How to Spot an Aspect

Yes, the whole celestial system is in motion! What we see before us in the chart is a freeze-frame of a continually moving thing, exactly as if we had pressed the pause button on a DVD. The chart as it stands no more tells us how the story will turn out than does that one frozen frame from a film. The villain has a gun in his hand; is he going to fire it? Mars is somewhere near Saturn; will they meet? From that freeze-frame alone, we cannot tell.

You need to be able to work out *if* a certain aspect will happen and, often, *when* that aspect will happen. First rule: faster planets catch up with slower planets. So you need to learn the usual order of speed. From fastest to slowest it is:

Moon   Mercury   Venus   Sun   Mars   Jupiter   Saturn

But, as discussed in the main text, the planets don't always move at the same speed. My Ferrari may be faster than his tractor, but if I'm pulling into a petrol station he may at that moment be travelling faster than me. The Moon is always very much the fastest. Apart from the Sun, whose speed never significantly varies, the others can all slow to zero and then click into reverse.

Finding aspects from the ephemeris

This is easy. Open your ephemeris to any month. You will see the planets marked along the top, with their daily positions in columns extending downward. The sign each planet is in is marked at the top of its column and elsewhere in that column whenever the planet changes sign.

You will see that in most columns the numbers get larger as you read downwards. If the numbers in a column get smaller, that planet must be retrograde. Except when the numbers jump from 29 to 0, which is when the planet is moving into a new sign.

Pick any two planets. You want to know if they make an aspect during this month. Run your eye down each of their columns to see if the numbers reach a point where they coincide. Example: maybe you see Saturn's daily position marked 9.02, 9.07, 9.12, 9.17. Mercury's position on those same days reads 7.13, 8.41, 10.09, 11.35. Mercury's number started out smaller than Saturn's; it then became larger. There must have been a point at which they coincided - when Mercury was at 9 degrees and something.

This point of coincidence may be an aspect. If there is no point of coincidence, there cannot be an aspect. But not all such coincidences are aspects. It depends which signs the planets are in. Now check their signs:

same sign:	conjunction
adjacent signs:	no aspect
next to adjacent:	sextile
next to that:	square
next to that:	trine
opposite signs:	opposition
adjacent to the opposite sign:	no aspect

NB: this is SIGNS, not HOUSES.

Done that? Good. You now know how to spot an aspect in the ephemeris. But checking these columns for every possible planetary pairing would be tedious. You do need to know how to do this, but you can cut out most of the work by looking for aspects in the chart itself.

Finding aspects from the chart

Believe it or not, after a while you will glance at a chart and notice all the aspects without even thinking about it. Much in the same way that a mechanic will listen to a car for a moment and know exactly what is wrong with it, not by running through a list of possibilities in his head, but because he can hear it and knows.

When judging a horary, you will usually be concerned with only a few planets and their possible aspects. But let's look at this chart and check all its aspects, as an example.

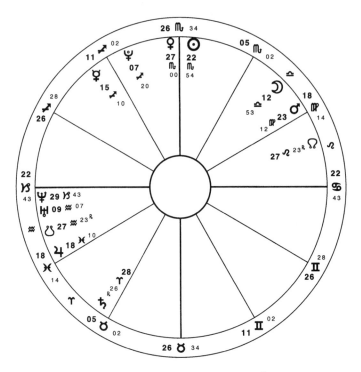

November 15th 1998, noon GMT, London.

Start with the fastest planet, the Moon.

What degree is in now? 12.53.

As it moves forwards, it will move into degrees of gradually higher number.

Which planet is at the lowest number of degrees that is higher than 12.53?

Mercury, at 15.10.

The Moon moves so fast it will soon reach 15 degrees of its own sign, by which time Mercury will scarcely have moved.

The Moon, then, will reach the same number of degrees as Mercury. ASPECT ALERT! We have a coincidence of degrees. Is it an aspect?

Mercury is not in an adjacent sign to the Moon, but in the next sign but one.

Yes, it is an aspect: a sextile.

What next for the Moon?

The planet with the next lowest number of degrees is Jupiter, at 18.10.

This gives a another coincidence. But the Moon is in Libra; its opposite sign is Aries. Jupiter is in Pisces, a sign adjacent to Aries. There cannot be an aspect.

Now what?

The Sun, Mars and Venus are all at degrees which the Moon will reach. But all of them are in signs adjacent to Libra, where the Moon is. The Moon cannot make an aspect to them.

Anything else?

Saturn is at 28.26 of its sign. The Moon moves so fast that it must catch Saturn before it changes sign.

Is Saturn in an aspectable sign?

Yes: it is in Aries, the opposite sign to the Moon's. There is an opposition.

That's it for the Moon. Now for the next fastest planet, Mercury. Mercury is at 15.10 of its sign.

Where's it going?

Mercury moves fast. It must catch Jupiter at 18 degrees.

Good - there is an aspect here. But only in potential. When looking at the Moon, we knew that it wasn't going to change course, but keep steaming forwards through the zodiac. The Sun, too, keeps plodding on its way. But all the other planets can change direction.

Yes, it looks as if Mercury will make an aspect with Jupiter, and then with Mars and then Saturn. But it won't. It is about to turn retrograde. Even though the 3 degrees it has to travel to aspect Jupiter at 18 Pisces is not a great distance, it fails to make it. There is no aspect here.

"How do I know Mercury will turn retrograde before it aspects Jupiter?" You don't. Now is the time to check your ephemeris, as described above. That will tell you whether the aspect will happen.

There is a clue in the chart. Mercury is almost a whole sign in front of the Sun: it must be turning retrograde soon.

Venus is at 27 degrees of its sign, and will soon reach 28 degrees, bringing it to the same degree as Saturn. But Saturn is in a sign adjacent to Venus' opposition, so there is no aspect.

The Sun is at 22 degrees. Mars is at 23. The Sun never turns retrograde or appreciably slows down, so will soon catch Mars. Mars is in the next sign but one to the Sun, so there is an aspect: a sextile.

Mars is at 23 degrees of its sign. Venus is at 27. But Venus moves faster than Mars, so there will be no aspect. But it is worth checking the ephemeris to make sure that Venus is not moving retrograde or moving so slowly that Mars might catch her. With Venus so close to the Sun, though, this will not happen.

Jupiter is at 18 degrees, Saturn at 28. They are in adjacent signs, so there is no possibility of an aspect.

APPENDIX 4

How to Read the Square Chart

Modern books on astrology, including this one, customarily print charts in a circular format. Older books usually print them as a square. I hope this book will inspire you to study some of the old texts, especially Lilly's *Christian Astrology*. Finding your way around in the square chart is not difficult.

This example is a chart Lilly cast to answer his own question about the recovery of some fish he had ordered, but which had been stolen from the warehouse before reaching him.[49]

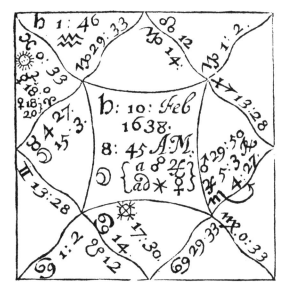

Where is my fish?

Start with the box in the middle of the chart. The Saturn glyph in the top left-hand corner of the central box shows the day of the week: Saturday. Sometimes

[49] *Lilly*, p. 397.

this is labelled *dies*, Latin for day. Often there is another glyph labelled *hor*, short for *hora*, Latin for hour. These are the planets that rule that day and that hour of that day. I have omitted all mention of them in this book, as after years of wasted time I have realised they serve absolutely no purpose in horary.

Then comes the time for which the chart is cast, in this case February 10th, 1638. If you want to recreate the chart on your computer you will need to adjust both time and date.

Lilly's England was still using the Julian calendar; his dates are known as Old Style. To convert them to the New Style that we use today you must add 10 days to them. Most software will not do this for you, so you need to do it yourself. Lilly's date of February 10th becomes February 20th New Style. The adjustment varies from century to century: 10 days is correct for the 1600s. Check the positions of the Sun and Moon to make sure you have got the right day.

The year was sometimes taken as starting on March 1st, so what Lilly calls February 1638 could be February 1639 by our reckoning (i.e. he could be regarding February as the last month of 1638, not the second month of 1639). Usage was never consistent, so be careful: for dates in January or February, check the positions of the outer planets to make sure you have the right year. In this case, Lilly's 1638 is our 1638.

The day was often taken as starting at noon, not midnight. This results in times in the morning being given as 'p.m.' Again, usage was not consistent: Lilly uses sometimes one style, sometimes the other. Look at the position of the Sun, remembering that it is on the Ascendant at dawn, near the MC at noon and on the Descendant at sunset. In this chart, the Sun has recently risen and is heading towards the MC: it must be morning. On another day Lilly could just as well have called this 8.45 pm.

He was not using any time zone recognised by your computer. He had no obsession with accuracy of timing, and used an approximation to local time. This is not the same as Local Mean Time. Start by entering the time he gives as LMT, then jiggle the time about about to find the closest fit with the chart Lilly gives. Do not expect to arrive at an exact match.

Below the time, Lilly has noted the Moon's most recent aspect and its next aspect. It is separating (*a* is Latin for 'from') from opposition to Jupiter and applying (*ad* is Latin for 'to') to sextile Mercury.

The four triangles sharing a side with this central box are the angular houses, in their usual arrangement: 1st house on the reader's left, 10th house at the top. The Ascendant is the uppermost side of the 1st house, so the Ascendant here is at

4.27 Taurus. The 2nd cusp is 13.28 Gemini, the 3rd 1.02 Cancer, the 4th 14 Cancer, and so on.

The glyph for the sign a planet is in is not usually given, the sign being shown by way the planet is placed within that house. The Moon lies parallel to the Ascendant, so is at 15.03 Taurus. Had it been in the early degrees of Gemini, it would have been placed parallel to the 2nd cusp, which is in Gemini. In the 12th house, the Sun and Mercury are both in Pisces, as shown by their being parallel to the cusp that is in Pisces.

Incepted planets, such as Saturn and Venus in this chart, are printed parallel to neither cusp, and usually carry the glyph of their sign.

Index

Only substantive references are listed here

ALSO BY JOHN FRAWLEY
and published by
APPRENTICE BOOKS

HORARY PRACTICE

The companion volume to *The Horary Textbook.* You've learned the
techniques   now give those astrological muscles a rigorous workout,
as John guides you step by step through a long series of judgements on
a huge variety of questions. This is your chance to stand at the elbow
of a master astrologer as he works, absorbing the thought processes
that will lead you to mastery of the horary craft.

Due for publication autumn 2005.

THE REAL ASTROLOGY

Winner of the Spica Award for International Book of the Year, *The
Real Astrology* provides a searching   and often hilarious   critique of
modern astrology and a detailed introduction to the traditional craft.
It contains a clear exposition of the cosmological background and a
step-by-step guide to method, accessible to those with no prior knowledge of the subject, yet sufficiently thorough to serve as a *vade mecum*
for the student or practitioner.

Philosophically rich – genuinely funny – written by a master of the
subject and informed with invaluable practical advice. – *The
Mountain Astrologer*

Wit, philosophy and a thoroughly remarkable depth of scholarship. I
will be ever thankful to John Frawley for this gem of a book. – *AFI
Journal*

Required reading for all astrologers – *Prediction*

ALSO BY JOHN FRAWLEY
and published by
APPRENTICE BOOKS

THE REAL ASTROLOGY APPLIED

This collection of notes and essays handles in greater depth subjects raised in The Real Astrology. It elucidates both technical matters and significant points of the philosophy that forms the basis of the practical craft.

An excellent book. Should be read and reread by all who intend calling themselves astrologers. – *Considerations*

Highly readable – a virtual fountain of knowledge and technique makes some of the most complex astrological material go down like a brandy snifter full of the smoothest amber elixir. – *The Mountain Astrologer*

THE ASTROLOGER'S APPRENTICE

The occasional magazine by John Frawley. This *is* the tradition as it lives.

The Apprentice includes astrological investigations of historical and cultural themes; articles on the background philosophy; tutorial sections – and even the football results!

To order books and magazines, and for details of future publications and John's worldwide lecture schedule, visit our website:

www.johnfrawley.com